# THE
# PRIVATE
# LABYRINTH
# OF
# MALCOLM
# LOWRY

# THE PRIVATE LABYRINTH OF MALCOLM LOWRY

## *UNDER THE VOLCANO* AND THE CABBALA

BY

# PERLE S. EPSTEIN

HOLT, RINEHART AND WINSTON

*New York    Chicago    San Francisco*

# *Acknowledgments*

Of all the many people who have in various ways helped and encouraged me in the writing of this book, I want to single out the following for special thanks: Professor Joseph Blau, of Columbia University, for the hours of his time spent teaching me the Cabbala and for reading the manuscript of the book; Mr. Basil Stuart-Stubbs, of the library of the University of British Columbia, for his guidance; Professor Vera Lachmann, of Brooklyn College, best teacher and friend; Mr. Don Weiser, of the Occult Bookstore, for his help and patience; Janet Thormann, for first introducing me to Lowry's work; Dr. and Mrs. Harold Leder, for reading my manuscript in its early days and for their faith in it; George Robinson, of Holt, Rinehart and Winston, Inc., for his editorial assistance and friendship; Mrs. Diana Blaikie, for typing the manuscript.

Mrs. Margerie Bonner Lowry has, from the first, generously allowed me to read unpublished material of Malcolm Lowry and throughout the entire project has been unfailingly available for help, criticism, correction and encouragement. In addition, in this book there appears material for whose reproduction she most graciously gave permission.

My brother, Lawrence Besserman, who took much time away from his own research to help me with Hebrew translations and to increase my understanding of Jewish mysticism; Cabbalists all over the world who have helped me through their letters and who deserve special thanks.

Above all, my husband has characteristically encouraged me at every point during the research for and the writing of this book.

Thanks are due to the following publishers for permission to quote from copyrighted materials: J. B. Lippincott Company for material from *Selected Letters of Malcolm Lowry,* edited by Harvey Breit and Margerie Bonner Lowry, © 1965 by Margerie Bonner Lowry, and from *Under the Volcano,* by Malcolm Lowry, © 1947 by Malcolm Lowry; George C. Harrap and Company Ltd. for material from Lewis Spence, *Myths of Mexico and Peru.*

PERLE S. EPSTEIN

*New York City*
*January, 1969*

*For my mother and father*

# CONTENTS

# PART
# I

# *Introduction*

... *that sixth sense mysticism of his and his eternal and so often verifiable adduction of Cabalistic correspondences—the evidence to him, of a mystic pattern [emerged to influence every facet of Malcolm Lowry's life]. ...*

—CONRAD AIKEN, *Ushant*

# Malcolm Lowry

MALCOLM LOWRY was born into the wrong family in 1909. His father, a wealthy Liverpool cotton merchant, assumed that the boy would graduate from Cambridge and join the firm. Only one of these assumptions materialized, but not before Malcolm had signed up for a one-year hitch as a merchant seaman. Under age and requiring his father's permission, the young adventurer was forced to agree to a family compromise: he was to enroll at Cambridge as soon as his ship returned to London.

To ensure the "safety" of his young son, the elder Lowry had the boy driven to the pier in his chauffeured limousine. It was this incident, along with some unfortunate publicity of the rich-boy-turned-sailor variety, that sparked the permanent hostility of the more genuine old salts that Malcolm was to face throughout his entire voyage. The misery and boredom at sea, as well as initiation into the alcoholism that was to plague him until his death, were all captured in the notes of a journal, which was later to become his first novel, *Ultramarine.*

His romantic wanderlust sated for a while, Lowry entered Cambridge, to leave with his degree after three years of guitar playing, wide reading, and equally wide drinking. Having filled his part of the bargain, and determined to write, Lowry adopted Conrad Aiken as spiritual father and literary mentor. One summer holiday while still at Cambridge, he descended upon Aiken and America carrying only a football boot, a bottle, and a collected edition of Shakespeare in his suitcase. So began a deep and lifelong, if somewhat turbulent, friendship between the two men.

In 1939, after an attempt at marriage and writing in Cuernavaca, Lowry suffered the first of the severe mental and physical collapses that were to recur throughout his life. A move to Los Angeles brought him better luck. It was here that he met his second wife, Margerie Bonner, a movie actress and something of a novelist herself. Together, they built a shack on the beach at Dollarton, British Columbia, which was to be their home for fourteen years (1940–1954), during which time he worked almost unceasingly on *Under the Volcano,* as well as on poems, short stories, and drafts of other novels. The atmosphere of this northern paradise pervades all his works and provides him with much of the imagery and symbolism of the Eden theme in *Under the Volcano.* But his personal "demons," as he called them, continued to torture him, and in 1957, while visiting England, he choked to death after a long night of drinking.

Lowry devoted his life to an enormous projected canon with one protagonist, the author's persona, at its center. A trilogy entitled *The Voyage That Never Ends* was to represent a twentieth-century *Divine Comedy,* with *Under the Volcano* (hell) as the first novel, followed by *Lunar Caustic* (purgatory) and *In Ballast to the White Sea* (paradise). In the end, however, he achieved only a fraction of his intended output. Beset by innumerable physical and mental difficulties and victimized by a compulsion to revise his manuscripts (for example, extending work on *Volcano* to eight years, and leaving literally thousands of pages of unpublished manuscripts still begging for editing), Lowry until recently remained the center of a small literary cult, essentially a "one-book author."

That he consciously derived much of his style from Joyce (by way of Conrad Aiken) is a critical commonplace; but what he personally strove to create was a poetic novel, something partaking of Sir Thomas Browne on the one hand and Wagner on the other.

Beginning on November 2, 1938, the action of *Under the Volcano* consumes no more than twelve hours in the life of Geoffrey Firmin, dipsomaniac, genius, Cabbalist, and former British Consul in Quauhnahuac (Indian name for Cuernavaca), Mexico. Both his estranged wife and his half brother "coincidentally" decide to return to him on this day—which turns out to be his last. The social climate is one of political unrest, crowded with fascist secret police, communist martyrs, and cloak-and-dagger melodrama—all surrounding and gradually enmeshing the perpetually inebriated Firmin.

Events are almost entirely unraveled by means of flashbacks and interior monologue, with third-person narrative reserved for the climactic scenes leading to the murder of the Consul by fascist police. Geoffrey harbors a deep, guilty secret concerning his role in the murder of a group of German war prisoners; Yvonne, his wife, has contributed to the couple's break-up by committing repeated adulteries with both his best friend and his half brother, Hugh; Hugh, romantic dreamer and communist sympathizer, bears his own burdens of jealousy and sibling hatred despite his burning desire to love his fellow man. The surface situations that loosely cover these inner turmoils are no less violent, ranging from a torment-laden bus trip during which an Indian is left to die in the sun to a kind of Lawrentian bullfight in reverse—during which Hugh, the young hero, urged by the promptings of his "blood" to throw the bull to the ground, proves himself no more than a bull thrower—and culminating in the violent trampling of Yvonne by a horse significantly branded with the number 7. With the Consul and Yvonne both dead, Hugh determines to go on a suicide mission for the Spanish Loyalists. His decision concludes what appears to be a hopeless and depressing tragedy.

Even a simple first reading of the novel uncovers the stream-of-consciousness technique used by Woolf and Joyce. Alcoholic hallucinations, trance states, bits of external reality are superimposed onto travel brochures, cinema posters, billboard announcements —all of these somehow merging into a complex symbolic substructure. Lowry establishes leitmotifs as signposts for recurring themes along the way. His use of interior-exterior dialogue, his purple passages imbued with Elizabethan imagery, and the perpetual becoming of poetry as opposed to the logical stasis of realistic prose narrative give the novel the sense of timelessness prevalent both in the unconscious and in the mystical experience. Further, because *Under the Volcano* partakes of the dream, the hallucination, the occult, its style must partake of the language native to those states: the use of symbolism, condensation, distortion, and displacement, while the inherent power of words apart from their ordinary uses is combined in a magical operation.

Fortunately, like Dante, Lowry has left us evidence of his symbolic intentions in his preface to the French edition of his novel, as well as in private correspondence, which includes references to Marlowe, Goethe, Dante, Aztec legend, the Cabbala, Swedenborg, Rosicrucianism, astrology, and alchemy. All the evidence points to a deliberate Cabbalistic framework for the novel wherein Lowry has employed his knowledge of the *Sefer Yetzirah* (Book of Formations), *Sefer Zohar,* tarot symbolism, *The Keys of Solomon,* the tree of life, and the writings of Cornelius Agrippa, Henry Vaughan, and other occultists.* It seems clear, therefore, that besides being a Bunyanesque novel of sin, redemption, politics, and contemporary despair, poetic metaphor and literary wit, *Under the Volcano* is consciously intended by its author to depict the ritual of mystic initiation. Thus Lowry says:

My novel consists of twelve chapters, and the main part of the narrative is contained within a single day of twelve hours. In the same way there are twelve months in a year and the whole book is enclosed within the limits of a year, while that deeper layer of the novel—or the poem—which derives from myth is linked at this point with the Jewish Cabbala, where the number twelve is of the greatest importance. The Cabbala is used for poetic ends because it represents Man's spiritual aspirations. The Tree of Life, its emblem, is a kind of complicated ladder whose summit is called Kether, or Light, while somewhere in its midst an abyss opens out. The spiritual domain of the Consul is probably Qliphoth, the world of husks and demons, represented by the Tree of Life turned upside down and governed by Beelzebub, the God of Flies.

In the Jewish Cabbala the abuse of magic powers is compared to drunkenness or the abuse of wine, and is expressed, if I remember rightly by the Hebrew word *sod* [sic]. Another attribution of the word *sod* signified garden, or neglected garden, and the Cabbala itself is sometimes considered as a garden (naturally similar to that where grew the tree of forbidden fruit which gave us the knowledge of Good and Evil) with the Tree of Life planted in the middle. In one way or another these matters are at the base of many of our legends regarding the origins of man, and William James, if not Freud, might be in agreement with me when I affirm that the agonies of the drunkard find a very close parallel in the agonies of the mystic who has abused his powers.

. . . My effort has been to clarify as far as possible whatever at first presented itself to me in a complicated and esoteric manner [i.e., the Cabbala]. . . . The novel can be read simply as a story during

* See Appendix A for books Lowry consulted.

which you may—if you wish—skip whole passages, but from which you will get far more if you skip nothing at all.*

In a letter to Derek Pethick that includes many valuable asides, Lowry claims that his hero is more than just a drunkard—a magician, perhaps:

As a protagonist on one plane [the Consul] is a faustian gent. The book somehow assumes . . . with some philosophic justice . . . that the ancestor of us all was perhaps a magician. The Consul has been a Cabbalist (this is where you get the Garden of Eden). Mystically speaking, the abuse of wine is connected with the abuse of mystical powers. Has the Consul perhaps been a black magician at one time? . . . a black magician is a man who has all the elements of the world (not to say universe) against him . . . this is what the Consul meant in Chapter X (written in 1942) enumerating the elements. In Chapter V (in the bathroom) you have a hint of similar dark forces in the background. The implication is that an analogy is drawn between Man today on this planet and a black magician . . . (The Consul implies his war, as opposed to any Hugh might be involved in, is far more desperate, since it is against the very elements themselves and against nature. This is a war that is bound to be lost) . . . The Consul has thus turned into a man that is all destruction . . . in fact he has almost ceased to be a man altogether, and his human feelings merely make matters more agonizing for him, but don't alter things in the least; he is thus in hell. . . .†

Twentieth-century symbolist literature developed in France of the 1890s. Coupled with theosophical fringe groups, ranging from the "evil" Satanists led by such figures as Joris Karl Huysmans in Paris to the benevolent Hermetic Order of the Golden Dawn (to which Yeats belonged), the literature associated with this movement often represented a reaction against the bourgeois realism of the mid-nineteenth century. Springing essentially from Théophile Gautier's preface to *Mademoiselle de Maupin,* the new doctrines centered originally on the beauty of artifact, and, when carried to their extreme, they focused eventually on the "beauty"of obscurity and ugliness. By the time Baudelaire had taken the critical reins away from the Parnassians, the writer had degenerated from high priest of classical ideals to drug-induced creator of diabolical delights.

* Lowry, "Preface to a Novel."
† Lowry, *Letters.*

Enid Starkie might be describing Malcolm Lowry's persona, Geoffrey Firmin, a descendant of this tradition, almost as much as Rimbaud, himself a Cabbalist, when she says:

> . . . he believed that like Faust, he had acquired supernatural powers through the agency of magic, that he imagined, like him, he had become the equal of God and eventually that his sin of pride and arrogance had been as great, as deserving of condemnation. Yet the study of Magic was not sinful in itself . . . it was the fount of all wisdom . . . a science of nature by which man could eventually possess a relative omnipotence. . . . But there were two kinds of magic—black and white; and two kinds of magicians—Joseph and Moses the good; Merlin and Julian the Apostate the bad. . . .*

The problem of black versus white magician fascinated Lowry too, but for a slightly different reason. He was interested in these figures as symbolic counterparts in man himself, that is, as psychological and spiritual paradoxes represented by id and ego, good and evil, Christ and Lucifer. "Black magician" is an occult term designating those highly gifted, often charming individuals who, for egotistical purposes, have elected to follow the left-hand path through the dense stages of matter that lead eventually to hell. White magicians, on the other hand, devote themselves to a life of self-control and an expansion of consciousness in order to serve all that lives.

The bridge between the symbolist writer and the art of magic is created by the power inherent in language. Thus, Baudelaire, for example, can easily make the literary transition from Swedenborgian correspondences between the spiritual and sensuous worlds to a poetic rendering of "Heaven and its wonders, and Hell." The technique applies equally to Rimbaud, Lowry, and all occult thinkers for whom ". . . there is a mysterious symbolism contained in the word itself, often in the separate letters of the word, and a secret meaning in each number." † To see through the "shells" into the "reality" of things became the goal of the symbolist poet, thus limiting his role as creator (in the traditional sense) and emphasizing instead his role as seer or medium. In order to induce visions many symbolist poets resorted deliberately to alcohol and drugs, thereby engendering, albeit unwittingly, the con-

---

* Starkie, *Rimbaud*.
† *Ibid*.

temporary obsession with art as disease. By the twentieth century, therefore, Thomas Mann could comfortably characterize the artist-magician as a man with a sick spot, a man predisposed by his neurosis to hallucination and a talent for magical operations.

The deliberate invitation to madness as a stimulus for creative power did not remain the property of the French symbolist movement alone. Writers like D. H. Lawrence picked it up to challenge, in a reversion to Rousseauism, a sterile society to return to the promptings of the "blood," or instinctual urges. The "beat" poets, still faithful to the trend, have experimented with mescalin and Zen to a similar end.

All these writers, however, were and still are merely echoing ancient symbolic parallels between drunkenness and ecstasy. Coupled with the infusion of divine (and therefore prohibited) knowledge is an enormous predisposition for suffering. Self-mutilation and mental and emotional torment are prescribed not only by Rimbaud and Baudelaire but by such esotericists as Eliphas Lévi and, in some instances, even by the legitimate Cabbala as well. Evil is not to be shunned. For the artist it provides secret knowledge unavailable to the plodding healthy man. He must know it and subdue it, employing equilibrium as his most powerful weapon. If he is successful, he will eventually learn that what he had, in his ignorance, originally perceived as evil is actually another aspect of God's multiple manifestations. Should he fail, the abyss awaits him.

Nevertheless, according to Cabbalistic tradition, there is a dual purpose in this deliberate self-immolation for it is considered that the Messiah himself will descend into the *Kelipah,* the pit of the demons, in order to release the holy power necessary for the redemption of mankind. This archetypal journey into the world of the shells becomes an example for men. They too must taste of sin in order to absorb the holiness locked inside until, at last, sin itself has disappeared forever and sanctity is all that remains.

Where Rimbaud dissociated himself completely from the religious overtones of this type of suffering, where Lawrence abhorred asceticism in any form, and where Yeats created his own occult vision of the universe, Lowry managed to endow his brand of magic with essentially Christian overtones of sin, purgatory, and redemption. Combining the influences of Kafka, Bunyan, Marlowe, Dante, and Dostoevsky with his own penchant for occult symbolism, he employed the Cabbalist's mysteries as a vehicle for the theme of guilt and separation from God. There was, therefore, definite literary value in his observation when he stated: "Even if they don't get the esoteric messages, there will be something of the universal in there [*Under the Volcano*] for everyone." * And what more colorful analogy to Lowry's basically Christian conception of the sinner than the occultist's "brother of the shadow"?

Influenced also by the theosophy of Jakob Böhme, Lowry conceived of man's evil as residing in the measure of his distance from God, in the total absence of the ability to love, rather than the actual committing of sacrilegious or criminal acts ( for example, the Black Masses of the French Satanists). The symbols he uses, such as misappropriated wine and irresponsible treatment of magical powers and incantations, merely conceal the more serious sin of spiritual isolation.

For the mystic the end and essence of evil is, after all, his transcendence of it. The magician sees only *particular* evils with their own particular magical remedies. It is thus a progression from the specific (limited) to the general (universal) view of the world that represents the turn from the left-hand (sinner's) path to the right-hand path of the saint. Lowry's multileveled vision of the universe proved a double-edged sword in that his peripatetic "Christian" magician always had one foot pointed toward heaven and the other always just poised above the *Kelipah,* which, in the form of drunkenness, was his constant obsession. This medieval (essentially black and white) view of man's moral predicament pervades *Under the Volcano.*

Having established that the Consul was a black magician, Lowry was faced with the problem of proving that his hero was also a holy sinner who had managed somehow to adopt the roundabout, nevertheless successful, path to God in accordance with his own more extreme Protestant tradition of kenosis, of coming to God the hard way, so to speak. It requires that the sinner experi-

---

* Mrs. Lowry, interviewed by the author in May 1964 in Los Angeles, California. At this time she also noted that her husband consciously derived much of the material for his novel (even including direct quotations and recurring motifs) from Dante, Marlowe, Goethe, Dostoevsky, and Bunyan. She also referred to the fact that he claimed an identification with Kafka both as a tormented individual and as a dabbler in Cabbala.

ence what Hegel called the "Golgotha of the absolute spirit" in all its starkness.

In the manuscripts for the ensuing novels, however, one senses Lowry's intention to create a man who is not basically evil, a man who will filter through into the other protagonists as white magicians and blundering but salvageable artists and jazz musicians (such as the characters in *Hear Us O Lord From Heaven Thy Dwelling Place,* a collection of Lowry's short stories). In this light the Consul assumes a subtler role, closer perhaps to that of the "mystic rebel" who must suffer humiliation, pain, and perhaps martyrdom before reaching his goal.

For the reconciliation of his Western religious dualism, Lowry turned to the religions of the Orient and to the Middle Eastern Cabbala, where the thousand faces of good and evil, beauty and ugliness are resolved in the paradox of the "I am that am becoming." In his vision of paradise, a short story entitled "The Forest Path to the Spring," he finally establishes the point where above meets below and so reconciles also the point where magician and mystic become one—the axis of love.

# *Lowry and Cabbala*

THE METHOD of the occultists has changed little since the days of Madame Blavatsky and her circle in the early part of this century. Centered largely in southern California, the theosophists, Yogis, and herb dieters continue to publish slender volumes of mystical advice supposedly derived from the Grand Lama himself. For this segment of those interested in magic, the Cabbala serves the function of no less than an official *grimoire,* authenticated by the fact of its age, exotic language, and Judeo-Christian foundations.

For serious scholars of Cabbala, the issue of practical theurgy remains a naïve and pointless stalemate. Men like Gershom Scholem, Louis Ginzberg, and Joseph Blau are not interested in the "miraculous" results of trances induced by mentally whirling the Hebrew letters of the alphabet for hours on end; they concern themselves rather with issues like the historical, social, and cultural affinities of Jewish mysticism with Egypt and the Gnostics, with eighteenth-century "enthusiasm," and with Christian Platonism. By confining their studies to such areas as linguistic changes in the Aramaic *Zohar,** they tend to maintain a safe and secular distance from the opaque and hazardous messages inscribed therein.

All magical-mystical traditions are united in the following basic premises of occultism:

1. The universe consists of one sacred substance;
2. There is a manifestation of this substance in an ethereal form;
3. There are degrees on the scale between the highest and the lowest order of things;
4. The world of opposites merges into equilibrium;
5. As above, so below;
6. Ultimately, all is resolved into One;
7. Man is a microcosmic reproduction of the macrocosm;
8. Sex is a divine mystery;
9. Man can transcend his condition and become divine through meditation on the spiritual self.

The last characteristic is indispensable to understanding the plight of the hero in Lowry's novel.

In addition, one might compile a number of general characteristics shared by all artist-magicians. The truly committed, regardless of school or intention, are:

1. Voluntarily asocial or antisocial and thereby often secretive
2. Viewed by their society as holy, afflicted, demonic, or neurotic
3. Attempting to imitate God in order to know him face to face (mystic), to create (artist), to obtain supernatural powers (magician)
4. Ritualistic by nature or discipline
5. Chaotic in their life habits

* Major book of the Cabbalist movement, written in the thirteenth century by Moses de Leon.

Unfortunately only a very small sampling of Lowry's personal library remains, but his personal correspondence, unpublished notes and journals, and other valuable information from interviews with Margerie Lowry about her husband and his work, along with the testimony of friends and biographers, all indicate that Malcolm Lowry was a voluminous reader with a special penchant for books of an occult nature. He began his voracious attack on anything in print during his seafaring days on extended, dull voyages around the world and continued to read through Cambridge well into even the worst times of his mature life. Therefore, the likelihood of his overlooking a book, especially one concerning his favorite topic of hermetic "correspondences," is negligible; the list of obscure books he did read is formidable—the more bizarre and exotic, the better.

His wife reports that while at work on the novel, he began to explore the theosophists' canon ranging from P. D. Ouspensky to Swedenborg to Blake, James, Böhme, and Yeats and further down into the arcana of A. E. Waite, Eliphas Lévi, Madame Blavatsky, and, through an amazing "coincidence," into the inner sanctum of Frater Achad's enormous collection of occult books. According to Mrs. Lowry: "He jolted up from his work one day to declare that his hero was a black magician." (Lowry had always been fascinated by Haitian voodoo, even before this "magical" period; and in an early 1940s trip to the Caribbean, he disappeared for three days in the company of a native witch doctor and supposedly attended certain secret initiation ceremonies, of which, having been sworn to secrecy, he never spoke afterwards. For him, voodoo was superior to all other religions because it was "based upon the actual existence of the supernatural.")

The next day the census taker appeared at the shack. When invited in, he introduced himself as Charles Stansfeld Jones—secret name: Frater Achad—Cabbalist, white magician, founder of a Chicago group of illuminati (now defunct), and owner of an enormous occult library. This white magician and author of Cabbalistic books and treatises announced that he had come to help the author with his Cabbalistic studies, and thus began a long and happy friendship during which, Margerie Lowry recalls, occurred daily experiments with astral body projection, *I Ching,* Yoga, and a detailed course on the Cabbalistic tree of life—a reproduction of which was hung on a wall in the shack. The esoteric books listed in Chapter Seven of *Under the Volcano* were actual titles included in Jones' library.

After months of immersion, Lowry insisted on calling a halt to the experiments for fear of "opening doors which should remain closed." He did, however, continue with the reading and research insofar as it pertained to his work.

Even his close friendship with Dylan Thomas, recalls Mrs. Lowry, was based almost as much on their common love of the grotesque and magical as on their mutual penchant for spirits of a more immediately obtainable order.

Harvey Breit's introduction to the recently published *Selected Letters of Malcolm Lowry* aptly characterizes Lowry's insistence on a magical view of life as follows:

Throughout the letters [the reader] will come upon a constellation of words revolving around a magical or fatalistic concept: *mystery, talisman, diabolic, cabbala, esoteric, demon, coincidence, luck, infernal, spell* and the *Law of Series.* Lowry held to some of this, not only as a writer. He was involved . . . with the invisible world.

. . . For his great novel has magic in it, achieving the fusion of opposites, containing the tranquility of a noble style and the fever of a contemporary vision.*

# *The Two Cabbalas*

WHEN LOWRY became more or less of an adept of Cabbala under the tutelage of Frater Achad at Dollarton Beach, he had little interest in the intellectual or historical aspects of the doctrine. Here at last, in the maze of colors, numbers, and heavenly worlds, he had found the mythopoeic framework for his novel. A convenient combination of Neoplatonism, pantheism, Orphism, Indian mysticism, and general occultism, Achad's "Cabbala" was a far cry from the original. Nevertheless, it provided Lowry with the paraphernalia he sought for his intended re-creation of the life and

* Lowry, *Letters.*

death of a Cabbalist. He had determined that the Consul's destruction should have the universal significance of the sacrificed god-man, or scapegoat. In addition, Lowry found that by combining the idea of the Jungian archetypal hero with the Faust legend, he could simultaneously indulge his taste for magic and mysticism. Moreover, he succeeded in creating a hybrid tragic form by crossing classical, medieval, and Protestant mystical concepts of human fate as Goethe did before him.

Notes and letters, as well as the books Lowry read, indicate that he leaned in the direction of magic as a means of human communication with the supernatural, or what scholars call practical Cabbala—the Babylonian influence on Jewish Cabbala of the fourth and fifth centuries A.D. emphasizing demonic magic and incantation. There is no evidence that Lowry ever studied the Hebrew language, but he was conversant with an English translation of the *Zohar* by MacGregor Mathers and with certain recurring Hebrew words and formulas, references to which are scattered through *Volcano* and the *Letters*. From his wife's information regarding their study of the tree of life, one can conclude that Lowry was in some way familiar with the Cabbalistic doctrines of emanation as presented in the *Sefer Yetzirah,* a Hebraic source written around the eighth century A.D. that is permeated with Gnostic influences. Lowry's acquaintance with the text, coming from Frater Achad, was probably limited to an English version.

In the late 1920s Frater Achad was the leader of a group of Chicago theosophists designating themselves brothers of the *Collegium ad Spiritum Sanctum,* who specialized in Cabbalistic manipulation of number and color symbolism with an eye toward prophesying future world events. His doctrines are propounded in two rare books privately printed in limited editions, *The Reception of the Bride* and *The Anatomy of the Body of God.* One reading of both is sufficient to classify Achad's doctrines as corruptions of the original Cabbala. And since he was Lowry's only immediate source of information, Lowry's knowledge of the Cabbala was probably limited to a mongrelized version. This did not prevent him from applying himself seriously to its study (actually, there are more readily available "illegitimate" than there are "legitimate" books on Cabbala) and interpolating its symbolism into his own work.

When one speaks of Cabbala, one can be referring to nearly anything of an occult, mystical, or theosophical nature, for the word has come to embrace the spectrum of mystical subjects. The Cabbala is regarded, in fact, as the conventional spearhead of occultism. There are, to start with, the "Jewish Cabbala" and the "Christian Cabbala." Then, as in a set of Chinese boxes, there are systems within the broader systems, and subsystems of those, and so on. For example, within the Jewish Cabbala itself we can discriminate between theurgical and speculative systems, between German and Spanish, between rationalist and pietist. When we extend our study further to the Christian Cabbala, we find that we must differentiate between Neoplatonists and hermetics, between Blavatsky and Böhme, between alchemy and medicine—in short, a historical complexity rivaled only by the doctrines of the Cabbala itself.

## JEWISH CABBALA: HISTORY *

Although its doctrines had been long in circulation, the name "Cabbala" appears for the first time in the eleventh century in the writings of Solomon ibn-Gabirol (Avicebron), a Spanish adept of the Jewish theosophy. The word is derived from the Hebrew *"kibbel"* ("to receive"). Therefore, "Cabbala" has become synonymous with "tradition," or information handed down orally. Only so general a term could possibly encompass theories as numerous and as profound as divine emanation, cosmogony, angelology, man and his role in the world, evil, ethics, and redemption.

Practicing Cabbalists pursue the origins of their tradition even further, tracing it all the way back to God, who supposedly taught it to a select company of angels, who bestowed the knowledge on Adam, who in turn gave it to Seth. From there it was passed on to Noah, who taught it to Abraham, who granted it to the learned of Egypt. Moses, of course, received some of this knowledge during the period of bondage in Egypt. But even more dramatically, he received the full message from God himself on Mount Sinai. After

---

* For the sake of convenience all practical magic will here be referred to as "illegitimate" Cabbala regardless of the religious distinctions established. Speculative or mystical Cabbala is generally considered "legitimate" by scholars although, admittedly, the boundaries are often obscure.

transmitting it to the seventy elders, Moses died, leaving the tradition in the hands of such successors as David, Solomon, Isaiah, Daniel, Ezekiel, Enoch, and finally Rabbi Simeon ben Yohai, who put it in writing for fear that it would be lost after the destruction of the temple during the second century A.D. To protect its precious contents from the unworthy, Rabbi Simeon ben Yohai codified the material in allegory and symbol. So runs the Cabbalists' justification for the existence of the *Sefer Zohar* (Book of Splendor), supposedly set down by the loyal disciples of Simeon ben Yohai exactly as he dictated it himself.

Opposing opinion claims that the *Zohar* is no more than a fabrication on the part of Moses de Leon, a thirteenth-century Spanish Cabbalist. In fact, Henri Serouya discounts the early Cabbalistic manifestations of the fifth and sixth centuries entirely, relating them to practical Cabbala and thereby dismissing them as bastardized Babylonian superstitions. However, we must consider also that it was during this very vague early period of Jewish mystical thought, infused with Persian, Neoplatonic, and neo-Pythagorean elements, that the seeds of theosophy as such were sown.

The earliest Jewish *Merkabah* (Throne) mysticism centers on the apocryphal Book of Enoch (c. A.D. 3–6). Throne mysticism is the Jewish counterpart to the Gnostic *pleroma,* the divine plane populated by angelic hosts and demiurgic powers. Derived essentially from Ezekiel's vision of God's throne and its surrounding ministering angels and spirits, *Merkabah* mysticism attempts to symbolize the various ascending stages of mystical experience in the form of the halls of a great palace. If successfully traversed, these halls lead to a subsequent passage through the seven heavenly palaces. The journey is usually completed in twelve days, during which the initiate must remain in a trance state.*

*Merkabah* mysticism also produced a controversial work considered most important by later Cabbalists, the *Shiur Komah* (Measure of the Body [of God]), consisting of cryptic numerical references to various organs, each signifying another mystery.

The Geonic period (c. A.D. 500–900) opens the doors on the earliest philosophical-mystical writings extant. In spite of the generally crude anthropomorphic descriptions of the deity that charac-

---

* This aspect of ritual suffering is relevant to Lowry's hero, who goes through twelve chapters of hell in an inebriated state to his martyrdom.

terize this period, the *Sefer Yetzirah* (Book of Formations) is traced to somewhere between the third and eighth century in Palestine or Syria. Though still heavily dependent on Christian and pagan Gnostic influences, the *Sefer Yetzirah* postulates the heart of Cabbalistic theory for the first time—namely, the doctrine of the *Sephiroth,* or "emanations," as they are commonly called.* Its major contribution to Cabbalistic thought lies in its description of the Creation by means of divine intelligence working through media akin to Plato's *logoi* (the *Sephiroth*). From Pythagoras perhaps, the author (or authors) derives the theory of "physical" creation of the world through numbers, hence the emphasis on mystical permutations and combinations designated as *notarikon, gematria,* and *temurah.*† The *Sefer Yetzirah* concludes, therefore, that God created the world out of form, number, and word. All of this is set in the form of an aphoristic monologue spoken by Father Abraham, who enumerates also the thirty-two mystical paths leading to communion with God (the basis for the Sephirotic tree of life).

Another characteristic derived from Neoplatonic sources is the articulation of the doctrine of metempsychosis, a belief that continued to permeate the entire Cabbalistic movement throughout the Middle Ages and beyond.

The more documented Cabbalism of the Middle Ages (c. 1150–1250) witnessed the growth of the first Hasidic (Pietist) movement under the guidance of Eleazer of Worms in Germany; the mystic school of Provence led by Isaac the Blind (c. 1200); and

---

* Though not sure of its precise meaning, scholars agree that the word "*Sephirah*" is derived from the Hebrew "*Saphar*" ("to number"). Certain Cabbalists have confused it with the Greek "*sphere,*" thus giving rise to the confusion between *Sephiroth* and "worlds" or "essences"; "powers" or "divine attributes"; "entities" or "planes of consciousness."

† Because the Hebrew alphabet represents both letter and number, the *Sefer Yetzirah* designates formulas based on the very intricate transmutations of *notarikon,* that is, interpreting individual letters of a word as an entire sentence; *gematria,* finding connections between Hebrew words and phrases with equal numerical value; *temurah,* interchanging letters by means of certain specified formulas—hence the preoccupation of later Christian Cabbalists and alchemists with magical codes and nonsense syllables supposedly derived from the original Hebrew or Aramaic. Such methods were ascribed to Saint John (a supposed Cabbalist) by those who, by means of *temurah,* read the numerical value of the Hebrew words for "Nero Caesar" as 666, the Beast of the Revelation.

the Spanish school of Abraham ben Samuel Abulafia (1240–c. 1292).

The school of Eleazer of Worms adopted all the intricacies and follies inherent in the practices of *notarikon, gematria,* and *temurah.* Concerned with metaphysical problems, they ignored the speculative trend of the Provençal Cabbalists and concentrated instead on magic, altruism, and asceticism. From their preference for theurgy there emerged the *Sefer Raziel,* a theosophical treatment of the "grand mysteries" of nature that justified the use of amulets and talismans.

Those who generally followed the doctrines of the Provençal Isaac the Blind were more concerned with the philosophical implications of creation through emanation. Isaac himself named the individual *Sephiroth* and wrote a commentary on the *Sefer Yetzirah.* Nachmanides (1194–1270), a disciple of the school, began to interpret the scriptures by means of mystical analogy. He concentrated on proving creation *ex nihilo,* but in more Platonic terms. He postulated the doctrine of God's voluntary contraction to a tiny point that, no longer capable of containing the elements, spilled over, thereby forming all created things. This theory of creation is referred to as *Tzimzum,* or contraction. From here Nachmanides, influenced by Gnostic trends, went on to state that God's original creature was androgynous. He too contributed to the growth of practical Cabbala by subscribing to belief in physiognomy, astrology, and mystical martyrdom. Continuing along the lines of the *Sefer Yetzirah,* he adopted the theory of metempsychosis, but limited the journey of the soul to three rounds (*Gilgul*). The trend implicit in the doctrines of mystics like Nachmanides (and, for example, his contemporary Rabbi Jacob Nasir, who established four worlds based on the four letters of the Holy Name) was a Neoplatonic reaction against the pervasive rationalism of Maimonides and his Aristotelian school of Jewish philosophy, which flourished from 1135 to 1204.

By far the most prominent text of the period is the *Sefer Bahir* (Book of Light), edited by Rabbi Nehonia ben Hakana around 1180 in Provence. Gershom Scholem considers this obscure treatise on the nature of man and the universe to be a compilation of earlier texts brought to Europe from the East along with works of

*Merkabah* mysticism. Here, for the first time, appears the Cabbalistic idea of physical man as an image of God: *Adam Kadmon* (Great Man) is, in essence, the physical reflection of God Himself; *Adam Tahton* (Small Man) is the microcosmic embodiment of the macrocosm. In the book *Bahir* we also find theories pertaining to the sexual origin of the universe—that is, God as masculine and his *Shekinah* (Supreme Essence) as feminine. The idea that the universe could not exist without the female aspect is typically Eastern and seems to justify Scholem's conclusion about the Oriental sources for the *Sefer Bahir*. Much of this material reflects the continuing bond between medieval Cabbalism and *Merkabah* mysticism, especially the exotic variety, with its attendant emphasis on magic.

Abraham ben Samuel Abulafia (1240–1292) achieved a synthesis between the metaphysical speculations of Isaac the Blind's Provençal School and the practical extravagances of the early *Merkabah* mysticism. Leader of the Spanish school, Abulafia inculcated his disciples with a Messianic approach to their studies, advocating meditation and mystical contemplation. This form of Cabbala emphasized gaining knowledge of God by means of communion with the *Sephiroth,* the "emanations," themselves through concentration, and achieving ecstatic visions and prophetic ability by contemplating the twenty-two Hebrew letters. Abulafia postulated seven stages of contemplation and seven methods of scriptural interpretation. He accepted the idea of an androgynous God; and from contemporary Christian mystics like Bonaventure, he adopted the belief in a trinity embodied in the three sacred names of the Divinity: JHVH, ADONAI, ELOHIM. However, the most important aspect of his approach lies in this emphasis on *contemplation* as the means to divine absorption. His leading disciple, Joseph ben Abraham Gikatilia, forsaking the speculative portion of his master's work, indulges entirely in the study of the intricacies and practical effects of *gematria* and *notarikon* and ushers in many of the superstitious and nefarious practices that later came to be designated as Cabbala.

The *Sefer Zohar*—written in Spain about 1290 and almost synonymous with the word Cabbala itself—is a pseudepigraphic compilation of homilies and commentaries on the Pentateuch written in Aramaic by Moses de Leon. Allegorical and bombastic in his stylistic approach, the author intended to represent his material as a genuine transcript of the doctrines set down by the faithful disciples of Rabbi Simeon ben Yohai during the second century A.D. The *Zohar* still remains, after seven centuries of dispute, a powerful and controversial text. Following the Gnostic trends of his predecessors, de Leon continued to stress the esoteric nature of the exoteric universe.

The *Zohar* is divided into eighteen unrelated books with such titles as "The Book of Concealment," "The Greater and Lesser Assemblies," and "Secrets of the Torah." Subject matter ranges from a description of the seven palaces traversed by the soul after death to a study of chiromancy, to an entirely Cabbalistic interpretation of the Song of Songs. Rabbi Simeon ben Yohai remains the leading figure throughout and whether he is rebuking a disciple insensitive to his cryptic analogies or calmly prophesying his own death in detail, he is the connecting link behind this seemingly heterogeneous theosophical collection.

Isaac Luria of Safed (1534–1572) founded what has been identified as the modern school of Cabbala. Entirely abandoning the speculative tradition in favor of practical Cabbala, he attracted a more eccentric following. His school is representative of a new phase of Jewish mysticism that would eventually evolve into alchemy. Luria's own theories have been passed down by his disciple Hayim Vital in a collection of notes entitled *Etz Chaim* (Tree of Life). They contain the master's personal interpretation of transmigration of souls: that there are male and female souls as well as "parent" and "daughter" souls representing weaker and stronger human personalities. For the most part he ignored the previous emphasis placed by the Cabbalists on the universe in general and centered his studies entirely on man. This led to preoccupations with the magical quality of the words employed in prayer and to the arbitrary creation of new holy days. His sect finally degenerated into a cult that prefaced the onset of the hysterical Messianism of the succeeding century.

Although the Sabbatian movement must be considered as only tangential to the mainstream of Cabbalism, it cannot be ignored, for it embodies all the darker elements of the so called illegitimate Cabbala. The theurgical dabblings of Abulafia and Luria are mere child's play compared to the demoniacal rantings of the Smyrnaborn Sabbatai Zevi (1626–1676). An impostor and psychopath who possessed remarkable powers of showmanship and persuasion, Sabbatai Zevi had convinced himself early in life that he was the Messiah. He had incorporated all the rags and tags of degenerated Lurianic Cabbalism as a young man, and, following in the practical tradition, he had determined to use it for furthering his own cause. In the name of Cabbala he imposed his own mania on the miserable persecuted Jews of the Middle East and incited in the process a mass hysteria that even his unmasking could not restrain. He perverted the sexual symbolism of the *Zohar* in order to justify the licentiousness in which he and his followers indulged. Uprooting credulous Jews from their families and homes (even as far as Eastern Europe), Sabbatai Zevi finally provoked the secular authorities of Islam, who eventually destroyed him.

This heresy, with its attendant disastrous effects on the Jewish community, had barely been extinguished when it was revived again in the following century. Joseph Frank, an eighteenth-century Polish self-styled Cabbalist, rationalized the orgiastic and sexual excesses of his cult by claiming the impossibility of evil in a world created by a perfect God. Like Zevi, he embraced the murkier aspects of Cabbalism and created such havoc both within and without the Jewish ghetto that his followers were eventually forced to convert to Christianity.

The Polish Hasidic movement of the eighteenth century, which grew, in part, out of earlier German Pietism, represented the last stronghold of legitimate Cabbalism. Designated as *Baal Shem* (Masters of the Holy Name), these Cabbalists supposedly possessed supernormal powers and were idolized and feared by the mass as magicians. They based their beliefs and practices mainly on the tenets of the older Provençal school of Isaac the Blind and Nachmanides. Although these great Hasidim have been brought to life in the tales of Martin Buber, the movement occupies only a minor place in contemporary Jewish thought. Today, almost all Jewish Cabbalism remains within the narrow confines of Hasidism. Set off once again from the mainstream of Jewish rationalism, its mysticism focuses mainly on the Messianic role of the Jewish people.

Strictly speaking, therefore, the term "modern" Cabbala refers to the school of Isaac Luria and his successors. From a literary

standpoint, however, there is more pertinent theosophical material in post-Lurianic Christianized Cabbalism. There were, then, seven major schools of Jewish Cabbala:

1. Isaac the Blind—philosophical, Neoplatonic
2. Nachmanides—theosophical, concerned with creation, emanation
3. Eleazer of Worms—Pietist, magical
4. Abulafia—contemplative, number mysticism
5. Nehonia ben Hakana—microcosm/macrocosm theories
6. Moses de Leon—*Zohar,* official synthesis of all schools
7. Isaac Luria—modern Cabbala, emphasis on magic, assumed by Christians as genuine

## JEWISH CABBALA: DOCTRINES

The doctrines of Cabbala are entangled in a labyrinth of mythology. The paradoxical language of the *Zohar* itself serves as a warning to the uninitiated. To begin a study of its systems is to set out on an immense and dangerous sea. "If thou desirest to mount thou wouldst not be able, and in descending, thou wilt meet an abyss without any bottom"—the abyss into which Geoffrey Firmin is finally tossed after a life of misapplied Cabbalistic study. Yet even the abyss itself is represented dualistically: it is the source of wisdom on the one hand and chaos on the other.

The intricacies of Cabbalistic symbolism can be unraveled only by restricting one's study to the areas of cosmology and natural law, sin and the problem of evil, man and initiation. These metaphysical categories and others are all subsumed under the structure of the *Sephiroth.*

The *Sephiroth* function as mediums between the infinite and the finite. They exhibit the results of the influence of spirit over matter, the relationship of God to His created universe. Although their exact nature is still contested, the *Sephiroth* are uniformly acknowledged as the means by which the *En Soph* (Boundless) is manifested in the universe. Some claim that they are distinct from God, merely agents by which He enacts His will. Others (like Luria) say that God is at the base of the *Sephiroth,* not outside, but that He is not identical with them for He is *One,* and they imply multi-

plicity. Azriel, a student of the school of Isaac the Blind, sees the *Sephiroth* as the beginning, the principle of all that is subsequent and limited. The pantheistic basis for this theory of emanation resides in the fact that God willingly left His fullness or self-sufficient being in order to be revealed to man.

It is in the doctrine of *Tzimzum*, "contraction," that we come closest to the negative or limiting force involved in the creation. God, by contracting to a tiny point, allows his essence to overflow its vessel, spilling out into ten worlds that can be mapped out in the form of a tree of life. The androgynous *Kether* (Crown, or First Manifestation) contains within itself all the succeeding *Sephiroth*. From *Kether* emanate the opposing male (positive) and female (negative) principles, *Chokmah* and *Binah* respectively. These three highest *Sephiroth*—often signified as father, Creative power; mother, Wisdom; son, Intelligence—represent the world of *Aziluth* (Supreme Intelligence). (This is a facet of Cabbalistic cosmology incorporated by Christians as representing the Trinity.) The energy emanating from active *Kether* to passive *Binah*, embodied in color symbolism as yellow-red to sky blue, represents the act of creation by sexual means. The essential mystery of this triad is that of three contained in one, projected into time as past contained in present, contained in future.

In the form of a zigzag lightning flash, the emanating energy continues, formulating the second triad in its path: *Chesed* (male, Mercy), *Geburah* (female, Severity), and *Tiphereth* (the sun, Beauty). These three *Sephiroth* represent the moral world, *Beriah*, which contains the divine throne and halls and also houses the souls of the pious. The opposing pillars of mercy and severity also symbolize the construction of matter, length, breadth, depth, and their positive and negative poles.

The next triad comprises the world of *Yetzirah* (Creation): *Netzach* (male, Triumph); *Hod* (female, Splendor), and *Yesod* (neuter, Foundation); all symbolize the dynamic world of energy. This world is ruled by Metatron, who presides over ten classes of angels.

The tenth *Sephirah*, *Malkuth* (Kingdom), represents our world of matter, *Assiah*, in which the angels called *Ofanim* intercede on man's behalf in the war against *Samaël* (Prince of Darkness, destructive energy). His kingdom is found in the abyss beneath *Mal-*

*kuth* and is designated as the *Kelipah,* or world of rinds and shells, the empty husks of matter. Thus, when King Solomon says, "I went down into the garden of nuts," he is referring to mystical speculation, which, of necessity, requires the trial passage through the shells, or the abyss.

All the worlds are characterized by individual systems of color, number, and sexual order somewhat resembling the Ladder of Jacob or Professor Lovejoy's great chain of being. Colors represent stages of development along the branches of the Sephirotic tree. *Kether* (Crown), the highest of the high, or the unknowable, is white, colorless, but contains all colors. *Tiphereth* (Beauty) is purple and contains all the potential colors of *Malkuth,* the world of matter. White stands for grace or mercy; red symbolizes justice; and green represents a union of the two. The admixture of colors and Sephirotic symbolism in general attains an important role in the experiments of alchemists and practical Cabbalists.

The Sephirotic worlds vary in their degree of distance from the *En Soph* (Boundless). Thus, the *Kelipah,* the world of rinds and shells, being farthest from the creative force, is subject to the grossest impurities of matter. For matter is the utmost limit of spirit.

Because sex is the primordial form of creation, harmony in life can only be derived from a properly functioning sexual union. *Kether* (male, Crown) and *Malkuth* (female, the Kingdom) symbolize the marriage between the ideal and real worlds. Therefore, the image of the river flowing through the Garden of Eden in Genesis, says the *Zohar,* is really an analogy for the fecundating power of God's light as it flows from the male to the female principle.*

Numerology, with special emphasis on the numbers 12, 7, and 3, plays a definitive part in the Cabbalistic cosmology. Twelve are the signs of the zodiac, the months of the year, and the human activities of seeing, hearing, smelling, tasting, touching, copulating, dealing, walking, thinking, becoming angry, laughing, and sleeping. When broken down into components of three, three serve love, three serve hate, three engender life, and three engender death.

---

* In later Christian and theosophical interpretations, God's light becomes synonymous with etheric or divine fluid. Sexual disharmony such as that suffered by Lowry's hero and his wife, the Consul's impotence, and the references to Yvonne's barrenness are punishments suffered by the unbalanced souls in *Kelipah.*

The heart, ears, and mouth are organs of love; the liver, gallbladder, and tongue, organs of hate. God rules over all—that is, One (God) over three (heaven, sea, land), three over seven (planets, days), seven over twelve (signs of the zodiac, tribes of Israel).*

The material world with its elemental qualities has been created essentially from the three mother letters M (the essence of water, which stands for guilt, earth, cold, the belly); A (the essence of air, which stands for equilibrating power, the atmosphere, temperate states, the chest); SH (the essence of transmuting fire, which stands for guilt, heavens, heat, the head).† The entire system is subject to the fundamental law of the Cabbala—the law of equilibrium.

Evil is therefore distinguished by means of good, and good is distinguished by means of evil. An ever-functioning system of opposites, mediated by harmony, rules over the mental and physical universe, whose new creations emerge from their fusion. Balance and harmony through creation are perpetuated by means of sex. Equilibrium is thereby equated with love, and love is personified in the female form of the *Shekinah,* or the mystery of God's everlasting presence. Love is the bridge between above and below; when a man crosses that bridge, he finds that he has arrived at a condition of oneness with all things. Only love, say the Cabbalists, is as strong as death.‡

It is the absence of the *Shekinah* that denotes the presence of evil. Supposedly, with the first sin of Adam, she ascended, away from man, withdrawing further into the seven heavens with each ensuing sin committed by six succeeding generations of men. Corresponding to the seven sinners are seven righteous men who bring

* Lowry methodically recapitulates the *Sefer Yetzirah's* emphasis on these numbers. He includes three protagonists, the recurring number 7 on the mysterious horse, twelve chapters and months of the novel's action. See the letter to Jonathan Cape in Lowry, *Letters,* for the author's own details.

† M is represented by Geoffrey, who is drowned in the barranca, affiliated with the water sign of Scorpio and with secret guilt; A, by Yvonne, the equilibrating power between the brothers, temperate in contrast to Geoffrey's alcoholism, identified with space and the stars, who finally meets her death by being carried up to the seven Pleiades; SH by Hugh, a guilty adulterer, passionate hothead, who suffers death by fire. The three protagonists are representative of three elemental states of existence.

‡ Thus, the greatest human punishment resides in the incapacity to love. This accounts for the terrible isolation of Lowry's hero.

her back to earth.\* But if a man cuts himself off from God, the *Shekinah* will leave him to Satan, who will drag him further into the pit until he suffers the torments of hell in his life. In this case the *Sephiroth* are reversed and form instead a "tree of death" whose roots emanate from the *Kelipah*. Evil in Cabbala is presented as a type of nihilism. Rejection of the divine spark within the self leads to self-hatred and self-exile. The *Shekinah* departs from such a sinner, who is then free to work out his redemption or to embrace his degradation. Although some Cabbalists regard incarnation into life on earth as a God-given opportunity to redeem one's soul, others regard human life as a continual struggle against the seductions of the demonic powers of the *Kelipah*. Still, in spite of its Gnostic affiliations, Cabbala does not subscribe to a strict dualism. Therefore, evil itself is said to exist for the hidden purposes of God. For man, however, evil is synonymous with imbalance (especially discord between masculine and feminine principles), with mistaking appearance for reality, and, finally, with emptiness. Anagogically, moreover, man's inner state is reflected in the outer world of nature. Adam's primordial sin is reenacted by the sins of each successive great soul. The banishment is therefore transformed into a symbol of something beyond the allegory of the Fall.† Herein lies the connection between sin and redemption discussed in Protestant terminology as kenosis. The Cabbalistic concept of the Messiah differs only slightly in that it recognizes no formal savior, regarding *each man* as a potential Messiah in his individual responsibility for sin and in his acceptance of suffering. It is no small wonder that such a doctrine could, in the hands of a Sabbatai Zevi, become a dangerous weapon.

These metaphysical abstractions for evil are all concretized in

---

\* Note also Lowry's identification of Yvonne with the female figure of *Shekinah*, especially in her ascent to the seven Pleiades upon being rejected by the Consul.

† Lowry's twelve chapters reflect the events of the twelve hours of Adam, who is created in the first, remains an unformed mass in the second, has limbs stretched in the third, is given a soul in the fourth, stands on his feet in the fifth, names all things in the sixth, is given Eve in the seventh (Geoffrey meets Yvonne at 7 A.M.), lies with her in the eighth (and on giving her up misuses his generative powers thus attracting succubi), is warned of God's prohibition in the ninth, transgresses in the tenth, is judged in the eleventh, and is expelled from the garden in the twelfth.

elaborate rituals. One of these is the scapegoat ritual performed on the Day of Atonement in order to exorcise the demonic forces. This magical ceremony consists of sacrificing a male goat to "Azazel" the incarnation of evil. The scapegoat propitiates Satan because of its power to transmute evil into good. The ritual, which also emphasizes ridding the world of "insolent dogs" runs, in part, as follows:

> The insolent dogs must remain outside and cannot come in,
> I summon the "Old of Days" at evening until they are
>     dispersed,
> Until his Will destroys the "shells."
> He hurls them back into their abysses, they must hide
>     deep in their caverns. . . .*

Judgment itself is rendered in metaphorical, almost allegorical terms. A cock cries, warning the man that he is about to die and be judged for twelve months in hell. Hell's chieftains wait to accuse him. If he is acquitted, then he may leave of his own volition. If not, then the magistrate of the *Gai-hinnom* flings him over a precipice into the chasm below. Then follows the storm, symbol of purification, announced by lightning flashes.

What place does man occupy in this system inhabited by angels, demons, and elementals? Comprising three natures—*Nefesh,* the earthy or animal soul; *Ruah,* the moral or ethical soul (seat of good and evil); *Neshama,* rational or divine soul—man is free to choose between good and evil and thereby determines his own fate. The purpose of life in this material world is to prove oneself worthy of higher Sephirotic stages by means of trial and retrial through reincarnation. Man's ultimate purpose is mystical reunion with the divine source. Nevertheless, there is only a dangerously thin line separating mysticism from magic—that is, selflessness from egomania. Should a man choose magic as his medium, he dares to assume God's place, exchanging the real world for an illusion. This entails a choice of evil on the part of the *Neshama,* and the siege

* Note Lowry's incorporation of the ritual animals throughout the story —the goat that follows Yvonne and Hugh and the pariah dog that attaches himself to Geoffrey and finally is cast into the abyss with him. The death of the Consul is in itself entirely ritualistic, combining many of the elements referred to above.

of the demons ensues. A magician like Sabbatai Zevi, for example, was subject to fits of depression, hallucination, and bodily pain engendered by the demonic forces he had called into play. The torments endured by the magician-sinner are matched only by those willingly undergone by the holy man during his initiatory descent into the abyss. The difference lies in the end result—whether one returns or remains in the darkness forever depends on the nature of the mission and the sincerity of the penitent. The mystic recalls that the Messiah himself will journey through the *Kelipah* to accomplish the redemption of Israel and mankind.

In direct contradistinction to *Shekinah,* God's positive female essence, the feminine principle is the indirect source of all the difficulties encountered by the race. In keeping with its Gnostic legacy, Cabbala traces severity, fear, and their demonic outgrowths to the *Sephirah Geburah,* which is central to the pillar of the left-hand side of the throne crowned by *Binah,* the first negative force. In her positive aspect, she is mother of all things. In her negative aspect, she is judge and accuser (compare the Indian goddess Kali). A man who neglects this "left hand of God" cannot hope to complete the ascent with success. In fact, the entire key to the mystery of initiation lies in the reunification of the male and female principles: joining *Kether* with *Malkuth* (God with His Kingdom) is a task only to be undertaken by a true Messiah, a soul capable of the direst suffering—again, a doctrine easily transformed by Christian Cabbalists. Symbolically, he must make his way through ruined gardens overgrown with poisonous weeds and thorns. He is often forced to live a life of apparent depravity among whores, gamblers, and thieves, taking their sins upon his own shoulders.*

His knowledge remains entirely secret, hidden from the world in the magical number 70, which simultaneously represents the number of elders to whom Moses himself passed the doctrine, the word *"Sod"* ("secret"), and wine. The Cabbalists regard wine as the outstanding symbol of creation, the guarded words that have never been revealed to man, the hidden spiritual energy underlying all things. The "grapes" are all created things emerging from the

---

* Cf. the Consul's repeated visits to the hellish cantina at Parián, perhaps derived by Lowry from Böhme's mystical enunciation of suffering as a condition of joy.

"vine"—an epithet for God.* From here it is only a short step to
the Zoharistic view of Noah's drunkenness as a blasphemous revelation of divine secrets and to Philo's view of man's union with God
as *sobria ebrietas,* sober drunkenness. No wonder such elaborate
precautions were taken by Rabbi Simeon ben Yohai and his disciples, who sought to conceal their secret knowledge from the uninitiated in a welter of paradoxical phrases and arcane allusions.
Small wonder too that these "initiates" lived in isolation or, more
commonly, that they suffered persecution and even martyrdom at
the hands of those very ignorant masses whom they sought to
avoid. (A fate shared by Cabbalists like Rabbi Simeon ben Yohai,
Moses de Leon, and, among Christian Cabbalists, Pico della
Mirandola and Giordano Bruno.)

Perhaps these strange rituals † and deviations from accepted religious practices served to estrange the Cabbalist. But we must
view the estrangement as deliberate in part, for persecution and
humiliation are the self-imposed lot of the dedicated Cabbalist.

## CHRISTIAN CABBALA

Unfortunately, a study of the Christian Cabbala does not lend
itself to an orderly history of schools or doctrines. Beginning ostensibly with the number and letter mysticism of Raymond Lully
(1225–1315), brought into Christian scholarly circles by Pico
della Mirandola (1463–1494) during the Renaissance, developed
along theurgical lines by Cornelius Agrippa (1487–1535), and
molded into Christian theosophy by Jakob Böhme (1575–1624),
the Christian Cabbala becomes a catchall for every variety of
hermetist, alchemist, visionary, poet, and fanatic from the four-
teenth through the seventeenth century, when Newton drew the
final boundary line between science and magic. After the seventeenth century it enjoyed a temporary popularity and subsequently
faded into obscurity. From the eighteenth century onward, philos-

---

* Lowry's source for the misused wine symbol is the *Zohar.* See his own
explanation in Lowry, *Letters.*

† For example, prefourteenth-century initiations into knowledge of the
Tetragrammaton (secret name of God derived from a complicated process
of *notarikon*) were practiced exclusively in water. Because the utterance of
this mighty word supposedly resulted in terrible changes in nature and the
elements, many Cabbalists were regarded as evil sorcerers.

ophers like Schelling, Hegel, and Schopenhauer as well as Free-
masons, theosophists, and charlatans like the Comte de Saint-
Germain, Alessandro de Cagliostro, and Eliphas Lévi borrowed
so-called Cabbalistic ideas that, for the most part, had nothing at
all to do with the Cabbala of the Jews.

The essential difference between the Jewish Cabbala and its
Christian derivatives lies in their opposing attitudes toward evil.
Whereas Jewish Cabbalists consider evil to be merely a temporary
state of privation, their Christian counterparts propose the existence of positive states of sin and damnation. Only this point of
difference can be clearly discerned; all the remaining doctrinal
changes were based on appropriately selective borrowings from
such corrupted Jewish sources as the school of Isaac Luria.

The first significant evidence of a Christian interest in Cabbala
are in Pico's nine hundred *Conclusiones,* written in 1486. Receiving
his information second hand from Flavius Mithridates, a converted
Jew with an eye toward pleasing the Pope, Pico freely imposed
Christian interpretations on Cabbalistic doctrines. Thus began an
intellectual fad that was to circulate among such illustrious Renaissance scholars as Johann Reuchlin, Erasmus, Robert Fludd,
and Henry More. Pico's purpose was twofold: as a scholar-mystic,
he wished to justify the current of magic and hermeticism underlying Renaissance Christian mysticism by aligning it with legitimate
ancient sources. As a Christian Hebraist, on the other hand, he
wished to reconcile Christian history with its Hebrew origins, proving their affinities by alleged comparisons between Cabbala and
Christianity. Moreover, he fervently believed that the Cabbala held
the key to certain conversion of the Jews once they had been convinced of its prophetic contents.*

His *Conclusiones* provoked condemnation on the part of church
authorities, especially for their emphasis on the belief that no science could prove the divinity of Christ better than the Cabbala. On
the other hand, orthodox Jews passionately rejected this sort of interpretation, maintaining that Christian doctrines like the Trinity
and incarnation were misinterpretations of Cabbalist symbolism.

---

* Pico's assumptions had been anticipated by Raymond Lully (1235–1315),
who, in the *Ars Magna,* had stated that Cabbala was the epitome of natural
revelation, finding its completion in Christian revelation. For this, he was
accused of heresy.

By forcibly distorting the Aramaic text in such possible translations of the phrase "the cross" to "His cross" or reworking the word "shadow" to read "cross" (a change dependent on missing vowel points), he altered the idea of a Jewish Messiah to fit a definition of Jesus as *the* Messiah. Employing such linguistic manipulations, he progressed even further into the symbolism of the *Sephiroth* (confusing the Hebrew *"saphar,"* to number, with the Greek *"sphere"*) and declared that the original triune world (symbolized by *Kether, Chokmah,* and *Binah*) was no less than the doctrine of Trinity itself.

Despite the fact that much of the material came from the forgeries of converts and deliberate misreading of original texts, such "scholarly" practice had not been limited to Cabbala only, for men like Pico, Postel, and Reuchlin had already Christianized Plato, Porphyry, and even Hermes Trismegistus by similar teleological means. They mixed Christian theology with principles that were foreign to it and, in some cases, even refuted it. They surrounded themselves with mystery, indiscriminately combining Cabbalism, Pythagoreanism, Platonism, Ptolemism, and Christianity.

Pico even went so far as to claim that natural magic was weak unless combined with Cabbala. He then divided Cabbala into two branches: the letter and number mysticism based on Abulafia's school and the natural magic aligned with practical Cabbala, which provides communication by means of written characters with supercelestial spheres beyond the stars. His distinction between "good" and "bad" magic—namely that it depended on the qualities of the practitioner—did not mollify the church, which condemned *all* magic. His declaration that the use of Hebrew, or words derived from the Hebrew language, was essential to any magical operation had an impact on magicians and theosophists that endures still. Pico also differentiated between what he termed "pure" Cabbala, equated with direct mystical communion with the First Cause, and "natural magic," which depended on intermediaries such as the stars during the process. Thus he widened the breach, already existing in the Jewish Cabbala, between practical magic and religious contemplation. Although both seek to accomplish similar ends, contemplation is relegated to the intellectual part of the soul (*ruah*), while magic is accomplished by the natural *spiritus* (*neshama*).

By means of this unqualified marriage between magic and Cabbala, Pico was the first to bring about an onslaught of obscure "Cabbalistic" treatises for generations to come.* From this point on, Renaissance white magicians dispensed with demonologic books of the Middle Ages, such as *The Keys of Solomon,* in favor of the newly sanctioned practical Cabbala.

Each of the key figures in the history of the Christian Cabbala during this period plays an important role in changing it: Pico, in accordance with his own Christian propensities; then Johann Reuchlin, who combines the Christian format with Pythagorean and Abulafian number and letter magic designed to communicate with angelic hierarchies; and finally, Cornelius Agrippa, in whose hands the entire system grew cruder and more practical, inclining toward alchemy and herb medicine. The results of their incursions on this obscure system of the Jews turned Pico's Cabbala into a complex system of Christian correspondences through which men could perform miracles, provided they possessed the ritual keys. And after Agrippa we come still closer to the idea of a magical religion held together secretly by its theocracy, characterized, for example, in the seventeenth-century beginnings of Freemasonry.

Followers of Luther also proved interested in Pico's theories, and there began a general correspondence between scholars of different countries and varying opinions. Prompted by his admiration for Pico's *Conclusiones,* John Pistorius, an English scholar, attempted to publish all extant Cabbalistic works but completed only one volume. Nevertheless, translations such as these influenced scholars like Robert Fludd, who brought astrology into Cabbalism, Henry More and the Cambridge Platonists, whose interest centered mainly on Cabbala as a means for converting Jews, and English writers of a mystical turn of mind like Vaughan, Browne, and Thomas Burnet. Even Erasmus makes note of the current fad in his correspondence.

Cornelius Agrippa (1486–1535), even more directly than Pico, merged Cabbalism with occultism once and for all. He carefully postulated a division between three worlds—natural, celestial, spiritual—with corresponding magical practices specified for con-

---

* Cf. the type of "Cabbala" that claimed Lowry's fascination in books like Agrippa's *Natural Magic,* and Thomas Browne's *Religio Medici,* to name a few of the saner varieties.

tacting each of them. Interested mainly in relationships between spirit and matter, he allotted theurgical qualities to each of the elements, attempting to separate the grossness of matter from the refinement of spirit. This naturalist philosophy, combined with elements of Christianized Cabbala, appears in the works of Paracelsus (1577–1644), gradually finds its way into German Protestant thought in general, and finally, through wandering scholars like the German Von Helmont, is disseminated throughout seventeenth-century Europe.

The last of the giants of seventeenth-century Christian Cabbalism is Jakob Böhme (1575–1624). Coinciding with a widespread revival of mysticism in Germany, evidenced by the simultaneous rise of Rosicrucianism and Freemasonry, both emphasizing philanthropy, toleration, Egyptian and Cabbalistic symbolism, Böhme's doctrines prove most influential on modern Christian Cabbalism. Heavily dependent on Agrippa, the Italian mystic Nicholas de Cusa, and Paracelsus, Böhme considered all life to be double, each state of nature implying its opposite—for example, there is no light without darkness. Therefore, what may appear one way to the gross senses is actually its opposite in the world of spirit. Through such reasoning he concludes that suffering is the condition of joy. In one supreme moment (presumably during illumination), they merge.

Later German romantics like Novalis, Schelling, and Goethe transposed Böhme's theories in accordance with their own. Novalis postulated the doctrine of the three natures of man: terrestrial, sidereal, and divine, building an entire masonic mythology in his *Klingsohr's Fairy Tale* and *Hymns to the Night*. Goethe, who for a time read widely in eighteenth-century German Pietist literature under the tutelage of Susanna von Klettenburg, adopted similar theories about nature and incorporated them into *Wilhelm Meister* and *Faust*. And Mozart's *Magic Flute* is, of course, constructed of Masonic and mystical symbols. We also owe an indirect debt to Böhme for inspiring subsequent idealistic philosophers like Leibnitz, whose acquaintance with Cabbala is documented in his correspondence and is illustrated by his conception of world creation as an emanation from a divine monad.

An uneducated shoemaker, Böhme was an isolated individual with relatively limited influence on his contemporaries. His Christian brand of Cabbalism, with its emphasis on ectasy and illumination, came into prominence only with the rise of the romantics, to whom his simple, obscure life must have appealed more than to the sophisticated German Pietists of his own period. But it is Baron Knorr von Rosenroth (1636–1689), worldly German scholar and Pietist, who provides the real bridge between "legitimate" and "illegitimate" Christian Cabbala of the modern period. We might say that he was the Christian Isaac Luria (from whom, incidentally, he derived his *entire* view of Cabbala). Somewhat conversant with Böhme's view of *Adam Kadmon*, Rosenroth claims unreservedly that this is a metaphorical term for Jesus Christ. The microcosm, macrocosm, higher and lower worlds, as well as demonic spirits—in short, all the elements of magic and practical Cabbalism—are now incorporated into "Cabbala."

In 1684 Rosenroth published the *Kabbala Denudata* in Latin, a book that, although based entirely on Christian interpolations and interpretations of the already degenerated Lurianic Cabbala, continues to exist as *the* great theosophical textbook of Cabbalism. Although he did study the Cabbala with a Jew in Holland, his interests gravitated toward proving that Jewish and Christian beliefs were identical at the core.

Oettinger, Rosenroth's eighteenth-century disciple, followed his master's example and studied Cabbala with a Jew at Halle, a new center of the Christian German Pietist movement that had begun at Frankfurt early in the century. He found that Luria and Böhme were compatible and also subscribed to the belief that the Cabbala is a prophecy of Christianity.

It was then only a short step from scholarship to wild speculation ranging as far as extensions of Christ as *Shekinah* and to claims that both Saint Paul and Saint John were Cabbalists, with the Apocalypse representing a kind of Christian *Zohar*. By the mid-eighteenth century, German Pietism, already engulfed in the stream of religious enthusiasm sweeping all Europe, reached men like Swedenborg, who entirely reconstructed an already reconstructed Cabbalistic system in conformity with his own very personal visions of heaven and hell. Blake, his natural successor, introduced a new literature of vision and prophecy, and the now totally unrecognizable Cabbala was fully assimilated into the mainstream of romanticism.

In addition to Sturm und Drang mysticism, the Oriental craze caught the imagination of Europe and gave opportunities to such enterprising charlatans as Cagliostro and the Comte de Saint-Germain. Primarily involved in amusing the aristocracy for their own fun and profit, men like Cagliostro and Saint-Germain employed personally created exotic versions of "Cabbala" and dubious "Oriental" rituals of debatable value. Court de Gebelin had carved a path for these practices by creating a synthetic *Book of Thoth*, a purported transcription of the original Egyptian tarot; and in 1670, Abbé de Villars had delighted readers with his novel, *The Count de Gabalis*, a *jeu d'esprit* treatise on practical Cabbala. Even Pope had had his share of fun with this type of material, on which he based his "Rape of the Lock."

The eighteenth century was split in its attitude toward Cabbala; on the one hand there were the Christian Pietists influenced by Hasidism, Swedenborg, the tradition of Böhme, and Sturm und Drang poets influenced by every type of Cabbalist springing from the Agrippan school. On the other, there was the aristocracy, part Freemason, part dilettante, courting the exotic for its own sake.

In the nineteenth century occurred a reversion to the scholarly seriousness that characterized the Christian Cabbalism of the Renaissance. An 1820 translation of Hindu scriptures evoked general interest in Eastern religion and thereby temporarily overshadowed the Cabbala. After 1850 the investigations of scholars like Max Müller in Germany brought about much of the enthusiasm for exotic material that eventually resulted in distortions of Eastern philosophies identical with those previously committed on Cabbala. The theosophical movement is such an example. Emerson and his fellow transcendentalists in the late 1830s and 1840s are another —both trends being extremely representative of the spiritual temper of the mid-nineteenth century.

Although by now Cabbala had become unrecognizable amid the bric-a-brac of Oriental philosophy, members of the Theosophical Society (founded in 1875) like J. F. Molitor and MacGregor Mathers made an attempt to legitimize their beliefs by translating "Cabbalistic" works. In 1890, Mathers condensed Knorr von Rosenroth's enormous Latin canon into one volume entitled *The Kabbala Unveiled*. Spurred on by new revelations such as these, scholars in different countries once again grew busy, and traffic in Cabbalistic correspondence expanded. With Böhme and Paracelsus now available in English and French, theosophists like Eliphas Lévi, Papus Encausse, and Madame Blavatsky were free to promote occult "scholarship" in spite of their very uncritical, often invented sources. Twentieth-century Rosicrucian and Masonic scholars like A. E. Waite and Wynn Westcott make a valiant attempt to edit the works of their predecessors with objectivity; but they neglect to investigate the actual Hebrew sources, relying instead on the by now totally unreliable versions of Renaissance productions. During the Blavatsky period, however, Hebrew scholars like Adolph Franck, Isaac Mayer, and Christian Ginsburg did make some valuable contributions to knowledge of the Hebrew Cabbala.

Still popular in the twentieth century, the theosophical movement continued to advance, with headquarters opening around the United States. Works like William James' *The Varieties of Religious Experience* and Bucke's *Cosmic Consciousness* had established a current of popular American interest in such spiritual matters.

When compared with its multiple Christian derivatives, the general scheme of the Hebrew Cabbala appears relatively simple. Post-Renaissance Cabbalists did not stop with such erroneous assertions as the identification of the angel Metatron (guardian of the throne) with the spirit of Christ or equating the *Shekinah* itself with Christ. Interested more in the practical aspects emphasized in astrology, numerology, and the like, they created an even more elaborate cosmology than that found in the *Sefer Yetzirah*. Obsession with intricate symbolic systems characterizes the Christian Cabbalist movement from Agrippa onward, so that by the time Eliphas Lévi makes his magical declarations in the nineteenth century any resemblance between older Cabbalistic symbols like the tree of life, *Adam Kadmon,* or emanation and the new theosophy is coincidental. In spite of, or even perhaps *because* of, their synthetic systems, the new Cabbalists insisted on their legitimate foundations. Pico, in the spirit of scholarship, had based his doctrines on "ancient Hebrew sources," thereby establishing a tradition that extended from Paracelsus to Blavatsky. Legitimacy once established by the customary tribute to the Jewish sources and heresy hopefully avoided by a nod in the appropriately Christian direction, the individual Cabbalist felt free to pursue his particular path into the unknown.

With the years, however, the admonition against magic seems to vanish, or at least it begins to weaken. Eliphas Lévi (defrocked Catholic priest), high priest of mid-nineteenth-century theosophy, incorporates magic rather easily into his occult framework by merely ignoring the idea of history altogether. Beginning with the relationship between Cabbala and the Chinese *I Ching*, he goes on to state that ". . . The *Sepher Yetzirah,* the *Zohar* and the *Apocalypse* are the masterpieces of occultism; they contain more meanings than words. . . . The *Apocalypse* summarises, completes and surpasses all the science of Abraham and Solomon. . . ." * Note the continuance, however, of the traditional Christian gesture.

The seventeenth-century English writer Thomas Burnet devotes volumes to a discussion of the origin and end of the earth.† His work entitled *The Sacred Theory of the Earth* is particularly relevant to a discussion of Lowry's symbolism, for it is here that we come across the major images of volcano, abyss, water, and fire that so haunted his twentieth-century successor. In Burnet's view, the original world (analogous to the Zoharistic reference to the world of the kings of Edom, which God created and then destroyed before his creation of our world) was smooth-surfaced. With God's decision to destroy it came the opening of the great abyss, which lay, quite literally, under the volcano. From this turmoil emerged our world—scarred and pockmarked, with the infernal world (*Kelipah*) just below. After elaborating on such "scientific" points as allegorized in Genesis, Burnet speaks of the results of this initial upheaval, which, for him, is identical with the flood story: ". . . for in the new form'd Earth, the Sea is cover'd and inconspicuous, being an Abyss, not a Sea. . . ." He goes on, in the apocalyptic fashion of his times, to prophesy the destruction of *this* earth by fire, in contrast to the previous destruction by water. The survivor of this second upheaval is, in the words of Saint John, "to eat of the Tree of Life, which is in the midst of the Paradise of God."

* Lévi, *History of Magic.*
† See Appendix A.

Even more important, Burnet provides a further clue to the Cabbalistic identification of Lowry's hero. In declaring Noah to be the key figure in the continuation of the race of Adam, he makes a side reference to the Zoharistic interpretation that later becomes a significant theosophical symbol of initiation. Noah's drunken nakedness is interpreted as an allegorical reference to his careless revelation of divine secrets. Like Adam made drunk by the fruit of the tree, Noah is intoxicated by the vine he himself planted. Like Adam also, he recognizes his shameful condition too late and is punished immediately after.

A favorite metaphorical carry-over from the Hebrew *Sod* (Secret), the Noah story continues to represent a lesson to all would-be Cabbalists. Two modern versions of the story follow:

1. Noah plants a mystical vineyard and partakes freely of its produce, but his determination all through is to try experiments with a view to discovering wherein consists the sin of the world, and if possible to find a remedy. Noah's humiliating state while intoxicated refers only to his destitution of adequate knowledge, even after much research, and this ignorance was exposed by his failure to have found the sought-for remedy. . . .*

2. The fact that Noah pressed the grapes—as Eve is said also to have done—partook of the juice and so became drunken, is affirmed to contain a mystery of wisdom. . . . So also Noah was concerned with an experiment, having set himself to fathom that sin which had caused the fall of the first man. His intention was to find a cure for the world, "in place of Eve and her poison"; but he became drunken in laying bare the Divine Essence without having the intellectual strength to fathom it. This is why Scripture says that he was drunken and was uncovered within his tent. The meaning is that he raised a corner of the veil concerning the breach of the world which ought always to remain secret . . . the tent of Noah was really the tent of the vine.†

Although they do adopt the original Sephirotic scheme, Christian Cabbalists are more preoccupied with the architecture of the bibli-

---

* Colville, *Kabbalah.*
† Waite, *The Holy Kabbalah.* The entire allegory, with its references to drunkenness and ensuing humiliation, corresponds to the condition of Lowry's hero. Burnet even refers to Noah as the responsible captain of the ark containing the last remnants of the world. The Consul too is an alcoholic shipmaster; and Hugh, his alter ego, boards a ship in order to "save the world."

cal world, the setting for the Fall. They go into great anachronistic detail about the names of the paradisal rivers (Hiddekel, Euphrates, Pison, Gihon), contrasting them with the rivers of Hades (Phlegethon, Acheron, Lethe, Cocytus) and assigning to them qualities of negative and positive spiritual power.

From their assimilations of Persian mythology, they create a religion of "light," claiming that the whole process of creation is the evolution of light, thus evoking later allusions to "etheric fluid" as a physical embodiment of the abstract *Shekinah*. They even go to the extreme of declaring that the Garden of Eden actually represents that virgin area of the self that unconsciously contains divine secrets and waits to be explored.

One outstanding feature of Christian Cabbala is the tendency toward value judgment, attributing positive and negative qualities to mythological visions like that of Ezekiel, for example. Where early Jewish Cabbalists like Isaac the Blind were content merely to speculate on the meaning of such mysteries, Knorr von Rosenroth felt free to make specific interpretations. To him, the vision of Ezekiel coincided both with the Apocalypse of Saint John and with the astrological forces of the zodiac. Therefore, the sphinxes of the first vision are equal to the beasts of the second, which are characterized by the zodiac signs of Taurus, Leo, Scorpio, and Aquarius. Scorpio has two aspects: as a good emblem it is represented by the eagle, as an evil emblem by the scorpion.

Thus becomes clear the eclectic, almost compulsive course of logic typical of Christian Cabbalists, who began with Sephirotic concepts and concluded by burying them under a variegated mass of mythological assimilations.

In the general cosmogony of the Christian Cabbalists, there is great concentration on *Malkuth,* the *Sephirah* representing our own world, and *Kelipah,* the demonic world beneath it. This is to be expected in view of the greater dichotomy between good and evil and the specifically Christian problem of original sin. Our world is regarded as a fallen one, cut off from the tree, barely poised above the abyss. The lower, demonic kingdom personifies unbalanced force and is ruled by the serpent whose coils surround *Malkuth.* The *Kelipah* contains its own inverted *Sephiroth* created by destructive force, God's creation turned upside down, as it were. Each of the archangels of the higher worlds has his counterpart in "the shadowy waters under the earth." With the evolution of human consciousness, however, these demonic forces became organized as a force of positive evil and so brought hell into existence.

Usually embodied as the war between light and darkness, evil must not be conquered but brought into cosmic harmony. Satan is therefore the *Shekinah* of *Assiah,* the dark world of action and matter. The secret of the Cabbala is to transmute the darkness. Pico even equated the letters of the name of Satan with those of the Tetragrammaton, claiming that one who could effect the transposition of letters would find each in the other, a process that entails the conquest of chaos. There can be no entry into the world of spirit until both good and evil are overcome.

The Messianic man is identified with the *Aleph* (first letter of the Hebrew alphabet) card of the tarot, the fool followed by a hound. The fool is actually supreme intelligence, or God's representative, and the dog represents inferior intelligence, or the mere earthly reflection of God.* Great mystics and redeemers go straight up the middle pillar of benignity, suffering no temptation from the *Kelipah.* They do not receive magical powers. The wise fool must experience every stage of existence along the Sephirotic tree. He, however, is subject to the terrible destructive powers. But when he achieves his goal, magical power is conferred upon him.

The ordeal takes place over a twelve-month period. Three chieftains of hell act as overseers who torment the victim with the extremes of fire and ice, the first ordeal representing the equilibrating of *all* the opposing forces within himself. Then he must totally isolate himself from his surroundings; and finally, he must meditate and force himself to become one with the spirit of his meditations. Should he succeed in his vision, he is master of an awesome power that he is free to use as his heart directs. But he must beware, for those who precipitously thrust themselves into the spirit world may be crushed under the weight of their own evocations and ultimately plunged into what Eliphas Lévi has called "the abyss of madness."

* Again relevant to Lowry's novel, the symbol of the fool followed by the dog is beautifully incorporated in the scenes where the Consul, both drunk and foolish, unwillingly befriends the pariah dog who is cast into the abyss with him. We must also take into consideration Lowry's close literary association with Dylan Thomas, whose pleasure in reversing the words "God" and "dog" stemmed from his own fascination with things occult.

Should the powerful spirit be drawn into a weak or debauched being, it will blind and eventually destroy him.

The perfect celestial man (what Agrippa refers to as the grand solar man, replica of the entire zodiac), or what Jewish Cabbalists called *Adam Kadmon,* is depicted as a kind of titan. Because he is regarded as such a figure, the biblical Adam becomes a personification of the entire creation. This persistent emphasis on man's role as that of a magician destined to seek beyond good and evil causes the Christian Cabbalist to dwell on the significance of his natural surroundings. By compiling a veritable bestiary based essentially on hermetic, Apocalyptic, and mythological writings, the Christian Cabbalist has codified many recurring Cabbalistic themes. The serpent, for example, represents both extremes of good and evil. From Genesis is derived the image of accuser, perpetrator of imbalance, and seducer. As Leviathan, the serpent is identified as the destructive force that awaits the initiate in his descent under the waters, the sea being a glyph of initiatory wisdom. The caduceus, or serpent staff, normally an equilibrating force, can also be transformed into a three-tongued brazen serpent (cf. the destructive power of the trident—*Shin* become pitchfork), whose number is 666, the beast of revelation.

However, Blavatsky continually recalls the symbol of wisdom characterized by the snake that coils about the earth grasping its tail in its mouth. Along similar lines, Lévi gives us a more specifically valuable insight into the meaning of the reiterated animal references in Lowry's novel when he characterizes the beneficent Jehovah as a magnificent horse and *Chavajah,* the demon, as a horse gone mad that overthrows its rider, tumbling him into an abyss. Three other animals play a symbolic part in ritual magic: the bull symbolizes the earth; the dog is Hermanubis, or Mercury; the goat is fire, the symbol of generation. Derived from the Mithraic rites, the Spanish bullfight is considered by theosophists to be symbolic of the death of the beast (666 again), whose blood issues forth in ten drops representing the ten *Sephiroth.* The entire process is supposedly an allegory of regeneration. Although overladen with Egyptian and alchemical symbolism, the importance of the dog and the goat is related to the exorcism ritual of the Jewish Cabbalists discussed previously.

Later Cabbalists also found the vagaries of *notarikon* to be amenable to their esoteric ramblings. In the maniacal search for correspondences, Christian Cabbalists of the French school went so far as to equate the four tarot suits with the four letters of the Tetrad: wands = *Yod;* cups = *He;* swords = *Vau;* pentacles = final *He.* They claimed that he who became adept at manipulating the names was possessed of the original keys of Solomon—that is, knowledge of the universal mysteries. Certain powers inherent in the *Sephiroth* could be withdrawn and imbibed, so to speak. The powers evoked, however, could be tricky, even vindictive.

The new Cabbalists believed that in separating the *Yod* from the Tetragrammaton, God had created Eve, the active, and thereby demoniacal, force—hence the preoccupation with the nature of woman and the threefold nature of *Yod* (note that three *Yodin* form the magical letter *Shin*) as severity, mercy, and mildness, a trinity in unity. The three *Yodin* come to represent the three trunks of the tree of life as well as the further attributes of activity, passivity, and equilibrium.

In her capacity as seductress, Eve gives the fruit (believed by Lévi to be intoxicating grapes) to Adam. She is associated also with the serpent as a Messianic force in her capacity of the *Matrona,* or merciful one. Her positive symbols are gardens, springs, the moon. But she is also represented as *Geburah,* the *Sephirah* of severity and judgment. In her demonic aspect she is symbolized by ruins, deserts, and deep and tangled forests. The final mystery of the *Sephiroth* consists in the union of the harsh female and the merciful male branches.

From the time of Pico, however, the important philosophical implication beneath this blanket of Sephirotic symbolism is the Christian Cabbalist's conclusion that "the sin of Adam separated the *Shekinah* from the other branches of the tree of life." The central problem for the magus is, therefore, the restoration of integrity to the universe. The unleashing of chaos resulted from the indiscretions of Adam and Noah (both archetypal grand failures) as conveyed by their allegorical drunkenness. The task of all Cabbalists thereafter is to repair the breach between God and man by symbolically rejoining His absent *Shekinah* with the Sephirotic tree. The procedure is perilous, consisting of superhuman trials and the ever-present possibility of damnation. In each case the undertaking is solitary, the magician's life lonely. The slightest mis-step results in unbearable torments, the slightest self-indulgence in immediate divine and demonic recrimination. The guardian of the sacred vine wears the mask of the fool and is therefore subject to humiliation and martyrdom. Yet he willingly accepts the risks, for the restoration of order to the universe supersedes all self-concern.

In many ways Malcolm Lowry personally identified himself with this God-intoxicated hero. The Cabbalist's battle with the elements represented for him both the inner war that takes place in the soul and the outer war against the forces of the universe itself—from his terrible fight against alcoholism and insanity to the cry against world war and the potential atomic destruction of the race. In the story of the Consul, he embodied these concerns in an emblematic language derived largely from the legends described throughout this chapter. Geoffrey Firmin has discovered many divine secrets; he is, in fact, intoxicated with them. He has acquired a type of clairvoyance, and he foresees the calamity approaching in the form of a world war. He is, unfortunately, not a savior; he is not des-tined to restore the order but is, instead, the scion of Adam and Noah, one of the epic failures whose pathetic-heroic attempt to overcome the chaos results in his own destruction. Still, we cannot claim total defeat, for his creator prefaces his story by claiming: "Whosoever unceasingly strives upward . . . him can we save."

# PART
# II

# THE SYMBOLISM
# OF
# *Under the Volcano*

*For the book was so designed, counterdesigned and interwelded
that it could be read an indefinite number of times and still not
have yielded all its meanings or its drama or its poetry: and it is
upon this fact that I base my hope in it, and in that hope that,
with all its faults . . . I have offered it to you.*
                                                —Malcolm Lowry to Jonathan Cape,
                                                *Letters*

*The Consul's awareness encompasses an astonishing range of
image and symbol, from the Greeks and Elizabethans to the
cabala and jazz. . . . Lowry wove these references not to
bewilder his audience, but because he was always haunted by
what he took to be the occult correspondences among events
and ideas.*

—CONRAD KNICKERBOCKER

# A General View

FOLLOWING IN THE TRADITION of the Christian Cabbala, Lowry
freely incorporated myths and symbols from many other cultural
sources. However, still intent on maintaining the Cabbalistic substructure, or what he referred to as the "poem" of the book, he
utilized the stylistic method of the *Zohar* itself, a book that is entirely composed of allegorical correspondences.* Take, for example,
the external world of nature as a representation of inner states of
consciousness; the Consul's alcoholic bliss is denoted by his idyllic
descriptions of the cantinas; his anguish is symbolized by the vultures, dogs, and overgrown gardens. Then there are the seemingly
casual references to themes like anti-Semitism that later emerge as
motifs of great significance with regard to the plot structure itself.
Each of the twelve chapters is really one degree in the twelve
stages of initiation, as Lowry attests in his explanatory letter to
Jonathan Cape. In addition, each tarot suit is embodied in its own
particular symbol: wands—the Consul's ever-present walking
stick; cups—the drinking theme; swords—a razor and later a
machete; pentacles—the zodiac.
A magical aura is diffused by the heightened awareness, the sen-
sitivity to an animistic nature featuring astrological coincidences
and spirit messages that characterize the Consul's state. These supernatural components are bound together by the central image of
initiatory wine, which bears the property of divine and demonic
communication; in this case, mescal, about which Lowry says:

* *Under the Volcano* is, therefore, a novel of many levels, and can be
read from perspectives as far-ranging as history and politics as well as
mysticism and religion.

But mescal is also a drug, taken in the form of buttons, and the transcending of its effects is one of the well-known ordeals that occultists have to go through. It would appear that the Consul has fuddledly come to confuse the two, and he is perhaps not far wrong.*

The "occult ordeal" is carefully framed not only in traditional numerological detail but is equally evident in the dominating symbolism of the volcano (or the pilgrimage of ascent) and the barranca (descent into the abyss). Archetypal in its significance, the volcanic peak usually symbolizes the home of the god or gods from which emanate thunder and lightning. Located at the base of the volcano is the cavernous abyss that represents hell.

In view of the ambiguous overlapping of above and below, the initiate cannot be sure of attaining his goal. He may be ritually tortured nevertheless, his only reward being a glimpse into a new dimension.

By way of Böhme and the Cabbala (especially in its Messianic emphasis), the Consul found that evil and self-sacrifice must be accepted before they can be rejected. Largely incorporated in the last three chapters of the novel, the culmination of the initiation in ritual sacrifice is presented in terms of the Mithraic bull sacrifice, the Eleusinian mystery feast, and the Kelipathic accusers.

Keeping in mind that the microcosmic initiation process is directly related to the external world, we learn that Geoffrey's destruction mirrors the coming destruction of nations by war, that Hugh's commitment to the democratic cause foreshadows American intervention in the war, and that Yvonne's barrenness, her denial of femininity, corresponds to the destructive nature of modern woman. Encompassing these characters and events is the ominous Mexican setting chosen because ". . . It is the ideal setting for the struggle of a human being against the powers of darkness and light." †

Mexican lore, with its death preoccupation, which goes to the point of devoting an entire day to the dead on November 2, contributed its share to the darker aspects of the novel. Certain Indian tribes in Mexico outline an elaborate seven-day journey to be taken by the souls of the newly dead, which involves a trial descent

* Lowry, *Letters.*
† Lowry, "Preface to a Novel."

into the darkness of the abyss. In the novel, we accompany the Consul on this downward journey from 7 A.M. to 7 P.M. by means of M. Laruelle's opening reflections from the heights overlooking the barranca in Chapter One, all the way through to Geoffrey's final plunge in Chapter Twelve. The route the Consul follows is derived largely from Lévi and Dante, whose vision of hell is that of a narrow end of a conical pit at the center of the cosmos. Here lie Satan's quarters. For one to find one's way out it would be necessary to discover the secret path of the initiate, the path where hell meets heaven and where God and Satan are one—hence the double significance implied in the Consul's assertion as he heads down the path to Parián: "I like hell."

The astronomical setting of the initiation process is also of great importance. Inextricably combined with astrology and numerology, the novel is loaded with zodiacal significances. Included, for example, in the references to the action taking place "in Scorpio" (the death sign) are reminders of Agrippa's contention that Christ's statement "Are there not twelve hours in a day?" alluded to favorable or unfavorable astrological times for self-purification. Lowry gives us a corresponding insight into his astrological intentions:

. . . the Consul remembers a make of golfball called the Zodiac Zone, a lot more evidence in [Chapter] XI. . . . The scorpion is an image of suicide: (Scorpions sting themselves to death). . . . I now see the whole book takes place "in Scorpio" . . . the action of the book is one day, exactly 12 hours, seven to seven; the first chapter takes place 12 months later on the same day, so is also in Scorpio. . . .*

As for the numerical reiterations, we find emphasis primarily on the numbers 666 (the beast in Revelation, but also, in occult circles, symbolic of completion of the "great work of initiation") and 999 (666 seen upside down by the Consul), a number of Zoharistic importance. The number 7 can stand for nearly anything, but in *Volcano,* it becomes the Pleiades, a traditional Old Testament number designating sacrifice, as well as the number of heavenly palaces and tower steps to heaven or to hell, and the ledges of purgatory. Moreover, 12 can be magically transposed into a form of 7; both contain 3 and 4, and both control time and events in our

* Lowry, *Letters.*

universe by means of the seven days of the week and the seven planets, twelve hours of the day, and the signs of the zodiac.*

The characters are interrelated, as are the cosmic correspondences. Geoffrey is surrounded by wife, half brother (Hugh), and childhood friend (Laruelle); all are connected further by Yvonne's adulterous liaisons with both Hugh and Laruelle. At some point in the novel the protagonists are or have been alter egos to Geoffrey or lovers to Yvonne. Magically speaking, therefore, people who have had contact in the past maintain an underlying magnetism that enables them to continue to influence, and even to symbolize, each other. In this fashion, Geoffrey often seems to be willing the actions of the others, and Yvonne can "plead with" Geoffrey to extricate himself from danger when she is not physically present.

The Consul is, in effect, the central figure of two interlaced triangles. In alchemy, the interlaced triangles stand for the fundamental elements of transmutation: fire and water. The magician's function is, of course, to maintain the equilibrium between the opposing elements. Geoffrey, victimized by "fire water," has lost his balance. Through familiarity with Achad's books, Lowry would know that Jewish Cabbalists consider the triangle representative of the triune worlds of the tree of life, a concept that Christian Cabbalists have added to that of the Trinity.

The names of the characters give interesting sidelights on their roles, for names are of utmost importance to the Cabbalist: "Geoffrey" (Teutonic) ironically means "God's peace," "peace of the land," which is ultimately what he dies for. "Firmin" (Anglo-Saxon) is "a traveler to distant places" (and, perhaps, Lowry's anagram for "infirm"). Both Geoffrey and Hugh are world travelers. "Hugh" (Teutonic) stands for "mind," "intelligence." "Yvonne" (French) is an "archer." She is characterized by Lowry as "the eternal woman . . . angel and destroyer both," † which would substantiate this image. However, her name is even more likely derived from the film *Mad Love* (*Las Manos de Orlac*), whose heroine is also named Yvonne. "Laruelle" (French) is a

---

* Lowry's preoccupation with number symbolism was stimulated by Achad's works, Westcott's translation of the *Sefer Yetzirah*, and Mathers' *Kabbala Unveiled*. According to a recent article by Knickerbocker ("Malcolm Lowry in England"), Lowry was also familiar with Aleister Crowley's work.

† Lowry, *Letters*.

narrow passage space or a small gap between a bed and a wall—very appropriate for a marital interloper. "Dr. Vigil" obviously stands for the guardian, and as a doctor (whose sign is the caduceus) he qualifies as guide and master of initiation. This figure disappears, as does Vigil after Chapter Seven, as the adept becomes involved in the experience of transition.

The most compelling symbol by far is, of course, the Consul himself. Overtly compounded of parts of Faust, Dante, and Bunyan, the roots of his mysterious nature reach deeper into the legendary levels of the book. Morally, he is identified with the strange William Blackstone, a seventeenth-century believer in witchcraft who came from Cambridge to New England much as Lowry himself had done, a man whose writings, like Lowry's, were destroyed by a fire similar to the one described in Yvonne's dying vision of Geoffrey's burning "great work." And it is as "William Blackstone" that the Consul meets his death.

From the occult angle Geoffrey can be identified with many other famous initiates who began as "white" magicians and were diverted to the wrong path. Apollonius Tyaneus and Agrippa are two whose stories seem to have directly influenced Lowry. A legendary hero of the late Greek romances esteemed by Blavatskian theosophists, Apollonius was a Pythagorean philosopher, sage, and mystic who, in a past life, had been guilty of mishandling his ship and averting positive political commitment in the process. Still plagued by guilt surrounding this episode, he openly admitted his crime and became involved in opposing the political tyranny of Nero. Apollonius is also famous for having become drunk on the "draught of Tantalus," a metaphor characterizing his lifelong search for the divine by means of magic.

Agrippa struggled to maintain a hold on Christianity while dabbling in magic. He was reputed to have fallen into the hands of the demons, however, when he was discovered in the perpetual company of a black hound. These are only a small portion of the legendary masks assumed by the Consul.

# A Specific View

LOWRY'S BASIC scheme generally, though not entirely, coincides with that of Frater Achad's tables of correspondence, as, for example, the number twelve, which symbolizes the death of the redeemer who is suspended over the abyss; the use of the image of the blasted tower; and the color symbolism. Each of the twelve chapters follows the hermetic scheme in which human punishment is projected by the twelve zodiacal signs, with suffering decreasing as the initiate ascends by abandoning the seven vices, and increasing as he descends to lower stages of matter. The first ten chapters represent the Sephirotic stages, while the eleventh and twelfth chapters symbolize the culmination of the undertaking in death. Because events actually occur on two levels—the earthly and the astral planes—the dialogue often appears to be ambiguous, the inner monologues confusing or seemingly irrelevant to the exterior action. On these occasions, particularly with regard to Geoffrey's "hallucinations," the reader is usually being presented with some form of Cabbalistic reference. One of the clearest examples of this technique occurs in the scene during which Geoffrey's rumination about his spiritual life is reflected by his lovemaking.

Each interior monologue becomes a form of meditation befitting the individual character's concern with his salvation, or more specifically, with his progress on the tree of life. All four protagonists are, therefore, allowed at least one long contemplative monologue. Hugh is concerned with his true political and humanistic motives; Yvonne, with the problem of regaining paradise through love; Jacques, with his lifelong effort to emulate the Consul in order to gain Geoffrey's knowledge; and Geoffrey, with regaining his lost innocence. Each character is, in his own right, a lost soul, another aspect of the human race that has been cut off from the tree of life, as symbolized by their common expatriate exile. Geoffrey, Lowry informs us, is in the *Kelipah*,* but the other three characters are

---

* Lowry, *Letters.*

probably located in *Malkuth*—our world, which is the antithesis of sanctuary, where, for twelve hours, the *Shekinah* is exiled (for Jewish Cabbalists consider the Hebrew exile as occupying the space of one day in eternity).

In his letter to Jonathan Cape, Lowry admits to being influenced by the Zoharistic allegory of the garden. But he does not explain it in full detail. Nevertheless, the fate suffered by his four characters indirectly corresponds to that of the four sages who, according to perhaps the most famous of the Cabbalistic legends, enter a garden. One looks upon it and dies, a second goes mad, a third turns away from it and becomes an atheist, while the last looks upon it and returns home. For to the Cabbalist, the Garden of Eden was actually no more than the human mind, in which God had planted the choice between good and evil. And as Geoffrey states himself at one point, "equilibrium is all" in this garden where the life is balanced between two scales of opposing forces. Destruction resides in such unbalanced forces as the fascist police who rule the Mexican gardens. Positive power resides in the hands of the world restorers (in this case, the socialists) who reconstruct the ruined world from the remnants of the primordial world of the seven kings of Edom whose possessions had been broken up and dispersed after their destruction. Herein lie the Cabbalistic underpinnings of the novel's political theme.

The ruined, infertile state of Geoffrey's garden, with its thorns and weeds, indicates that there is a breach between upper and lower planes, that is, between God and man. Therefore, in the recurring allusion to the ruined palace of Maximilian is implied not only the death of earthly love but also the forfeiture of communion between the heavenly palace and the kingdom below.

Only man himself can seal this breach, and because the Cabbalist regards all mankind as one great totality, "one great united stream of life," the suffering of one man atones for all. It becomes the responsibility of this man to penetrate the secrets of the terrestrial, the astronomical, and the undefined worlds by means of his own corresponding channels of communication in order eventually to reunite those worlds. The Consul has apparently accomplished the first two stages, but by misusing his power he has lost control of the undefined world, becoming victimized by it instead. From this world emerge all the haunting demons and hallucinations that overcome him. Here too lies the territory for the ecstatic experience that is likened by Cabbalists to a sense of drowning or sinking (the manner in which the Consul ultimately ends his life).

Geoffrey Firmin is the embodiment of the "world fool" of the tarot, who has attained supernatural knowledge and who, when he attempts to reveal it, renders himself a magician. Practical Cabbalists regard the beard as a symbol of the covering of truth, whereas the mariner represents one who has been instructed and enlightened. Geoffrey is portrayed as a bearded former ship captain who, in a moment of nostalgia immediately before his death, recalls the days before his fall when he had been "lean, bronzed, serious, beardless, and at the crossroads of his career."

Another striking and appropriate symbol alluded to in Rosenroth's *Kabbala Denudata* is the allegory of Cain and Abel. Related to the sacrificial deaths of the two brothers in *Volcano,* especially with regard to the sea/abyss motif, the legend claims that God placed Cain into the mouth of the "great abyss" and then immersed his brother in the "great sea" in order to temper the divine tears. In his detailed description of Geoffrey's death in particular (Hugh's death at sea is only hinted at, the details left to the reader's imagination), Lowry has followed the Cabbalistic design of ritual torture almost in full, even down to the Zoharistic detail of having the Consul, and *he alone,* hear the crowing cock of death at his last hour.

The central struggle between light and darkness is embodied in various images of contrast, but the single most persistent image of this struggle is that of the Farolito, or "the lighthouse that invites the storm"—a paradoxical center where light and dark meet and merge. The lighthouse is also an outgrowth of the tower symbol of the tarot and Achad's tables, as well as the Tower of Babel. But it assumes even deeper symbolic connotations considering that alchemists attribute powerful supernatural influence to the Pharos of Alexandria, the lighthouse reckoned among the seven wonders of the world.

Two more appropriate background references with Cabbalistic roots demand special mention: namely, the volcanoes themselves and the lightning and thunder frequently associated with them. Popocatepetl and Ixtaccihuatl seem to bear special significance for Yvonne, who repeatedly identifies "Popo" as a dangerous, smoke-belching symbol of retribution, while "Ixta" is pictured as a soft profile bearing gentle feminine contours. In *Kabbala Denudata,* Microprosopus and Macroprosopus represent, respectively, the lesser and greater countenances of the *En Soph* (Boundless). Smoke belches from the nose of Microprosopus, which contains both a good and an evil aspect; whereas Macroprosopus is seen only in profile and bears the merciful, gentle countenance of the Ancient of Days.

Lightning and sometimes thunder appear at the peak of nearly every major crisis in the novel. Usually seen and heard in the area of the volcanoes, the lightning flash is depicted in the *Sefer Yetzirah* as a sign of emanation relating to transmutation. The angle of the lightning flash is used to indicate the course of the emanations upon the Sephirotic tree that the initiate must follow.

# PART
# III

# *Under the Volcano*
## AND
## THE CABBALA

# Chapter One

The story begins with a long physical description of Quauhnahuac (Cuernavaca) on the Day of the Dead, November 2,
1939. Jacques Laruelle is having a parting drink with his Mexican friend Dr. Vigil; after a long exile in Mexico, the French
movie director has decided to return to Paris. The two men
make oblique references to the tragedy of a mutual friend,
Geoffrey Firmin, who died precisely one year ago to the day.
Jacques retraces a sentimental course through familiar landmarks
and reminisces about the dead British Consul, his childhood
friend. We learn that Laruelle's love for the Consul's wife in
some way helped to precipitate the tragedy. Jacques ruminates
about the strange childhood of Geoffrey Firmin until he is
forced by an oncoming storm to duck into a cantina that bor-
ders on the town cinema. To his surprise, the same ominous
motion picture that played there a year before is being repeated. Struck by further coincidences, such as the reappearance
of Geoffrey's book of Elizabethan plays and his personal correspondence, in addition to such "supernatural" manifestations
of the Consul as a wild, drunken man on horseback, Laruelle
passes the time in conversation with Señor Bustamente, the
cinema proprietor. By this time the storm is raging in full force
and all the theater lights are out. Jacques contemplates Geoffrey's "mysterious" role as a sea captain and former Consul and
compares him to Faustus. Finally, driven by the forceful though
invisible presence of his friend, Laruelle begins to read Geoffrey's letters to his estranged wife, Yvonne. As a result, we learn
that Geoffrey had been a confirmed alcoholic as well as a Cabbalist and a mystic. In one letter he talks of having fallen into
hell and pleads for Yvonne to return and save him. When he
has finished reading, Laruelle burns the letter as the bells announce the end of the Day of the Dead and the beginning of
the flashback that will explain the past year's events as symbolized by the image of a ferris wheel revolving backward into
time.

This opening chapter establishes nearly every major theme and symbol of the book, for it is intended as an introduction to and a recapitulation of the past year's events. Despite Lowry's meticulous blueprint of the setting, the precise locations in time, and the cut-and-dried numerical facts, the reader is immediately plunged into the eerie realm of timelessness. Each symbol of importance in this chapter, even whole phrases, is reiterated throughout the remainder of the novel until all are gathered together in full force during the intense climactic events of the last three chapters.

The first page of the text is devoted to an enumeration of seven factual details about an area soon to be recognized as *Malkuth,* the *Sephirah* containing the ruined earthly palace. Quauhnahuac has two mountain chains, two volcanoes, is six thousand feet above sea level, on the nineteenth parallel, possesses eighteen churches, fifty-seven cantinas, four hundred swimming pools. The Hotel Casino de la Selva (Selva being "the dark wood of Dante") is "built far back from the main highway. . . . Palatial . . . [but of a] desolate splendour." It is haunted by "the ghosts of ruined gamblers." The "Olympic" (gods') pool is empty of swimmers. Here is the ruined garden, God's palace on earth, vacant because it is cut off from its source. The setting sun, the year beginning with world war (1939), the Day of the Dead with its sounds of mourning—all warn of the doom that hovers over this place.

Laruelle and Dr. Vigil are meeting for the last time—Laruelle, the only survivor of the year's events, plans to leave the "garden." Vigil is referred to as a doctor and an "apostle" who carries a "triangular" tennis case, which establishes him immediately as a healer and guide as well as a master of the elements. The two men, enclosed in a reddish glow, are drinking from a bottle of anis whose label bears a devil brandishing a pitchfork. The pitchfork is the fiery *Shin* in its destructive aspect, which recalls Geoffrey as a direct contrast to Vigil, who guards the light and "conjure[s] a flaring lighter out of his pocket" so quickly that he seems to have "drawn a flame out of himself."

The first reference to the Consul's alcoholism is ambiguous in that he is characterized as being *perfectly* drunk (a statement that will be repeated by his accuser), yet "sick in soul"—a clue to the paradoxical condition effected by overindulgence in the mystic wine. As though in response to mention of the Consul, the lights go off suddenly and on again as Jacques remembers his friend's last message: "No se puede vivir sin amar" ("Life without love is impossible")—for only love is as strong as death.

The landscape the two men are in plays an important part in the action to come: the two volcanoes to the left, "ten miles distant" the village of Tomalín, the bus, the prison watchtower, and the purple foothills. All are features of Geoffrey's initiation: the volcanoes on the left indicate the left-hand path of ascent; the ten miles are the ten *Sephiroth;* arena Tomalín is where the bull sacrifice occurs; the bus is the same one that will encounter the dying Indian; the watchtower is the blasted tower of the spying evil forces; while the purple foothills stand for *Yesod,* the first plane leading out of *Malkuth* into higher worlds—the magical sphere whose color is purple.

Jacques recalls his first and last meetings with Hugh, Geoffrey's younger half brother, exactly twelve months before, and indicates that in three nights they had become as father and son, Geoffrey's and Yvonne's deaths being the unifying principle. Jacques had dreamed of changing the world through illusion (cinema), the younger man through politics. Both would go to Vera Cruz ("True Cross"), neither one sure of reaching port. The interrelatedness of their fate is established when, after many false starts, Jacques and Hugh set out one year apart on the dangerous initiatory sea as Geoffrey had done before them. Jacques is alone and frightened; he longs for Paris, his home, which, "If God willed," he would see again. Mexico, the strange "Earthly Paradise," he notes, is actually Everywhere. And he realizes that each man must prove himself here before "going home" (an echo of the Abbé de Villars' internal garden within each man). Dissatisfied with his progress, Jacques regrets not having come to grips with the place, having enmeshed himself with trivia instead. He feels like a "wanderer on another planet," a lost soul surrounded by external conflicts between the forces of good and evil. "Though if the Allies lost [the war] it would be harder. [But] in either case one's own battle would go on."

Partly because of his secondary role, partly because he is set up as a foil to the Consul, Jacques has not really reached any significant point of comprehension of Geoffrey's supernatural quest. Basically a materialist, he can catch only a glimpse of the truth about the soul's struggle. Cabbalists would characterize him as the average type of man living in *Assiah,* the gross world of matter, who is blinded by greed, egotism, and materialism. This aspect of his character is evidenced by his flabby waistline and dandyish style of dress. His spiritual grossness is portrayed especially in his insensitive and provocative confrontations with Geoffrey in Chapter Seven.

At this moment, however, Jacques Laruelle is experiencing a sort of spiritual awakening. He notes the approaching out-of-season storm and wishes to walk in it, perhaps even desiring to be cleansed as his tennis clothes get "wetter and wetter." Relating the rain to love itself, he introduces the theme of "Huracán," the paradoxical creator-destroyer god, by noting that the thunder of God "slake[s] no thirst," thereby equating the Consul's alcoholic thirst with the mystical quest that had ended with "the love which came too late."

"Walking gradually downhill," Jacques comes upon the revolving Ferris wheel and hears the "despondent" sound of the "St. Louis Blues." This wheel is of course the wheel of life and time, which continuously rolls on accompanied by the sad music of man's lot on earth. The blues theme, continued throughout this chapter, is ingeniously tied in with the Consul when Laruelle later comes across a ruined blue Ford and when Geoffrey is referred to as the man with the blue eyes. (Blue symbolizes the magician and the *Sephirah Chesed,* mercy, toward which, we learn, Geoffrey is striving.) As he walks along, Jacques recalls the Consul's delight in scaling the ruined pyramid in Cholula, which he had "proudly insisted was the original Tower of Babel." The blasted tower is another form of the fallen world of *Assiah* that is intended as the reversed image of the Consul's dying vision of climbing the volcano. The Tower of Babel theme recurs most effectively in Geoffrey's evaluation of the moral atmosphere of the Cantina Farolito. The Tower of Babel is a Cabbalistic metaphor for the fact that an attempt to lay hold of the secrets of heaven to pass them on to the uninitiated on earth ends in misunderstanding and anarchy, confusion of tongues, false symbols.

Tired of walking, Jacques decides to pursue a new path back to the center of town. He soon realizes that he is wandering through the realm of the shades, for he suddenly encounters two Indians

whose features and bearing suggest they are Aztec princes, resur-
rected dead nobility of the land who, in keeping with the legend of
the Day of the Dead, have arisen. They too are apparently involved in a conversation about the Consul, for they reiterate
Vigil's astonished assessment of Geoffrey's alcoholism—"perfec-
tamente borracho . . . completamente fantástico"—in an astral
commentary on the Consul's condition that seems to Jacques to
come from beyond the grave itself. But all vanishes and Laruelle
looks to the west (death) and meditates once again on the soul
and its battles. Almost subliminally driven by a force outside himself, Laruelle turns left despite his desire to take the path on the
right, motivated by "an obscure desire on his last night to bid farewell to the ruin of Maximilian's Palace."

As he labors down this left-hand path the scenery grows nightmarish, threatening signs of the storm surround him: "To the
south an immense archangel, black as thunder, beat up from the
Pacific. And yet, after all, the storm contained its own secret
calm . . ." Jacques is now approaching the Consul's territory, for
the *Kelipah* (hell) is situated in a southerly direction on the earth
and is guarded by its own ten mighty archangels—mirror images,
so to speak, of those who guard the upper regions. The "secret
calm" pertains, of course, to the successful transition of the initiatory path that runs through the center of the *Kelipah,* soon to be
mentioned by the Consul. For Laruelle, however, the calm is identified with his own love for Yvonne, which reminds him in a way
he cannot explain of the sanctity of Chartres Cathedral. Here is the
first of the symbolic references that identify Yvonne with the divine *Shekinah.* She had fled north, leaving both Geoffrey and himself still under "enchantment." Yet neither of them had been capable of retrieving her though there had been reason enough "for
putting the whole earth between themselves and Quauhnahuac!"
(To regain the departed *Shekinah,* it is *literally* necessary for man
to transcend the earth.)

The entire atmosphere is pervaded by an air of sorrow, as
Jacques is guided toward the "total wreck" of the blue Ford—an
image loaded with allusions to the Consul, who, we learn, is a
frequent car wrecker. The front wheels of the car are prevented
from any "involuntary departure" by bricks. "What are you waiting for, he wanted to ask it, feeling a sort of kinship, an empathy

for those tatters of ancient hood flapping . . ." Jacques is looking
at the fantastic remains of the black magician, a wreck who can no
longer make the ascent up the slope, for his wheels are eternally
stuck, blocked by stones—a fate directly opposed to that of the
mystic, who, in his ascent, would arrive at the vision of the eternally rotating wheels within wheels. Geoffrey, like the wrecked
Ford forever stuck on the slope of the mountain, could not ford
the breach between God and man.

Perhaps as a result of contemplating the sadly symbolic scene
before him, Laruelle is again reminded of Yvonne's departure and
its part in enforcing the Consul's hopeless condition, which, in its
intensity, had been equal to the utter degradation of the man who
is abandoned by the *Shekinah*. But he recalls in amazement that
"the Consul had calculated it all, *knowing* M. Laruelle would discover [Yvonne's plea for life written on a postcard] at the precise
moment that Hugh . . . would call from Parián [announcing
their deaths]." In other words, Geoffrey's last tragicomic act is a
comment on both his and Yvonne's failures to achieve love, in addition to its being a prescient indication of the coming tragedy.

As though in reflection of Laruelle's thoughts of Parián, its
agents suddenly appear, the spying evil forces, the military police
who forever watch from their tower, followed by a swarm of
"small, black, ugly birds . . . like monstrous insects. . . . Shat-
terers of the twilight hour . . . with their incessant drilling mechanic screech. . . ."

When Jacques reaches Maximilian's Palace the sun has set, and
he is left alone in hellish darkness so that ". . . he immediately
regretted having come." His fear of the ruined garden is too great
to be overcome even by the memory of his love for Yvonne. Like
the crumbling Sephirotic pillars that had flanked the destroyed
symbolic temple of the Rosicrucians, the decaying pillars are about
to fall in "this place where love had once brooded." Covered with
weeds, urine, excrement, green scum, and scorpions—that is, with
all the symbols of death and decay—it is a grotesque remnant of
love's mansion, which resembles the lowest pit of the *Kelipah* itself. The sadness of the place is heavy with recollections of the
"two lonely empurpled exiles . . . lovers out of their element—
their Eden." Although ostensibly Maximilian and Carlotta at first,
the ghostly lovers merge identities with Adam and Eve and

Yvonne and Geoffrey, who were also lovers in exile, "empurpled" once in the sense that *Yesod* (the purple *Sephirah*) represents "foundation" and "fertility" on the earthly plane. Maximilian (Geoffrey, Adam) had been "unlucky in his palaces too," for the place had begun to smell like a "brewery" after the drunkenness that led to his final fall. Once again Jacques hears the voices of the dead. This time they are the sounds of a quarrel between the spirits of his two friends.

Noting the imperturbable presence of the "burning" wheel, Laruelle trudges farther downward on a terrible road and suddenly finds himself confronted by the abyss. "It was too dark to see the bottom, but: here was finality indeed, and cleavage! . . . wherever you turned the abyss was waiting for you round the corner." Regarding it as Moloch's "dormitory" of death, he is reminded of the "sea-borne" legend that the earth here had opened, becoming an abyss at the moment of the crucifixion—sea-borne because secret to all but those "mariners" initiated into the mysteries of the abyss. And he recalls the time when Geoffrey had attempted to pass the very secret on to him, speaking of "the spirit of the abyss, the god of the storm, 'huracán,' that 'testified so suggestively to intercourse between opposite sides of the Atlantic.' " But he had not understood Geoffrey's meaning in spite of the fact that it was really no more than a foreshadowing of his own previous vague observation about the calm at the storm's center: namely the path of loving self-sacrifice. The Consul had even suggested that Jacques make a film about the sunken Atlantis—that is, seek his own paradise through art, thereby transforming the negative spirit of the abyss ("huracán") into a positive force.

By an inversion of meaning Lowry lets us see that the abyss also refers to a golf course sand trap (like the sea, the golf course becomes a metaphor for the initiatory path) where Jacques had discovered the young Geoffrey, who, in turn, was himself discovering the secret of sex. The "Hell Bunker," as it was called, therefore, bears "some obscure relationship to the later one in Maximilian's Palace" where the evil spirit lurks, waiting to poison love. Even an absurd boyhood ditty entitled the "wiblerlee wobberlee WALK" recurs as a mocking reminder of the Consul's alcoholic stagger.

For twenty-five years (which could be Cabbalistically read as $2 + 5 = 7$) the two friends had been parted, and then by means of a correspondence "that might be labelled: 'favourite trick of the gods,'" they had found each other again in Mexico.

Having met Geoffrey at *sea*side in 1911 ($1 + 9 + 1 + 1 = 12$), Laruelle gives a full description of the Consul's mysterious origins and his singular adolescence. Brought (like the Cabbala itself) from the East by Abraham Taskerson (Father Abraham, also a "tasker of sons"), the young Geoffrey could not hear the words "mother" and "father" without weeping. (The *Zohar* states that, cut off from the triune world inhabited by divine father and mother, the son, or wandering soul, longs to return and weeps at the thought of being born again in the lower world.) Geoffrey is the *seventh* relative of six "older" and "tougher" sons (cf. the seven generations of men required to reunite *Kether* [Crown] and *Malkuth* [Kingdom], those of the lower *Sephiroth* [planes on the tree of life] weaker because of the greater distance between themselves and the *Aziluth* [archetypal world]).

The Taskerson home is as strange as their family habits. It is situated on an island bounded by the *seven*-mile "estuary . . . of a river: white horses [marking] where the real sea began." Surrounded by mountains "with occasionally a snowy peak to remind Geoff of India," the boy is continuously aware of his task: to climb the figurative mountain in search of the father who so mysteriously disappeared among the peaks of the Himalayas (the soul's reunification with the Father being the primary function of the Cabbalist's life).

Jacques recalls that there had also been "an old stubby deserted lighthouse"—to recur later in the form of a cantina called the Farolito ("Little Lighthouse")—set in a landscape of "space and emptiness." This light that invites the storm, which, we later learn, is a parallel motif to that of Huracán, is also the theosophist's interchangeability of the light of God with the fire of Satan.

Geoffrey had "expertly" handled a *twelve*-foot yacht in those days when they had sailed on the inlet leading to the sea—and indication of his innocence and primordial powers before the first (sexual) stage of the fall in the Hell Bunker. Further, although the Taskersons had attempted to include him in their "unprecedented, portentous" drinking, the boy had hated the taste of alcohol. Perhaps his weakness in this area is an early failure to acclimate himself to the heady mysteries borne by the wine. The healthy young

Taskerson boys pity the fellow who cannot drink seven pints in fourteen minutes—again a ritualistic reminder. But old Abraham himself, brooding over the loss of his favorite son, begins to take a liking to young Firmin, whose " 'nose was always in a book,' so that 'Cousin Abraham,' whose work had a religious turn, should be the 'very man' to assist him."

But Jacques is driven always to the recollection of the Hell Bunker, the "dreaded hazard, fairly near the Taskersons' house [the relativity of the *Kelipah* to *Malkuth*], in the middle of a long sloping eighth fairway." It is "far below" the fairway and "slightly to the left." "The abyss yawned in such a position as to engulf the third shot of a golfer like Geoffrey, a naturally beautiful and grace-ful player. . . ." This is the path of the *Sephiroth*, with its haz-ardous abyss to the left and below the green (*Netzach*—Venus and victory), which engulfs the initiate after his third transgression; for God gives a man three chances in which to redeem himself. Up to this point Geoffrey has already sinned both sexually and aggres-sively. His third and last sin will be the denial of Yvonne. Jacques remembers the Consul's first transgression in the Hell Bunker and their attempt to cover it over by drinking in a tavern significantly called "The Case is Altered," an ironic commentary on both the condition of their friendship and Geoffrey's fate. "The holiday fiz-zled out in . . . equinoctial gales," for the loss of paradise en-genders the generation of the flood.

Laruelle is drawn back into the present when a drunk, swinging a machete, rides dangerously close to him on a wild horse— "somehow . . . this too, obscurely, was the Consul . . ." This vision of *Chavajah* (God's destructive power unleashed) will later be recapitulated when Yvonne sees the Consul atop the wild horse that kills her. The machete, a transition from "wands" to "swords," stands, like the pitchfork, for the destructive power of the magician, or the letter *Shin* in reverse. Geoffrey will actually wield a machete later in an attempt to fend off his accusers, but his action will be ineffectual, for he will have lost all his power by then.

The furious horseman appears just as Jacques is passing the Consul's house, "where there would be a light in the window . . . for long after Adam had left the garden the light in Adam's house burned on. . . ." Occultists often use "house" to denote "soul." This light in the Consul's window is Geoffrey's immortal soul, and the many natural disturbances that follow, including the spectral rider, are really manifestations of the Consul's restless presence. It is as though this tumultuous spirit, evoked by the intensity of Jacques' concentration, is responsible for the savage thunderclaps and the "scribble" of lightning (common occurrences during evocation of spirits) that follow.

As though to emphasize the timelessness of the events, Lowry has Laruelle notice that *Las Manos de Orlac,* the film of a year ago, is being shown again, and he makes an extended mental comparison between the nature of the film and its relevance to current political events. During the power failure that follows Jacques speaks with the cinema proprietor. "The rainy season dies hard," he says as they enter a cantina called simply XX, previously referred to by Vigil as "place where you know." The bar is lit by candles. "XX" (a Mexican beer trade mark), standing for the "unknown" as well as the number 20, is also 20 as a symbol of fire and regeneration, as Lowry saw in Achad's chart. It is, in fact, to be the place where Jacques will "know" what has been heretofore unknown to him when he is given Geoffrey's letters to read. Fire, embodied in the cantina's candlelight and associated with Dr. Vigil, as keeper of the flame, represents enlightenment.

Señor Bustamente, the cinema proprietor, complains that "every blessed week [*seven* again] something goes wrong with the lights . . . ," as though by still burning the light in his own house, the dead Geoffrey remains embroiled in the struggle with the elements. Persistent in declaring his presence (his book of Elizabethan plays and his letters are still in the bar), Geoffrey's spirit is connected with the film of which Señor Bustamente notes: ". . . we have not revived it. It has only returned." At seven o'clock the film is interrupted by thunder and rain and, as though to cap the occult correspondences, the cinema owner suddenly produces Geoffrey's copy of Elizabethan plays.

Another ghostly taunt at Jacques, the book that he had never given back now becomes "an emblem of what even now it is impossible to return." Laruelle had originally borrowed the book in order to create a modern Faustus based on Marlowe's model. He had toyed with the idea of using Trotsky as his hero (another correspondence designed to evoke the figure of the Consul, who is jeeringly called Trotsky by his accusers in Chapter Twelve). As Jacques opens the book thunder rumbles ominously outside, and he tries to give the book back to Señor Bustamente. As soon as the latter speaks directly of Geoffrey, identifying him here as the "blue-eyed one," the light within the cinema fails completely, and a "curious hush" befalls the theater while the screen is "suddenly illumined, swept, by silent grotesque shadows of giants and spears and birds . . . ," all projections of the major images involved in the Consul's death; the giants are the police chiefs, the spears are the machete and Kashmiri sword, and the birds are the cock of death. The cinema audience, meanwhile, is "waiting for the show to begin, for a glimpse of the murderer's bloodstained hands." The guilty hands are an allusion to all responsible for the world war, as well as to the reenactment of the Consul's life and death, which the audience waits to see on the screen, for the souls in *Kelipah* are doomed to relive their torment. When the lights go out, Jacques remarks that it is " 'raining, out of season,' . . . the dark waters rising outside to engulf . . . his useless tower against the coming of the second flood." The watery element is Geoffrey's province, and Laruelle realizes that his own spiritual "tower" is insufficient to withstand the destructive force of Geoffrey's invisible strength. The flood image serves the further purpose here of figuring Yvonne as the weeping Merope who floods the earth with her tears during the "Night of the Culmination of the Pleiades."

Continuing to mull over his dead friend's life, Jacques remembers that Geoffrey had been mistaken by many as a spy because he had no longer functioned officially as an English Consul but had continued to remain in Mexico with no apparent professional capacity. Instead, seedy, often wearing only one sock, wifeless, and drunk, Geoffrey had become prime suspect of every political group and, like the foolish and drunken Noah, also "spied" upon in his nakedness, was unaware of the danger. Living among whores and thieves, giving all his money to beggars, Geoffrey, the dilapidated Cabbalist, is recalled to have begged Señora Gregorio, the woman later identified with his lost mother, for "sanctuary," which, unfortunately, does not exist in *Malkuth* (our world), the home of husks and demons. Nevertheless, there had been something ambiguous about the Consul's absolute degradation, something that makes Jacques think that Geoffrey "might have actually proved a great force for good"—a kind of Messiah in *Kelipah,* perhaps. Not having done well as a diplomat, however, Geoffrey had been kicked "downstairs into even remoter Consulships . . . where he was least likely to prove a nuisance to the Empire . . . in which he . . . so passionately believed." Although ostensibly a reference to the Consul's career and his relationship to the British Empire, on a deeper level this observation serves as background information about the descending path of initiatory degrees reserved for transgressors within God's "empire." Laruelle immediately provides us with the answer to why all this had happened, when he remembers the second transgression that inspired the Consul's downward path, the episode of the S.S. *Samaritan:* "a stray sheep on the immeasurable green meadows of waters. . . . As if by magic the sheep turned to a dragon belching fire." The tanker had turned gunboat, and "in some obscure capacity" Geoffrey had been responsible for the mysterious murder of some German officers perpetrated in a manner violating the rules of war. In Cabbalistic terms, the Consul had either deliberately or unwittingly turned his power from that of a creator (lamb) to that of a destroyer (Leviathan) during a past initiatory trial (the sea).

Geoffrey's hidden guilt and suffering are immediately echoed by a random quote from *Faustus,* which Jacques reads or "sees" incorrectly as *"Then will I headlong fly into the earth,"* but which is actually "Then will I headlong *run* into the earth," for "to run was not so bad as to fly." The allusion here is both to the manner in which Geoffrey is literally flung into the abyss and to the fact that the evil of the ordinary man (that is, Jacques himself) is neither so grand nor so awful in its consequences as that of the black magician. Laruelle then momentarily has the "illusion" of the sacred Thoth (Hermes Trismegistus) while looking at the cover of the book. As god of magicians and writers, Thoth too would be affronted by the Consul's flagrant behavior; and as secretary of the gods, he would be the recorder of Geoffrey's disgrace. The image of Thoth as scrivener recurs in Chapter Two and in Chapter Twelve, at, respectively, the beginning and the end of the Consul's day.

Jacques is almost entirely enveloped by his friend's presence, and he now sees the correspondences "between the subnormal world and the abnormally suspicious." Each gradual discovery relating to this modern Faustus unearths a further illumination, a series culminating in an open confession from the Consul himself in the form of a strange letter written all "downhill . . . individual characters seemed as if resisting the descent, braced, climbing the other way." Such might be the description of the living, moving characters manipulated in secret messages by practical Cabbalists in a trance state, often for magical purposes, partly for communication with spirits, sometimes for prayer. In this case it is a kind of exhortation from Geoffrey to Yvonne in her role of *Shekinah*—a plea for release from the mental crucifixion of mystical delirium tremens. By having the Consul use Hotel Bella Vista stationery, Lowry puns on his own experience of writing from Bellevue Hospital, where he committed himself for a cure after a terrible siege of hallucinations.

The Consul writes that he had attempted to escape the nightmare of "daemonic orchestras . . . howling pariah dogs . . . cocks that herald dawn all night," by flying farther headlong into the earth to "unimaginable cantinas where sad-faced potters and legless beggars drink at dawn" (figures who will appear in the last hours of his life and who haunt his clairvoyant imagination). The letter continues with a description of a train journey to hell. Geoffrey is here himself the soulless corpse being delivered by express to Oaxaca. But he is also the "murderer" with the artist's hands when he saves the life of a child on that same train by rubbing its belly with tequila—the sacred wine as a life-giving as well as a life-destroying power. As low as he might have fallen at that point, then, the Consul had still retained some of his magical power: the belly being the organ corresponding to mastery of the zodiacal water sign, Scorpio, with which he is associated.

By the time the train image is picked up again in Chapter Ten, it is too late for salvation, for Geoffrey has reached the last degree of his fall. And there, the train is a one-way, no-stop express to death.

The consequences of the Consul's turning away from God's *Shekinah* are embodied in the metaphor of his "divorce" from Yvonne. In his isolation, he has fallen to the depths:

. . . my secrets are of the grave and must be kept. . . . I . . . think of myself as a great explorer who has discovered some extraordinary land from which he can never return to give his knowledge to the world: but the name of this land is hell. . . . This was as I invited it. [Having committed himself to death, therefore, Geoffrey tells her that he] shall perhaps go home but not to England, not to that home. . . . [An indirect reference to his search for sanctuary; this time in the hope of final annihilation in *Tiphereth*, the "home" of sacrificed gods.] But . . . worst of all [is] to feel your soul dying. I wonder if it is because to-night my soul has really died that I feel at the moment something like peace. [When the Cabbalist has broken away from *nefesh*, the mortal soul, he achieves the objectivity that is a necessary preparation for death as well as an insight into the divine plan. Thus Geoffrey can speak of the secret path.] . . . right through hell . . . as Blake well knew, and though I may not take it, sometimes lately in dreams I have been able to see it . . . [and still accept his inevitable martyrdom].

Lowry now introduces the paradise theme, which is to be repeated in consistent contrast with the *Kelipah* throughout the book. More than a burst of creative description, this section, a passage of the Consul's letter being read by Jacques, is devoted to a carefully detailed metaphor of the mystical experience. It contains information from Agrippa's elemental magic and astrology, Swedenborg's portrayal of heaven, Frater Achad's number and color symbolism, Ezekiel's vision, and the *Sefer Yetzirah*. He seems to see, Geoffrey writes to Yvonne, a path that leads on to "strange" vistas, promises of a renewed life he and she might one day lead together. The country he describes is northern, mountainous, with blue skies and blue water. Balancing these northern, and therefore cabbalistically spiritual elements of his vision, the Consul sees an oil refinery, whose jets of flame recall Agrippa's identification of fire as the purest element, and with Tiphereth, the Sun.

Firmin then describes a vision of *Kether* that rivals even Ezekiel's vision in its drama and beauty. It is introduced by the "gathering thunder" of a train "rolling eastward." This, in opposition to the hell-bound express, is the train that carries the soul to immortality emphasized by the triple repetition of the word "east," the "holy" point of the compass:

. . . and we face east, like Swedenborg's angels, under a sky clear save where far to the northeast over distant mountains whose purple has faded [ascending away from *Yesod*], lies a mass of almost pure white clouds, suddenly, as by a light in an alabaster lamp, illumined from within by gold lightning [*Kether* radiating through *Tiphereth*], yet you can hear no thunder. . . .

Then a silver boat (the moon) enters the vision as a reflection of the "remote white thunderclouds in the water," and the two merge in a symbolic reunification of masculine and feminine principles; ". . . silence, and then again, within the white white distant alabaster thunderclouds beyond the mountains, the thunderless gold lightning in the blue evening, unearthly. . . ." Each image is a stage in the inexplicable mystery of communion with *Kether*.

". . . [All] at once comes the wash of another unseen ship, like a great wheel, the vast spokes of the wheel whirling across the bay." Unable to sustain the vision any further, the Consul interrupts his meditation when Ezekiel's wheel of life reminds him of the wheel of time and its harsh reality, which can only be confronted by a consciousness influenced by "several mescals." Geoffrey is swiftly thrust back into the drugged state, where he agonizes over his desperate but ineffectual attempts to hold on to the roots and branches of the tree of life. Without Yvonne, he knows that he will never be able to traverse the abyss, so he begs her to return to him. He is pained by their diminishing communication, the letters that "came too late," for the greater the distance between a man and God's *Shekinah,* the weaker that man's control over the holy letters comprising His name. Yet Geoffrey cannot ask her to return outright: every cry for help in *Gai-hinnom* is a step deeper down, farther away from God. Even the telephone will not work for him since he is no longer capable of interpreting magical characters necessary for contact with the heavenly hierarchies.

Such an attempt is later to be portrayed when, in a moment of unbearable desperation, he will call for God on the telephone.

In an even more direct allusion to his lapse from his Cabbalistic function he tells Yvonne that he is no longer at work on his great Cabbalistic document entitled "Secret Knowledge."

Meantime do you see me as still working on the book, still trying to answer such questions as: Is there any ultimate reality, external, conscious and ever-present etc. etc. that can be realised by any such means that may be acceptable to all creeds and religions and suitable to all climes and countries? Or do you find me between Mercy and

Understanding, between Chesed and Binah (but still at Chesed)—my
equilibrium, and equilibrium is all, precarious—balancing, teetering
over the awful unbridgeable void, the all-but-unretraceable path of
God's lightning back to God? As if I ever were in Chesed! More like
the Qliphoth.

". . . [N]othing can ever take the place of the unity we once
knew and which Christ alone knows must still exist somewhere."
For the Christian Cabbalist Christ was *Adam Kadmon,* and thus it
becomes apparent that Geoffrey is appealing to Yvonne for a restoration not only of their marriage but of that union between microcosm and macrocosm—a secret "which Christ alone knows."
But because of his basic longing for goodness despite his tragic
commitment to evil, the Consul is still aware of the mystery of love
as "the only thing which gives meaning to our poor ways on
earth. . . . You will think I am mad, but this is how I drink too,
as if I were taking an eternal sacrament. . . . We cannot allow
what we created to sink down to oblivion in this dingy fashion—"
    Although he has a painful, actually supernatural, insight into his
fate, Geoffrey is unable to continue writing out his own story, as it
were, and he begins to *live* it instead. He perceives the dim outline
of the secret path but has no means by which to unify the fractured
themes of his life: the conflicts between love and death, creative
and destructive power, and, above all, the duality inherent in the
mystical wine. "Lift up your eyes unto the hills, I seem to hear a
voice saying," but he has sunk too far to act on it.
    In his mind Yvonne's return is associated with the little red mail
plane that comes over the hills each morning at seven, an unlikely
conveyance that nevertheless brings her back in exact accord with
his clairvoyant vision. She comes to him at seven, not out of the
blue (mercy), as it were, but out of the "red" plane of *Geburah*—
judgment, or *Binah* in her aspect of severity. Geoffrey sees her
being carried downward through the air as she is later to be borne
upward for the last time, and his letter ends with a heart-rending
cry that might still be echoing throughout the spirit world:
". . . come back to me, Yvonne, if only for a day. . . ."

    It is almost as though the Consul's spirit has been temporarily
appeased by Jacques' having read his mournful testament, for when
Laruelle stops reading, the storm ends. The ritualistic release of

the Consul's soul is enacted when Jacques burns the letter, and this
purifying fire is followed by the final tolling of the bell, which signifies that the dead can return to their rest and that the Day of the
Dead is ended. "The flare lit up the whole cantina with a burst of
brilliance . . . beautifully conforming it folded upon itself, a
burning castle, collapsed . . . like tiny red worms crawled and
flew . . . a dead husk now, faintly crepitant . . . Suddenly from
outside, a bell spoke out, then ceased abruptly: *dolente . . .
dolore!"* This last scene of this chapter parallels both Yvonne's vision of Geoffrey's burning book at her death and the bells that announce the Consul's death in the last chapter. Outside the cantina
the wheel of life and time turns twelve months backward, or is it
actually forward, or has it been standing still all along while only
the spectators themselves were deluded into motion? And in the
timeless fourth dimension where all things are possible, the Consul's story begins again.

# Chapter Two

It is 7 A.M. on November 2, 1938. Yvonne has just returned to
the Consul. She hears his voice coming from the bar of the hotel
where he has been drinking all night. Their confrontation is
deceptively casual, for neither wishes to disturb the fragile,
somewhat superficial nature of their first meeting in a year. In
the background, a noisy American fascist boasts about his battle
activities as a member of the Foreign Legion. Geoffrey is preoccupied with "a corpse that will be delivered by express," and
Yvonne is concerned about her "severance" from her husband.
The couple discuss trivial matters and automatically head toward
home, followed by sinister Mexicans in dark glasses. They pass
and read the billboard posters that announce a bull wrestling
that afternoon at Arena Tomalín and see the town scrivener
typing out on the street. In a printshop window, they look for
a while at an odd photo of a split rock that depresses Yvonne.
Geoffrey stops, ostensibly to buy eggs, at a dark little shop. The
Consul tells her that he has maintained a friendship of sorts with
his rival, Laruelle, and that his brother, Hugh, is staying at the
house. She responds to both these pieces of information with
disappointment inspired by her guilty past associations with each
of these men. Nevertheless, the Firmins manage to generate
temporary hope for healing the breach between them as they
enter the broken gate leading to their home—as a "hideous" dog
follows ominously behind.

The revolving "luminous wheel" of life turns backward into
Yvonne's consciousness, events past and present converging into
one day. The chapter begins with the words "A corpse will be
transported by express." This statement simultaneously relates to
the many different motifs presented in Geoffrey's posthumous letter
and, in the "roar of the great train" that climbs through the mountains of paradise, is later to become the train that will carry Hugh
to his mission; it is culminated in Geoffrey's final nightmare train

vision that climaxes in a repetition of the phrase "a corpse will be transported by express."

The voice making this statement is familiar to Yvonne, who overhears this singular remark—a kind of announcement made by Geoffrey or even perhaps by one of his "familiars." In an ambiguous answer to her question ". . . why should a corpse be transported by express, do you suppose?" the cab driver who has just deposited her outside the Bella Vista bar says: "Sí, señora—El Cónsul . . . Qué hombre!" as though in corroboration of the fact that it was the Consul who spoke or that it might even be the Consul's corpse that is in question. Yvonne, convinced that it might not be such a strange idea after all, hears "Absolutamente necesario" again, an ambiguous confirmation of the Consul's determined, self-imposed doom.

Geoffrey's letter had made clairvoyant reference to her wished-for arrival from Acapulco. Now she has in fact returned to give him another chance, arriving by the odd route he had imagined, by mail plane, a living message (quite literally) from heaven. Her trip downward is depicted as an astral descent from a higher plane (the *Shekinah* lodges in *Tiphereth*) to a lower one, which involves passage through the elements, ". . . her consciousness so lashed by wind and air and voyage she still seemed to be travelling, still sailing into Acapulco harbor yesterday evening through a hurricane of immense and gorgeous butterflies swooping seaward . . . at first it was as though fountains of multi-colored stationery were being swept out of the saloon lounge. . . ." Yvonne is apparently responding to Geoffrey's unposted pleas after all, since magical desires can often be accomplished as a result of deep concentration that takes the form of a message to higher spheres.

She arrives in the "seven o'clock morning sunlight" as a messenger of light who is both judge and lover, and eyes "her volcanoes," which rise "eternally," pondering at the same time the meaning of "Quauhnahuac, her town of cold mountain water swiftly running. Where the eagle stops! Or did it really mean . . . near the wood? The trees . . . massive shining depths . . . how had she ever lived without them?" Here is Eve returning to the scene of her lost innocence. But the underlying force of the images results from their association with her forthcoming death: the cold spring in which she will bathe, the eagle she will release, and the forest in which she will finally be trampled. Her recollection of the dawn includes the colors green, purple, gold, lapis (*Netzach, Yesod, Tiphereth, Chesed*), in the midst of which "the horn of Venus burned so fiercely," Venus meaning respectively love and victory in astrology and Cabbala. Yvonne is like the soul that, in regaining consciousness of the material world, passes through the individual *Sephiroth*. Yvonne, in her little red plane, breaks through the "peaceful foreboding" of this multicolored dawn, the plane's color coinciding with *Geburah,* trial and severity, in the metaphor of "a minute red demon, winged emissary of Lucifer." She emerges now as woman in her harsh aspect, harbinger of further trial for the Consul. But as earthly woman she becomes aware of her conflicting emotions of love and hate, and she can only fully accept her mission when she realizes that "her spirit had flown to meet this man's. . . ."

It is in fact the Consul's voice she hears. He has been speaking to the barman about the absolute necessity for a woman depicted in an advertisement hanging over the bar who is "wearing a scarlet brassière" (another connection with Yvonne, whose "scarlet" handbag is the first thing Geoffrey notices as she enters). His conversation is "ritualistic" and "one-sided," for he is still unaware that the object of his ritual has just materialized. When he finally does spy her, she is "blurred . . . because the sunlight was behind her." As an emissary from a fiery sphere, Yvonne is blurred to Geoffrey, who detests any vision of sunlight, even to the point of later denouncing a sunflower as a "spy." All he can see of her is the red bag—that is, the prospect of judgment—so that in spite of his desperate need for her, he mistrusts her and treats her coldly.

When they finally do speak, their conversation is interrupted by snatches of a boisterous American right-wing monologue filled with references to violence and war, which is to be repeated once again at the Farolito as an accompaniment to the events of the Consul's persecution. The symbols contained in this commentary foreshadow the couple's tragedy by including references to "sun parched lips" (the unslaked thirst theme), "kicking horses" (Yvonne's death), and "they shoot first and ask questions later" (Geoffrey's death). Yvonne speaks first: "I came by boat . . . from San Pedro" (St. Peter, heaven). Geoffrey is disconcerted by the fact that she came to him via Cape Horn, for " 'It has a bad habit of wagging its tail' "—an economical reference that combines his own cuckoldry, the scorpion who stings itself to death with its own tail, and the "Horn of Venus"—love, which stings and cuckolds its victims. " 'Or does [*hornos*] mean ovens?' " he goes on to ask, implying that cuckoldry is another contribution to his burning hell.

As a continuation of the underlying suggestion that Yvonne is a messenger of mysterious forces, her baggage is taken by a "dark god . . . who bowed and disappeared obscurely." Geoffrey, testing her allegiance, asks her to drink with him. She cannot and thereby evokes the old quarrel, with its reminder of their divorce as a "sundering, severing." Divorce is associated in Geoffrey's mind with Oaxaca, which becomes another metaphor for hell. When she learns that the Consul has, in fact, been to Oaxaca during her absence, Yvonne sees that he had gone "into the heart of the sundering, of the severance. . . . wandering over some desolate cactus plain far from here, lost, stumbling and falling, attacked by wild beasts, calling for help. . . ." The Cabbalist who is to reconcile the two kingdoms and restore integrity to the tree of life is committed to "go into the heart of the severance" in order to search among the ruins for the love lost with the banishment.

Almost in answer to Yvonne's thoughts, the Consul brings up the issue of the "little corpse," reminding her that "it must be accompanied by a person holding its hand"—an indirect warning against following him into hell at the cost of her own life. But he then ironically reassures her that it requires "a first-class ticket," indicating that he alone is qualified to make the journey. Yvonne, sensing his "ultimate denial," mentally pleads: "Must you go on and on forever into this stupid darkness . . . where I cannot reach you, ever on into the darkness of the sundering, of the severance!"—as the *Shekinah* would plead in order to draw the sinner back to the heavenly path. The mental telepathy by which they communicate reinforces the design of their interdependence, as Geoffrey wordlessly replies by rejecting her "sunlight" in an apology for his commitment to the darkness and to the secret mysteries of drink:

Forgive me . . . not even the gates of heaven . . . could fill me with such celestial complicated and hopeless joy as the iron screen [doors

of the cantinas] . . . which admit those whose souls tremble with the
drinks they carry unsteadily to their lips. All mystery, all hope, all
disappointment, yes, all disaster, is here, beyond those swinging
doors. . . . how, unless you drink as I do, can you hope to understand the beauty of an old woman from Tarasco who plays dominoes
at seven o'clock in the morning?

It is as though Geoffrey had evoked the old woman merely by
naming her, and although Yvonne cannot see her at first, ". . . it
was almost uncanny, there *was* someone else in the room. . . ."
     Continuously busy at dominoes (reading fate by means of
*gematria*), the woman carries a stick "made of steel with some
animal's claws for a handle [which] hung like something alive"
(the magic wand is literally alive when magnetized by its owner)
and a live chicken (the cock, indispensable in black magic, forms
the initial appearance of the cock of death motif), which "chill"
Yvonne's heart, for "It was like an evil omen." The old lady is, in
fact, an evil omen, for she spells death. Displaying his magical insight into the ramifications of this omen, the Consul says, "Talking
of corpses . . . ," and goes on to delineate his desire "to be buried
next to William Blackstone." This statement becomes a forecast of
his death, during which he merges identities with—and is, as far as
he is concerned, buried as—William Blackstone. As he speaks, the
Consul signs a chit book, a symbolic concession of his debt to the
oracular messenger service of the spirits who appear with the alcohol. Then aligning himself with his evil familiars, he puts on a
pair of dark glasses (the sunlight being anathema to the demons of
*Gai-hinnom*) and calmly acknowledges the spies on his trail such
as "the ragged young Mexican," also in dark glasses, who is joined
by "another man with a shade over one eye and bare feet."
     Geoffrey and Yvonne walk through the empty morning streets
watched over by the "motionless" great wheel of the fair. Has time
stopped to give them another chance at life? As they pass the billboards they are informed of a special event during which *The In-
vincible Indian of Quauhnahuac weighing 57 kilos will fight for the
championship title*. . . . This is another indirect reference to the
Consul, who, born in India, is fighting to escape the abyss and,
after twelve $(5 + 7 = 12)$ hours, dies inadvertently as a "cham-
pion" of the rights of man. Yvonne says, "I hate boxing," for she
detests his violent struggle. He suggests the bullthrowing match as

a substitute. A man carrying a long plank of wood passes by and taunts the Consul with a shout of "Mesca*lito*" * as a demonic reminder of Geoffrey's own form of crucifixion. Yvonne cannot look at the volcanoes now, for, in the Consul's presence, the "sunlight blazed down upon them," transforming them into harsh blinding mirrors.

As they pass the town scribe, who is "crashing away on a giant typewriter," the recording archangel of men's deeds, the Consul jokingly, but meaningfully, calls out: "I am taking the only way out, semicolon. . . . Good-bye, full stop. Change of paragraph, change of chapter, change of worlds—" an open announcement of his plan to "change worlds," that is, attempt to get out of *Kelipah* by dying. Sensing his underlying meaning, Yvonne retorts, "You might have made use of him to answer some of *my* letters," reminding him that communication can be used for positive as well as negative purposes.

Near the Cortez Palace "but divided from it by the breadth of a steep narrow street desperate as a winze" † is a little printer's shop. Here they stop to look into a window, actually a magic mirror that truly reflects the ominous curse of their marriage in the form of "a photographic enlargement, purporting to show the disintegration of a glacial deposit in the Sierra Madre, of a great rock split by forest fires. [Ranged by poignant bridal photos, the picture] . . . set behind and above the . . . spinning flywheel of the presses, was called: La Despedida" (the Farewell). The printer's wheel is another representation of the wheel of life, which will permanently impress the destruction of the rock by a fire so violent that it had "incited the destruction of each separate rock, cancelling the power that might have held them unities. . . . [Yvonne wonders] why—by some fanciful geologic thaumaturgy, couldn't the pieces be welded together again!" Geoffrey's persona in the other half of the rock answers: "That's all very well . . . but . . . I propose to disintegrate as I please" for the scorching fire that emanates from his own body will serve to split the doomed man away from any hope of regeneration.

Agrippa's influence on Lowry lies behind this passage, where

---

* The awesome and terrible Mexican-Indian god of peyote.
† In addition to being a vertical mine shaft, "winze" is also Scottish dialect for "curse."

Yvonne longs to draw the rock together by means of alchemy, for the symbol of the degeneration of the rock by fire encloses the al- chemical secret of the duality of fire, which, depending on its manipulator, can either purify or destroy. The Cabbalistic corre- spondences to the severance theme are brought into play when the images of fire and mystical thirst are intertwined as Geoffrey's demoniacal craving for drink causes him to tremble and draw away from Yvonne as they walk along the Street of the Land of Fire. Because he is associated with the watery element, he can bear the torment of the sun no longer and must enter a dark little shop where he can appease his thirst for the moment.

From the shop, Yvonne hears: " 'You-are-a-man-who-like- much- Vine!' [accompanied by] . . . incredibly good-humoured but ruffianly male laughter," a reference to Dionysus, the keeper of the sacred vine located by Christian Cabbalists in *Tiphereth,* home of the sacrificed gods. Then, calling the Consul "Diablo," the voice mimics Geoffrey's request for "eggs," repeating the word three times. Lowry later picks up this theme by referring to the cosmic egg and repeats it again in the bawdy mystery feast that takes place in Chapter Eleven. The "rotten egg" is a form of infertility or a perversion of Eros (cf. Yvonne's childlessness) and pertains to the corrupt condition of the world as well. To reinforce the images of infertility and death, Lowry has the couple pass a bizarre funeral of a dead child as they enter the district of their home. This will eventually lead to Yvonne's recollection of her own dead child, also named Geoffrey, of a previous marriage. Here, however, Lowry puts down still another omen generated by Geoffrey's fore- cast of himself as the little corpse to be delivered by express.

Even the grass near their home is not "as green as it should be at the end of the rains: there must have been a dry spell. . . ." Green being the practical Cabbalist's color of *Netzach* (Venus), and therefore fertility, a dry spell means disaster for the Consul, who, like the arid waste surrounding his house, is shortly to be- come impotent.

The severance, rottenness, and impotence motifs are strength- ened by the unavoidable, lingering presence of Jacques, who is personified by the figure of a "peon going into an alleyway" (*La ruelle* is also an alleyway) after gazing intently at Laruelle's house (the blasted tower, sign of the corrupted world). Yvonne has chosen to block all memories of Jacques from her mind. The Consul, sensing her discomfort but nevertheless deriving a kind of sadomasochistic pleasure from publicly declaring himself a cuckold, pursues the adultery theme anyway. He speaks jokingly of the bond between Jacques and himself and follows this up with the news that Hugh is staying with him. The external world responds accordingly, for at the moment of this announcement it is as though the billboards themselves speak through the advertisements for the Arena Tomalín (where Hugh will later prove his masculinity) and *Las Manos de Orlac* (in which a man is driven mad with jealousy). Geoffrey's sardonic comment is, "It seems everyone comes flying to see me these days," for Hugh, like Yvonne, has come to save the Consul. Whereas she comes from the sky, however, Hugh, being a reporter for the *Globe,* has come from the earth.

Although he seems to be superficially beating poppies with his stick as he walks along, the Consul is actually striking out at Hugh, whose proficiency as an herbalist is dedicated to straightening Geoffrey out by drugging him. Parallel to the serious mescal-drug motif is a wry subplot, which begins here with Geoffrey intimating that Hugh is poisoning him in order to cure him. (There is a subsequent humorous overtone in Geoffrey's encounter with his neighbor Quincy, who merges identities with De Quincy, the opium addict.) Hugh is here characterized by Geoffrey as an ambitious reporter who, having caught wind of a story, runs "after it here like a red rag after a bull." The inverted cliché is intentional, since Hugh is a communist who seeks positive earthly action and gets it when he later confronts the bull.

When she is reminded of her infidelity by Geoffrey's insinuating comments, Yvonne (now viewed as Eve, the source of sin, or the female in her negative aspect) assumes part of her husband's guilt over the failure of their marriage and sees Geoffrey as "living in the midst of her blame." This chapter closes with a false reunification, a simulated reprieve of suffering, as the Consul indicates with his stick the "lane to the right . . . the abandoned iron mine running under the garden," the silver treasure of their lost innocence buried under the original garden of paradise. They enter their gate, which hangs "off its hinges," and when Geoffrey calls, "almost home" we see that "A hideous pariah dog followed them in."

# Chapter Three

The Firmins enter the ruined garden, Geoffrey accompanied by accusing inner voices and Yvonne bravely restraining her horror at the condition of her home. The maid comes out with a bottle of whiskey, but Yvonne declines a drink. The Consul is antagonistic to her abstinence, and his tormenting voices grow spiteful against her. Husband and wife continue to talk about the past year of separation like two strangers, but the underlying tension comes closer to the surface. Finally, they argue over the nature of a little bird that has appeared on a nearby tree. The water trickling into the swimming pool provides Geoffrey with still another tormenting refrain until they are interrupted by the ringing of the telephone. The Consul has a hasty conversation and is so shaken by it that he takes to the street in search of a cantina. At the base of the hill at the street's end, Geoffrey falls on his face and suffers a momentary blackout, during which he mistakes an English tourist for his brother and dizzily contemplates the difficulties of their childhood. The Englishman helps him up and offers him a nip. Fully revived by now, the Consul returns to the house and enters his wife's bedroom. He talks about his unfinished Cabbalistic book and alludes to his alchemist friends in Chicago. Yvonne and he reminisce about their unhappy past attempts at getting together and then begin to make love. Proving impotent, the Consul leaves her and drinks to the point where he hallucinates the figure of a dead man by his swimming pool. Exhausted, Geoffrey falls into a deep, drunken sleep.

The Firmins return home to be faced with "the tragedy" of their fate mirrored by nature at her lowest: their ruined garden. Lowry continues the sterility theme by contrasting the once-fecund past with the barren present, as embodied in the "gaping potholes . . . tall exotic plants . . . perishing on every hand of unnecessary thirst, staggering, it almost appeared, against one another, yet struggling like dying voluptuaries in a vision to maintain some final attitude of potency, or of a collective desolate fecundity. . . ."

Geoffrey, again telepathically, hears Yvonne at his side as the pleading *Shekinah* wishes to draw him back to God:

"Regard: see how strange, how sad, familiar things may be. Touch this tree, once your friend [the tree of life that grows in the midst of the garden now becomes the tree of death]: alas, that that which you have known in the blood should ever seem so strange! Look up at . . . where Christ is still suffering, who would help you if you asked him. . . .* Consider the agony of the roses. . . . Regard: the plantains with their queer familiar blooms, once emblematic of life, now of an evil phallic death. [On the tree of death sex is transformed into lechery.] You do not know how to love these things any longer. All your love is the cantinas now . . . a love of life now turned to poison . . . and poison has become your daily food. . . ."

As he enters the garden, the Consul "amiably" addresses the pariah dog who appears "familiarly at heel," perhaps as Hermanubis, the magician's "familiar," in order to shut out the pleading voice in his ear. Then he comments on Hugh's determination to clean up the garden: "We've been virtually without a gardener at all for months. Hugh pulled up a few weeds. He cleaned out the swimming pool too . . ." Obviously, Hugh's work at restoring the garden gives the Consul all the more reason to resent his earthy constructive/active alter ego who opposes his own "watery" lassitude, especially since the water in the garden is a symbol of divine fluid and therefore more properly Geoffrey's attribute, not Hugh's. Then Geoffrey launches into a biblical enumeration of the catastrophes that befell his house, which is described as "a pretty little ship lying at anchor" overcome by a flood that "left us with something that smelt like the Cosmic Egg. . . ." When Yvonne asks him what became of the flowers she had planted (that is, life), Geoffrey replies, "God knows," thus providing a climax to their investigation of the ruined garden; for only God himself knows the circumstances behind the fall.

At this moment, the maid, Concepta, appears. Lowry uses her as one of Abbé de Villars' earth spirits, whose sole delight is to work for men who can evoke and control them. They live under the earth and are called gnomes. Perhaps still another manifestation of the mysterious old woman with the dominoes, Concepta is

---

* The Christian Cabbalist looks to the *Sephirah Tiphereth*, where Christ as *Adam Kadmon*, the direct image of God, can intercede on behalf of *Adam Tahton*, the microcosmic man.

described as having "the face of a highly intellectual black gnome . . . (mistress to some gnarled guardian of the mine beneath the garden once, perhaps). . . ."

When the Consul had begun to despair of a drink, he merely willed, and "as in answer to his prayer Concepta was approaching them" with a tray of Scotch and Hugh's "poison" (paraldehyde). He must now fight off the hideous chattering of his voices, his pursuing "familiars," for the false security of the alcohol of the morning is beginning to wear off. One demon is "a pleasant and impertinent familiar, perhaps horned, prodigal of disguise, a specialist in casuistry." This is, actually, another aspect of the Consul himself, who is also charming and "horned" as a cuckold. He takes the "sinister" medicine, which fools him into thinking his redemption is sure. No sooner does this thought cross his mind than he is confronted by another tormentor who mocks him and tries to turn him back to wine, the product of Yvonne's ancestral country, "the throat-smarting fire of your wife's ancestors." This is Lowry's first direct allusion to the ancient magical potency of the gods subsumed in the combined images of fire and wine, or the theosophical "divine light" or "divine fluid."

On the other hand, the 1820 $(1 + 8 + 2 + 0 = 11)$ label on the bottle of Scotch is a dangerous sign, for the *Zohar* specifically emphasizes that there are *ten* and not *eleven* paths to redemption, the final object of Geoffrey's quest through alcohol, eleven being ascribed to the *Kelipah*. As though sensing the danger, Yvonne subverts the tormentors momentarily by gently urging her husband to drink the Scotch. In that split second, love, in the form of "a swan, transfixed [which] plummeted to earth," reenters and they embrace for the first time that morning. Yvonne is to be equated here with the white bird of the Pleiades legend since she too has descended from heaven to bring love.

But driven by his familiars to thoughts of the cantina, the Consul can no longer endure sanctioned love. In his mind's eye he sees "the doomed men . . . crowding into the warmth of the sun, waiting for the shutters to roll up with a crash of trumpets . . ." (that is, the judgment of those who derive life from the false warmth of intoxication). He absent-mindedly locates Dr. Vigil's card in his pocket and brings it "to light," thus continuing the identification of Vigil and Yvonne with light, as opposed to the demons and the cantinas, which draw him toward darkness. The card reminds him that there is still hope, that time is being extended: Vigil's office hours beginning at *twelve* and ending at *seven*—an offer of initiatory assistance. Annoyed by the intrusion of light, the demons inside him persist with their lies and fool Geoffrey into thinking of himself as being "Still strong as a horse . . . strong as a horse!" a false alignment with Lévi's symbol of divine strength, for he is unaware that it has by now begun to turn toward destruction.

Now ensues a double-edged exchange about Yvonne's condition, which Geoffrey starts by saying: "You look as though you've had plenty of sun . . . There's been plenty of sun here too of course . . . As usual . . . Too much of it. In spite of the rain . . . Do you know, I don't like it."

"Oh yes you do, really. . . . We could get out in the sun, you know." Coming out of the region of *Tiphereth,* Yvonne represents sun, light, love, warmth. Geoffrey, committed to the darkness, rejects it, preferring rain. Sitting on a "broken green rocker" (*Netzach* = the green *Sephirah,* Venus or broken love), he contemplates their suffering from a Cabbalistic point of view: "Perhaps it was just the soul, he thought . . . that grew older [*Gilgul*]. . . . And perhaps the soul thrived on its sufferings. . . ." This last reflection is a thought derived directly from the *Zohar,* which claims that God only permits great suffering to those souls on earth who will, as a result of the "maturation" process, be rewarded after death. The Consul considers his wife to be such a soul as he muses over her past, her dead child—also significantly named Geoffrey—her bad luck in marriage, and he concludes: "She was no longer his: someone had doubtless approved her smart slate blue travelling suit: it had not been he." No longer in control of the *Shekinah* Geoffrey has lost his balance somewhere in the region of *Chesed* (blue), manifested in the outer world by his loss of positive magic power, which he compares to "the demoted skipper's lost command." Like Vigil, however, Yvonne continues to extend symbols of hope, for she is still wearing her wedding ring. The Consul wonders if it was "merely for his, for *their* benefit? The swimming pool ticked on. *Might a soul bathe there and be clean or slake its drought?*" Geoffrey rejects the validity of the wedding ring as a symbol of reunification, but continues to seek a possibility of quenching his spiritual thirst, the pool here assuming in his mind the meaning of the paradisal rivers.

Yvonne, "leaning against a pillar," the pillar of severity, now chastises him: "Geoffrey, this place is a wreck!" Angered by her attack and "winding his wrist watch" (the first indication of his preoccupation with time), he flings back at her: ". . . [You] can't very well expect to invite your soul into quite the same green graces, with quite the same dear old welcome here. . . ."

This retort starts a covert spiritual struggle that manifests itself in the form of a disagreement about the nature and color of a bird that suddenly appears. In her harsh aspect, Yvonne is an agent of *Geburah* (Severity), which Geoffrey fears and resents. She, correspondingly, sees the bird as red ("a bit of flame"). Haunted by the thought of judgment, which he associates with the extreme damnation represented in the image of "hellish Wesleyan breath," Geoffrey contradicts her by saying: "He's a coppery-tailed trogon. . . . And he has no red breast. He's a solitary fellow who probably lives way off in the Canyon of the Wolves . . . so that he can have peace to meditate about not being a cardinal. . . . the ambiguous bird!" Geoffrey intends this flat contradiction as a sarcastic reminder of his own ambiguous fallen state, his willful isolation, and the negation of her attempted intercession between himself and God.

All the while the water is "still trickling into the pool—God how deadeningly slowly . . . ," reminding him once again of the passing of time and of his own unbearable thirst. Thirst leads him immediately to thoughts of Parián, the place where the illusion of grace is sold in the form of mescal. Again falling prey to hallucinations, the Consul hears and yet does not hear the celestial music, which, when converted by black magic, becomes a source of madness: "It was doubtless the almost tactile absence of the music, however, that made it so peculiar the trees should be apparently shaking to it, an illusion investing not only the garden but the plains beyond, the whole scene before his eyes, with horror, the horror of an intolerable unreality."

In the sunlight, brought even closer by Yvonne's presence, his perception is of terror. He sees the sunlight as antipathetic and alien. A neighbor's gardener at work becomes a menace. His nerves are attacked by the erratic flashing of small red birds, as though they were connected to his nerves by "sensitive wires." Suddenly the wires come to life: the telephone rings, introducing the first of the book's tortured phone conversations, each one Lowry's device depicting another attempt at communication from above. So hypersensitive is Geoffrey to the possibility of the "Wesleyan" retribution embodied by the red birds that he hurries frantically through the call, "apprehensive lest at any moment boiling oil pour into his eardrums or his mouth," for the torments of the *Gaihinnom* turn even the quotidian world into a vast nightmare of expected punishment. The call is a warning about his diplomatic position, perhaps even an attempt to get him to leave Mexico, to which he ambiguously responds: ". . . Christ. What does he want to ring me up at this hour of the morning for. . . . [From] Erikson 43 [4 + 3 = 7]. Christ . . ." And he hangs up the receiver "the wrong way," presumably in order to forestall any further efforts in his behalf on the part of the Savior.

Hell-bent, the Consul leaves the house on the prowl for another drink. "It was as if he were toiling up some endless staircase between houses ["house" = "soul"]. Or perhaps even old Popeye itself. . . . The road with its tossing broken stones stretched on forever into the distance like a life of agony." This is the trial ascent that is later to be relived at his death. In a foreshadowing of that final fall, Geoffrey does not complete this ascent, aiming for the cantina on the path "branching to the left" then "to the right." This unsuccessful short cut to the top of the volcano through the evil path indicates what is actually happening in his soul. The little jaunt to the cantina results in a literal fall. A blackout follows, during which he imagines that Hugh is helping him up. Removed from time and space by unconsciousness, Geoffrey has a vision of his childhood, succeeded by Hugh's betrayal and his own forgiveness and a resurgence of his incurable longing to reunite with the father up in the White Alps. In preparation for the Consul's later association with "Il Papa," Lowry describes Geoffrey's fatherly but unsuccessful attempts at initiating Hugh to the "high seas," for novices of the occult must make their own way independent of their guides, a principle Lowry knew from many sources, the most explicit in Ouspensky's *A New Model of the Universe* in the chapter "Christ and the New Testament." Hugh had misunderstood the enforced separations, the "guardians," "surrogates," "establishments," and "schools" that had kept them apart. Now, in his trancelike state, Geoffrey gives his younger brother the supernatural reason for his own alcoholic condition by describing the "war" that each is waging, Geoffrey with his bottle and Hugh with his "dangerous" ideas. The Consul hopes, he says, that the ideas will not prove as dangerous to Hugh as they were to their father, nor, for that matter, as dangerous as the Consul's own are to himself. More than that, he goes on, there exist certain reasons, which shall be revealed only at the "day of reckoning," that Hugh must not press him for. This cryptic "explanation" of the stupefied Consul refers to the secret mystical burden entailed in descending into the *Kelipah,* its repercussions not justifiable or indeed capable of justification in earthly terms. He speaks of the apparent "clownish" nature of his actions in terms of the voluntary assumption of suffering on the part of the tarot fool: "Yet does this help, what I am trying to tell you, that *I* realise to what degree I brought all this upon myself?"

. It is not Hugh helping him to his feet, however, but an Englishman wearing a Trinity College tie, which bears a symbolic fountain immediately associated in Geoffrey's mind with *"Might a soul bathe there and be clean or slake its drought?"* The man with the Trinity tie, like Vigil or Yvonne, is another agent of the first triune world, which sends aid and extends mercy, in this case, a resuscitative drop from the "fountain of life," here as a bottle of Irish whiskey.

Once revived and grateful to the forces of human decency, Geoffrey can return home and enter Yvonne's room with renewed good intentions. He finds her reading an astronomy magazine. After a short discussion of the Mayan calendar, Geoffrey reflects on the nature of time and the relative unimportance of human intellect in the universal scheme: ". . . [Where] does it all get you in the end? . . . The knowledge, I mean. One of the first penances I ever imposed on myself was to learn the philosophical section of *War and Peace* by heart. That was of course before I could dodge about in the rigging of the Cabbala like a St. Jago's monkey." Magicians must indulge in certain ascetic practices in order to prepare themselves for the "great work." Thought control in the form of concentration, even philosophical meditation, prepares them for greater telepathic powers. The Consul is therefore referring to the early phase of his initiation, the time when he was still in complete control of his mind. Soon after, his acquaintance with Cabbala very broad, he had achieved powers beyond that of the merely intellectual realm. There is also a certain sadness inherent in this type of knowledge that does not make up for the inability to live within the world of time, but serves, in fact, to isolate the adept from other men.*

When Yvonne questions him about money matters, Geoffrey talks about a diplomatic colleague whose property in Tlaxcala, the capital of magic in Mexico, has been confiscated, and he hints at his own precarious position, since he is now resigned from "the service." No longer a servant of the "Empire," Geoffrey is stranded in the midst of the struggle between fascism and democracy (black and white magic); he has decided to blindly fight it out alone: " 'They haven't my number yet, I'm not sure where I really do stand in that regard. . . . I'm thinking of becoming a Mexican subject, of going to live among the Indians, like William Blackstone. . . . all very mysterious to you [who are] . . . outside looking in. . . .' " This train of thought leads him to a sudden vision of "what was—Good God!—his salvation . . ." This is his first realization that his coming martyrdom in the person of Blackstone could bear with it some hope of salvation: he cannot, therefore, accept Yvonne's request to leave Mexico. Again grasping the meaning of his thoughts with their underlying danger, Yvonne, who is always on the side of life, says, ". . . [This] house has become somehow evil—" To this Geoffrey retaliates: "What's the use of escaping . . . from ourselves?"

Bolstered by his new discovery and conscious of the enormity of his mission, he marvels at his own mystical "Sober drunkenness" — "And even if he were not sober now, by what fabulous stages, comparable indeed only to the paths and spheres of the Holy Cabbala itself, had he reached *this* stage again . . . so arduous to maintain, of being drunk in which alone he was sober!" Disgusted with the world's inability to comprehend the "importance" of a drunkard's life, he threatens to stop drinking, resume work, and

---

* Lowry was probably talking from experience here, for Mrs. Lowry described a period in their lives when Frater Achad drilled them according to a strict schedule, testing their powers of concentration, memory, and so forth.

finish his book (that is, give up the quest and settle for being a mere chronicler of the secret knowledge). In still another death fantasy, he continues:

Yes: I can see the reviews now. Mr. Firmin's sensational new data on Atlantis! The most extraordinary thing of its kind. . . . Interrupted by his untimely death . . . Marvellous. And the chapters on the alchemists! Which beat the Bishop of Tasmania [mentioned again in Chapter Ten as an exemplification of the victim of a mirage that leads to his death] to a frazzle. . . . I might even work in something about CoxCox and Noah [the Noah-wine secret]. I've got a publisher interested too; in Chicago [Frater Achad's *Collegium ad Spiritum Sanctum*, which he goes on to describe]. . . . [It's] amazing when you come to think of it how the human spirit seems to blossom in the shadow of the abattoir! How—to say nothing of all the poetry . . . people can be living in cellars the life of the old alchemists of Prague! Yes: living among the cohobations of Faust himself, among the litharge and agate and hyacinth and pearls. A life which is amorphous, plastic and crystalline. . . . Or perhaps I might get myself another job, first of course being sure to insert an advertisement in the *Universal:* will accompany corpse to any place in the east!

This speech describing the lives of the modern Cabbalists in Chicago runs the gamut from alchemy to necromancy. It is, in addition, a justification of the Consul's own spurious spiritual survival in the "shadow of the abattoir," for he is at odds with himself and is still diffident about his alchemistic purpose.

By proposing to change his "job" (inquiring first into the "universal" scheme of things), he manifests his willingness to die if that is what is entailed in a return to the east—that is, both home and immortal life. On hearing his declaration, Yvonne makes a "gesture of supplication" epitomizing the "loyalties and eternal hopes of their marriage." (In the *Zohar,* prayer and the sex act are equivalent in marriage.) In the face of his wife's appeal, the Consul replaces his dark glasses and immediately, as if the glasses were a magic looking glass into tragedy, sees not the prospect of union and hope but images of forlorn lost love—Oscar Wilde in handcuffs, "a butterfly flying out to sea: lost," all leading to painful reminiscences of past attempts and failures to find Yvonne.

With the street of sorrow as his mental backdrop, Geoffrey once again wanders "homeless," mistaken for a wrestler in Mexico City because of his beard, "wandering around from place to place, wrestling, and thinking all the while I could prevent you from

going . . . if I could only find you!" * Still conscious of the abattoir, the Consul recalls identifying Yvonne and himself with
"two little fawns shrieking with fright" as they are dragged in for
slaughter by "an executioner," and he compares the present state
of his soul to that of the fawns, who are "dragged . . . as at the
tail of a runaway horse," the punitive force of *Chavajah,* Lévi's
destructive power of God.

Sorrow suddenly overcomes them both, and there is an attempt
at lovemaking described in accurate Cabbalistic terms, which
equate the sex act with the symbolic entry of the soul into *Yesod*
(the *Sephirah* corresponding to the genitals of microcosmic man).
". . . [He] could feel now, too . . . the image of his possession,
like that jewelled gate the desperate neophyte, Yesod-bound,
projects for the thousandth time on the heavens to permit passage
of his astral body, fading, and slowly, inexorably, that of a cantina . . . taking its place." The Consul's break in concentration is
analogous to the disturbance from the outside for the meditating
Cabbalist, who must place himself in a state of suspended dissocia-
tion from all distractions, focusing his attentions entirely on the
wish to join with his chosen *Sephirah.* This attention often entails
the recitation of "preparatory phrases" designed to aid in the
process of autosuggestion. But once again pulled down from
heavenly anticipation by his contrary longing for hell, the Consul is
distracted by visions of his haunts, where he can see the ac-
countant "gloomily" surveying accounts, where exiles lurk in cor-
ners and "a brigand" with an "iron scorpion" all gather, "people
eructating, exploding, committing nuisances . . . the debris from
the night before. . . . vendors of *La Prensa* and *El Universal.*
. . ." These are symbols of the material world that prove the most
effective hindrances to completing the mystical ascent: namely the
attachment to the lower bodily needs, the criminal element in the
initiate's own character, which he projects onto the outer world,
the temptations of obsessive thoughts (*La Prensa*) and worldly
concerns (*El Universal*).

In Geoffrey's mind it is "a little past nine," for *Yesod* is the
ninth *Sephirah,* and he is mentally working his way down into the

---

* In Cabbalistic terms, Jacob wrestles with the spirit in order to maintain
its power and sustenance; further, the magician must expect to wrestle with
the spirit he wishes to evoke.

illusory Gate of the Sun cantina, where sunlight is "flooding the bar
. . . in a single golden line as if in the act of conceiving a God
. . ."; *Yesod* and sex being identified with the moon, his sunlight
vision is out of context here and a sign of his reversed position on
the Sephirotic tree. Thus, both the lovemaking and the meditation
are unsuccessful, for they end in an abrupt struggle between the
elements of fire and water when he sees the illusory cantina sunlight fall "like a lance straight into a block of ice—" and the tortures of hell are resumed once again. He craves a drink so badly at
this point that he accidentally resorts to Hugh's "strychnine" and
then hopes that maybe this will act as an "aphrodisiac" that will
restore his lost potency.

Falsely identifying love with drugs as he does life with alcohol,
he drinks the 1820 (*Kelipathic*) whiskey again and *sinks* down
through the *green* cane rocking chair, thereby totally destroying
the corresponding image of their love, which had been heretofore
only broken. As he says, "I love you," to the whiskey bottle he can
hear Yvonne crying in the next room. His deliberate abandonment
of love for intoxication enables the "other" to appear with the
power to prophesy death in the form of a corpse "lying flat on its
back by his swimming pool, with a large sombrero over its face.
. . ." * Frightened by this grotesque vision, with its underlying
connotations as to his own condition, he attempts to convince himself that he is in complete control, that he can "carry the eighth
green in three" (that is, achieve meditation on the eighth level of
the tree in only three stages). Then, as if in sudden recognition of
his actual physical and spiritual impotence: "I am tapering off.
. . . What am I talking about? Even I know I am being fatuous.
. . . I am too sober. I have lost my familiars, my guardian angels." The dangerous process of contacting one's guardian angel is
outlined in Mather's *The Book of the Sacred Magic of Abra-melin,
the Mage,* which, according to his wife, Lowry studied very carefully. Much advance preparation is outlined in that book for the
procedure, which entails losing oneself to this world for a time.
The ritual, if incorrectly handled, can, apparently, lead to insanity.
The Consul can only manage to avoid this insanity by remaining

* "The dead man with hat over head the Consul sees in the garden is
man by the wayside in Chapter VIII. This can happen in really super D.T.'s.
Paracelsus will bear me out. . . ." Lowry, *Letters.*

drunk. He rationalizes his sexual-spiritual failure by claiming: "One must never forget either that alcohol is food. How can a man be expected to perform his marital duties without food?" In a final excess of mock-Faustian blasphemy before the inevitable unconsciousness to follow, the Consul proclaims: "The will of man is unconquerable. Even God cannot conquer it." Then, after making a mental note of the ironic harmony between the two volcanoes in "perfect marriage" (as opposed to his own) and the vultures circling in wait, "he [falls] asleep with a crash."

# Chapter Four

Hugh, a reporter for the *Daily Globe*, is reading the cable he intends to dispatch to his paper. It concerns the anti-Semitic propaganda being spread by fascist elements in Mexico. In the midst of his reading, he suddenly catches sight of Yvonne working in the garden and is taken aback by her unexpected presence. They indulge in a strained conversation, and he places the telegram in his brother's jacket, which he had borrowed earlier that day. He is obviously still in love with his sister-in-law but makes a valiant effort to restrain his feelings. He informs her of some of his communist-affiliated adventures and drops some hints about a Loyalist mission to which he is committed. They both decide to hire some horses and continue their conversation on horseback. (Hugh is appropriately dressed in cowboy boots and ten-gallon hat, for he has flown down to Mexico from a Texas cattle ranch.) Their mood relaxes as they ride through some lovely pastoral scenery—particularly a quiet dairy farm, where they pick up a friendly little white dog, who follows them the entire way. As he rides, Hugh mentally muses over his ideals, his hero and mentor, Juan Cerillo, his Loyalist mission (which includes blowing up his own freighter along with the enemy's ammunition boats), until they stop for a drink at a little brewery. Here they notice an Indian peon sleeping against the wall; his horse, branded with the number 7, is tethered nearby. As they move on, Yvonne and Hugh begin to talk about Geoffrey, who seems enigmatic to both of them—perhaps he is a black magician! Yvonne discusses her plan to salvage what is left of her relationship with her husband by taking him up to the Canadian woods. At first Hugh is skeptical, but he grows enthusiastic as he starts to spin an elaborate fantasy of a life of rustic peace and simplicity for his brother and sister-in-law. For a moment, he even redeems himself by obscuring his adulterous guilt feelings about Yvonne. But immediately after his cheerful note of hope is sounded, they ride into the ruined territory surrounding Maximilian's Palace, and now only the tragedy of Maximilian and Carlotta pervades their thoughts. In the wild landscape and in the crags of the moon that Yvonne points out to him, Hugh's dreams of peace are replaced by a terrible longing.

The initial reference to Jews and anti-Semitism, later so vital to Geoffrey's misidentification by the fascists, occurs here. More than just a device for depicting Hugh's character, the Jew-versus-fascist theme becomes part of the general white-versus-black-magician political plot. The Consul will even remark that Hitler's obsession with exterminating Jews stemmed from his fear of their secret powers.* Hugh is wearing "his brother's jacket" into the pocket of which he places the incriminating telegram, which cryptically reads: ". . . *headcoming antisemitic campaign . . . pamphlet asserts jews influence unfavourably any country they live etemphasises quote their belief absolute power etthat they gain their ends without conscience or consideration unquote stop Firmin.*" The passage is entirely in italics and lacks punctuation and thereby leaves itself open to nearly any type of interpretation. Generally, however, it relates to the Consul, who, as a Cabbalist, is actually associated with Jews and is therefore subject to a similar coming disaster; hence the underlying warning implied in the "stop Firmin."

Hugh, as Geoffrey's alter ego, is also spiritually bound to Yvonne, so that when he sees her working in the garden after a year's absence, the world literally stops for him. She is "clothed entirely in sunlight . . . [and is] wearing yellow slacks" so that she serves to bring his past into the light as she had done for the Consul that morning on her appearance in the dark cantina. He even experiences a similar reaction to Geoffrey's—"an instant's paralysed confusion, and reluctance to meet the past"—and hands her the cable "for some reason" as he shakes her hand in greeting (an unconscious warning of danger for her husband, which she, just as unconsciously, returns). Hugh is extremely tanned, "more black than brown with sun," and is identified from the beginning with the earth, for he had come to Mexico "disguised as a cow." In spite of his avowed disgust with life (he has resigned his position on the *Globe*), Hugh is representative of the life force.

Yvonne appeals once again for assistance in returning order to their lives: "Isn't the garden a *wreck?*" Hugh, always literal and

* Cf. Lowry, *Letters.*

earthy, avoids the implied plea: "It looks quite beautiful to me, considering Geoffrey hasn't had a gardener for so long." In the midst of the strained conversation Hugh feels as if he "had mastered the branch" (of a bougainvillea tree that she is working on). He then immediately associates the gesture with the thought that ". . . they are losing the Battle of the Ebro because I did that—" a strange commingling of thoughts ostensibly referring to his newspaper resignation, but actually related to his own position on the tree of life. Hugh feels guilt about his spiritual vacancy, for, once having mastered *Malkuth,* the Earthplane, he is now aware of responsibility for more than just himself and consequently seeks the brother with whom he vaguely associates the answers to his problems. He describes his troublesome flight *"down"* to the *Kelipah,* on which he had been accompanied by "an American semi-fascist . . . in the Foreign Legion," actually the man who has kept up the running commentary of the morning in the cantina and who is to show up again at Parián that night. ("Coincidentally," then, Hugh is traveling with one of the legion of devils who is "flying in" to join the assembly of accusers at the Farolito.)

Noticing that Yvonne wears a "blouse embroidered with birds and flowers and pyramids . . . bought or brought for Geoff's benefit . . . [he feels] a pain in his heart. . . ." These symbols on her blouse are all positive aspects of Yvonne's mission to remind Geoffrey of his past hope and innocence: the pyramid is the triune worlds of the tree of life; birds are herself; flowers are the promise of fertility. Hugh, sensing that they are not intended for him, feels pain in the organ corresponding to the reception of the *Shekinah.*

"My God, this used to be a beautiful garden. It was like Paradise," she insists again. Hugh, still coveting his brother's wife, counters with: "Let's get the hell out of it then," only to be confronted with Geoffrey's presence through a very loud snore, which represents both English political inaction and Geoffrey's own deliberate passivity toward his wife. Yvonne fears that ". . . Geoff might come catapulting out of the window, bed and all . . . ," in an allusion Lowry intends to the common power of magicians to make sudden and surprise appearances. Nevertheless, they leave the garden, Yvonne "floating rather than walking." As they turn left ". . . the road decline[s] sharply below them. At the bottom rose purple hills." Passing down through *Yesod,* the purple *Sephirah* representing sex, they descend to the material world, where the scenery grows rougher. Here they come under the vigilant gaze of the secret police on the watchtower, and their conversation appropriately turns to war. Hugh's concern with the war is actually the exterior reflection of the demonic battle fought by the Consul. He too longs for the East, in his case the future worker's "paradise" of communist "China," as Geoffrey longs for the more unearthly India.

Suddenly a goat enters the scene as a living embodiment of Hugh's desire for Yvonne—perhaps a manifestation of Geoffrey himself—and regards Hugh and Yvonne "with patriarchal contempt."

". . . [They're] the lowest form of animal life . . ." Hugh barely gets out, when the goat starts to charge. And as the animal comes toward them he reaches for Yvonne only to be overcome by "the sudden intoxicating terrified incidence and warmth of Yvonne's body." * Still unwittingly referring to Geoffrey's destructive power, and his own lechery, Hugh continues: "Goats. . . . Even when there are no wars think of the damage they do. . . . [Catching himself] I mean journalists, not goats."

At this moment, they come upon the barranca, which Hugh claims is the only punishment for "them," referring to journalists. Yet his statement stands as an ominous foreshadowing of Geoffrey's death, especially when viewed in light of the Cabbalistic goat sacrifice. Still pursuing his double-entendre monologue, Hugh describes a friend who "was killed by a stray shell before seeing any action" in the Spanish Civil War, which is precisely how he himself will die. The discussion turns from the war to Geoffrey, who is seemingly politically unconcerned, for he *knows* that the fascists are going to win. He [Geoffrey] "says *when* the fascists win there'll only be a sort of 'freezing' of culture in Spain—by the way, is that the moon up there?" The allusion to Geoffrey's accurate prediction is coincidental with the appearance of the moon, because *Yesod* (Foundation), as lunar *Sephirah,* also stands for magic power and clairvoyance.

Where Geoffrey has become a man of destruction, Hugh sees

---

* In his letter to Jonathan Cape, Lowry says that the goat is intended to represent lechery, cuckoldry, and tragedy.

himself as a potential savior. When Yvonne asks him about his "mysterious purpose," he says:

. . . I'm going back to sea. . . . If all goes well I'll be sailing from Vera Cruz in about a week [seven initiatory days]. . . . I've always wanted to take a look at Trinidad [a pun in keeping with his Christ identification]—might be some real fun coming out of Trinidad one day. Geoff helped me with a couple of introductions but no more than that, I didn't want to make him responsible. . . . Try persuading the world not to cut its throat . . . like me, and it'll begin to dawn on you that even *your* behavior's part of its plan.

Geoffrey has introduced his brother to the method of saving one's soul by means of martyrdom by initiating him to the sea and by "introducing" him to the triune worlds along the path emanating from the True Cross. No longer needing his brother as a keeper, Hugh wishes to make the remainder of the journey alone in an attempt to improve on the "world plan"—a concept probably derived by Lowry from Achad's *Anatomy of the Body of God,* which deals primarily with forecasting and manipulating the course of world events.

In his stream-of-consciousness monologue that follows, Hugh reenacts Geoffrey's sea experience in reverse, perhaps in atonement for his brother's murder of the German officers. He sees himself as a Samaritan who steers the ship on which ". . . the officer on duty had changed from white to blue for winter [*Kether* emanating to *Chesed,* mercy being the appropriate *Sephirah* for a Samaritan]. . . . for it was not a ship he was steering now, but the world, out of the Western Ocean of its misery." It is as if his noble thoughts cause a change in the scene around them, for beginning with the sighting of some peaceful horses rolling playfully in the grass and "in the distance a few rather large cows," more reminders of Hugh's earth sign, the terrain changes—"A sweet smell of milk and vanilla and wild flowers hung about. . . . And the sun was over all."

Here Yvonne is in her element. As she and Hugh ride through on horseback they are followed by "an affectionate scrubbed woolly white dog," the direct antithesis of the black pariah that had been following Geoffrey. Because they are now in a higher sphere looking down at the descending paths to the abyss below, they can see the Consul's house "to their left . . . parallel with which on different levels obliquely climbing the hill, all the other gardens of contiguous residences . . . also descended steeply toward the barranca. . . ." Purposely avoiding "the entrance to the public garden . . . they trotted into another lane that inclined to their right." Hugh is pleased that Yvonne rides "cowboy-fashion . . . and not 'as in gardens.' " At this moment, then, she is identified with him, with his ten-gallon hat and Texan boots, rather than with Geoffrey. All the accompanying images counteract Geoffrey's destructive influence. It is as though the little dog has been specifically sent by divine forces to guard Hugh and Yvonne from evil and to promote thoughts of hope for the future. The little dog is therefore "evidently trained to detect snakes. . . . It was certainly hard to reconcile this dog with the pariahs . . . those dreadful creatures that seemed to shadow his brother everywhere." Protected by the dog this time, they laugh as they pass the same goat again. But the Consul is still at work, for Lowry adds the goat's unheard thoughts to the scene: *"I may have missed that time. I am still on the warpath however."*

During this momentary reprieve, Hugh experiences an epiphany that explains the dual mystery of the Day of the Dead as a backdrop for Yvonne's return (that is, love), which will bring Geoffrey to life only in order that he may die again. For Hugh himself, she will act as the motivating force toward his search for selflessness in death and rebirth at sea. The unifying principle underlying the brothers' deaths is that each, in a way, dies for his other half. For a moment, then, Hugh is capable of reflecting on the enigma of love and death: ". . . [It] is as if, upon this one day in the year the dead come to life . . . this day of visions and miracles . . . we have been allowed for one hour a glimpse of what never was at all . . . the image of our happiness. . . ."

Losing the evanescent vision, Hugh is about to despair when his guardian angel appears in the form of a memory of his friend and mentor, Juan Cerillo—a white magician who, like the soon to be martyred Indian, is involved in helping the poor. "Trained as a chemist . . . delivering money on horseback . . . [his every] glimpse of the mysterious mountains seemed to mourn this opportunity lost to Geoff. . . ." In direct contrast with the Consul, the white magician utilizes his alchemy and "horsemanship" (mystical power) constructively. Because he had been enslaved at the age of seven, Juan's life had developed early into a long bout of suffering, but every man, "Juan seemed to be telling him . . . must ceaselessly struggle upward. What was life but a warfare and a stranger's sojourn? . . . No peace but that must pay full toll to hell—" which Lowry may, perhaps, intend as an astral extension of Geoffrey's previous explanation of the necessity for suffering. As they approach a little bar called La Sepultura, Juan is again recalled by and embodied in the figure of an Indian, "with his back against the wall . . . resting outside in the sunshine. His horse, or a horse, was tethered near him to a tree . . . the number seven branded on its rump." Two emblems of the Indian's approaching martyrdom surround him: the advertisement for the *Orlac* movie, with its emphasis on the murderer's guilty hands, and a toy windmill, which will recur later when Geoffrey will compare Hugh's efforts to aid the dying Indian to jousting at windmills like Quixote. In expectation of the afternoon's events, as well as in regard to his past betrayals, Hugh contemplates the bloody hands of the film murderer and, recalling his involvement with Yvonne, identifies himself with Judas and his brother with the betrayed Christ. The Consul, having willed this guilt suffering on his half brother, has had his vengeance on Hugh for his adulterous betrayal.

"And here indeed it was again, the temptation, the cowardly, the future-corruptive serpent: trample on it, stupid fool. . . . Have you not passed over the river? In the name of God be dead. And Hugh actually did ride over a dead garter snake. . . ." Hugh's private abyss resides in his fight against the snake as tempter. Although he has conquered one trial (having "passed over the river" between Sephirotic worlds) at sea, the danger of the serpent is always present for him in the form of his adultery with his brother's wife.

While Hugh is thus reliving and projecting his life into the future, he and Yvonne ride past what is to become his path of salvation in a repetition of the image of Geoffrey's paradisal train that runs through the mountains: ". . . [A] railway track, raised above scrub-land, gleamed through the trees to their right. . . ." In another positive mirror image of Geoffrey's negative experience (the ride to come, later, on the great wheel), Hugh and Yvonne stop for a beer at a pleasant mill, which casts "reflections of sunlight on water." Unflinching in projecting his presence, Geoffrey manifests himself once again in animal form when Yvonne develops a spontaneous sympathy for an armadillo being sold at the roadside by a little girl. She regards it as "soft and helpless" at first. But when she turns it upside down it appears that it had once been "some engine of destruction [which] after millions of years had come to this." Her reflection on the armadillo's evolution is, of course, pathetic analogy to the Consul's metamorphosis and what he has "come to." Hugh warns, "You don't really want it . . . if you let the thing loose in your garden it'll merely tunnel down into the ground and never come back. . . . It'll not only never come back . . . but if you try to stop it it will do its damnedest to pull you down the hole too." As if in answer to this gloomy prediction, a leaf falls behind them "with a crash," which is how Lowry had described Geoffrey's falling asleep earlier. Hugh, sensitive to his brother's presence, whether actual or magical, asks Yvonne if she and the Consul are divorced. As if in reply, "her horse gave a small lurch forward," Lowry's demonstration of the use of sympathetic magic to control nature and animals.

Because the environment is by now totally infused with the Consul's presence, their thoughts and conversation take a turn toward Parián, and Hugh says that there seems to be something sinister about Parián. Yvonne describes it as a ruined monastery, "rather like Oaxaca in that respect. . . . even the cantinas are part of what were once the monks' quarters." This comment resumes the "drinking as a sacrament" theme begun earlier, but it further explains the Consul's persistent identification of Oaxaca with Parián: both are varying stages of his hell. The Farolito, the brothel in Parián, with its seemingly infinite chambers of horror is, like the Cabbalist's *Gai-hinnom,* a gruesome reversal of heaven. It is a monastery turned into a combination bordello and death house. Lowry's purpose here includes a symbolic clue to Geoffrey's overriding need to return to Parián and the Farolito, for only there can he locate the secret path that leads to heaven. In still another sense, the Farolito is the destroyed temple of Solomon, battleground for the war between good and evil, a mythical place that harbors secrets that only devils and intoxicated men dare to investigate. Although Hugh wonders aloud about what attraction Parián has for Weber, the American fascist, he is probably actually wondering what Geoffrey sees in it. And he worriedly contemplates at that moment a crooked, wide left turn of the railway track, which Yvonne identifies as English in construction. Hugh laughs at the fact that it is "laid out in this cock-eyed fashion just for the sake of the extra mileage," which is another parallel to the Consul's cockeyed, drunken choice of the long "leftward" way around to heaven.

Yvonne articulates the Consul's, by now, almost palpable presence: "What do you think about Geoffrey?" Hugh mentally responds by regarding the blue forget-me-nots that grow vulnerably along the railroad tracks. For a moment he even feels that they incarnate his brother's danger, and in a sudden rush of identification that foreshadows Geoffrey's hell-train vision in a later chapter, he thinks, as the flowers might, ". . . what is this frightful dark sun that roars and strikes at our eyelids every few minutes? . . . Hours more likely. Perhaps even days. . . ."

Because he is at this point capable of comprehending the essential nature of his brother's plight, Hugh can argue, "[But] . . . after a while one begins to feel, if a man can hold his liquor as well as that why shouldn't he drink?" To Yvonne, however, this rationalization is obviously out of the question, for she can only be concerned with preventing her husband from the drinking that she knows ensures his doom:

". . . Geoffrey said something this morning about going on with his book—for the life of me I don't know whether he's still writing or not, he's never done any work on it since I've known him, and he's never let me see scarcely any of it, still, he keeps all those reference books with him . . ." [Lowry's playful comment on his own book, with its hidden Cabbalistic affiliations].

"Yes . . . how much does he really know about all this alchemy and cabbala business? How much does it mean to him?"

"That's just what I was going to ask you. I've never been able to find out—"

"Good lord. I don't know . . . Maybe he's a black magician!"

This exchange indicates that even his closest relatives are unaware of the extent of the Consul's involvement in the magic art, in great part because of his secretiveness, his eccentricity, his isolation; and it is the reason for much of his misunderstood, enigmatic conversation, which only confuses and excludes the uninitiated. Although these attitudes are unsociable, they are a necessary part of the magician's character, a mask he *consciously* cultivates in order to put outsiders off the track. Only Dr. Vigil, an initiate himself, can catch a glimpse of what is actually going on in Geoffrey's occult life. Hugh is closer to Geoffrey's secret than is Yvonne, for he has been partially "introduced" to it as a child. Later in the book, he will actually be permitted to see the arcana, which will corroborate his half-joking assumption. Geoffrey *has* inadvertently become a black magician; but Yvonne, with only one thought in mind—to save the ruin of their marriage—tells Hugh that she hopes to take Geoffrey off to a farm. Hugh retaliates with a sharp reference to the Consul's distaste for cows—that is, the earth symbol, or Hugh himself.

This is the first time Lowry mentions Geoffrey's property in the north—"the most terrific place in the world," or paradise. Hugh warns her that "Geoff's liable to be vague on the subject" since he has disengaged himself from the northern, or Yetziratic, regions of the tree of life. His land is characterized as a place abused by man, where people "Mine the country and quit. Blast the land to pieces, knock down the trees [the activities of greedy alchemists who misuse paradise in their ignorance]. . . . You have to drink at home, and when you run short it's too far to get a bottle—": there is no place for the bottled illusions of the Farolito once the spirit has located its proper home.

In repeating Geoffrey's earlier remark about being "strong as a horse," Hugh implies that there still remains enough divine strength to turn his brother back into a constructive force. He recommends a "shack . . . on the sea," with "No phone. . . . And perhaps he'll be able really to get down to his book and you can have your stars and the sense of the seasons again. . . . And get to know the real people . . . the last truly free people left in the world." If the Consul, Lowry means here, were to retrace his steps "Northward," he could finish his "great work" among the "truly free people" who have been liberated from materiality, those who live in closest sympathetic touch with nature, in harmony with the esoteric knowledge. Here in the "south," Geoffrey does not have that contact. With this new hope, Hugh feels that "Judas had been, somehow, redeemed." But his feeling is short-lived, and the momentary contemplation of paradise regained is dispelled as the two suddenly confront the barranca and the ruined palace. Hugh has once again "lost his bearings," not only with regard to their immediate surroundings, but by envisioning hope for the doomed pair, Geoffrey and Yvonne.

Once again Lowry conjures up the province of hell and sorcery as Hugh and Yvonne "secured their mares to a broken pink pillar that stood apart from the rest of the desuetude, a meaningless, mouldering emblem." Yvonne feels "ill at ease," for the broken emblematic pillar signifies the shattered remains of the tree of life and her blasted hopes. The sudden appearance of the moon in mid-morning, "a fragment blown out of the night by a cosmic storm," magnifies the mood of despair. It is out of place here, as Geoffrey's blazing vision of sunlight had been during the lovemaking scene, and is another symptom of the upside-down nature of their situation, in which active and passive forces are malfunctioning and even contradictory. The moon is a reminder of the Consul's earlier unsuccessful attempt to scale *Yesod,* whose abysses and harbors are enumerated here as the Marsh of Corruption, Sea of Darkness, and Sea of Tranquillity, all transformed by Hugh into an echo of his own soul's longing for paradise, which he conceives of as "the desire to be, to do good, what was right. . . . feeling it in his heart still . . . the immeasurable longing!"

The chapter closes on this sad note of the soul's longing for completion of its earthly missions, which Hugh still unconsciously associates with crossing the mystical sea leading to one's own proper Atlantis. But as Geoffrey's other self, Hugh must pay his debt to the sea before he can reach his destination.

# Chapter Five

Geoffrey is dreaming. He sees himself climbing Mount Himavat in a vision of lilac, white, green, and blue paradisal images.
Suddenly the heavenly vision becomes a rainstorm. Now, surrounded by cattle, he is lying face down in a stream, but he
cannot assuage his thirst. The dream now changes to a nightmare; Geoffrey finds that he is drinking only "light." He
awakens with a hangover and decides to find a tequila bottle
hidden somewhere in the undergrowth of his garden. As he
stumbles along, he sees a snake and a new sign there that he
mistakenly translates as "You like this garden? Why is it yours?
We evict those who destroy!" At this point he sights his American neighbor, Quincey, and the neighbor's cat. Working his
way toward Quincey, the Consul comes across the terrible
barranca that cuts through the entire town. Although tempted
to "pay a visit" to the bottom, Geoffrey changes his mind and
begins a rather one-sided conversation with Quincey instead.
The Consul here compares himself to William Blackstone (an
English exile living among the American Indians during the
colonial period), as he is to do repeatedly throughout the book.
The striking of a clock brings him back to his senses, and he remembers that Yvonne is home. Dr. Vigil suddenly appears, reading the newspaper *El Universal*, which Geoffrey interprets as a
spy sheet directed against himself and his own questionable past.
He joins Vigil, and together they walk toward the Consul's house,
but not before Geoffrey has attempted to save an insect from
Quincey's cat, to whom he refers as, "my little snake in the
grass." Back at the house, Hugh and Yvonne engage the doctor
in conversation while Geoffrey drinks alone in the bathroom for
a while. A few moments later, he emerges and is urged by Vigil
to stop drinking. The doctor warns him of "soul" sickness and
invites all of them to Guanajuato, his home town. The Consul
refuses the invitation, claiming that he has decided on an excur-
sion to Tomalín and Parián. He returns to the bathroom; this
time he is enlisting furious apocryphal abominations against the
world. He emerges in time to catch Vigil before he leaves and

yet again returns to the bathroom, where he is haunted by hideous insects and demonic voices.

In a dream/nightmare vision (italicized by Lowry), pervaded throughout with mystical references, Geoffrey Firmin opens this chapter as his astral presence had closed Chapter Four. Lowry begins with a meditation, during which the Consul's spirit is at first ascending upward into the Himalayas, where he wishes to join his father (*Kether,* Crown) *"with heaven aspiring heart."* He makes the climb in seven degrees, surrounded by varying scenery and with vastly differing results at every stage. At first he finds himself in the world of *Beriah* (Creation), where lilacs bloom, where *"mountains were glistening . . . spring was green . . . snow was white . . . sky was blue. . . ."* * On the astral plane, therefore, this dream is occurring simultaneously with Hugh and Yvonne's ride and, on a still profounder level, with another attempted ascent up the Sephirotic tree: *"And by degrees they reached the briny sea. Then, with souls well disciplined they reached the northern region, and beheld . . . the mighty mountain Himavat . . ."* This passage anticipates Hugh's desire to climb Mt. Popo and is later to be reincorporated into Geoffrey's dying vision.

Like the astral journeys outlined by Böhme, the Consul's dream follows a prescribed route, each stage represented by the colors and scenery encountered by the initiate. The farther from the material world, the more refined and ethereal the elements. However, the distance between each stage is spanned by a trial, personified, in Geoffrey's case, by the ability to withstand the desire to quench the aridity in his soul; but *". . . he was still thirsty. Then the snow was not glistening, the fruit blossoms were not clouds, they were mosquitoes, the Himalayas were hidden by dust, and he was thirstier than ever."* This trial is succeeded by a dry wind, which blows everything in its path. As the initiate ascends he must pass through and absorb into himself all of the elements, seasons, and ages of man, so that

*now the rain was falling. But this rain, that fell only on the mountains, did not assuage his thirst. Nor was he after all in the mountains. He*

---

* Lowry's repeated use of the colors red, blue, white, and green can be traced to *Kabbala Denudata,* which prescribes these to the four emblematic beasts of Ezekiel's vision.

*was standing, among cattle in a stream. He was resting, with some ponies, knee deep beside him in the cool marshes.* . . . [For the Consul's astral body is actually present] *lying face downward* [in the lake which reflects] *the white-capped ranges* . . . [above].

At this point, Lowry makes a direct reference to the "divine fluid" of the theosophists: *"Yet his thirst still remained unquenched. Perhaps because he was drinking, not water, but lightness, and promise of lightness* . . . *not water, but certainty of brightness.* . . . *Certainty of brightness, promise of lightness, of light, light, light, and again, of light, light, light, light, light!"*
Having reached the eighth plane on the upward climb ("light" having been used here eight times), the initiate would enter into the world of *Aziluth* (*Arch*etypes), finding there the *Sephirah Chokmah* (Divine Wisdom). He would be almost blinded, like Moses on Mount Sinai, by the strength of the sublime light that emanates directly from *Kether.* Geoffrey, too unstable to complete his journey, is overwhelmed by the light and is immediately catapulted back in "an inconceivable anguish of horripilating hangover thunderclapping about his skull, and accompanied by a protective screen of demons gnattering in his ears. . . ." With the unsuccessful spiritual attempt at climbing out of the abyss through meditation, the Consul finds himself once again in hell—his ruined garden.
Lowry hints at this point that Geoffrey may even have attempted to leave his own body in order to merge with that of "William Blackstone . . . or . . . his friend Wilson [who disappeared] . . . in a pair of dress trousers [magician's outfit], into the jungles of darkest Oceania, never to return. . . . [But] any such visioned escape into the unknown must shortly be arrested by what was, for him, an unscalable wire fence." Trapped by the demons of his own making, Geoffrey is once again overcome by his familiars: " 'Do not be so foolish as to imagine you have no object, however. We warned you, we told you so, but now that in spite of all our pleas you have got yourself into this deplorable— . . . condition.' " They communicate their taunts to him "through the metamorphoses of dying and reborn hallucinations," which eventually lure him on to a bottle of tequila hidden in the garden. Rationalizing, in spite of his feeble protests otherwise, that tequila is not mescal (mescal is the sacramental liquor that even *he* fears),

he drinks and ritually murmurs: "God . . . Ah. Good. God. Christ. . . . Bliss. Jesus. Sanctuary . . ."

In immediate recompense for his sacrilege, the demons begin again, for he is now confronted by a talking snake, which sardonically advises him to stop drinking and scuttles off.

The snake—a form often assumed by Bael, a ruler of "inferior spirits"—is followed by a reappearance of the hound, whom Geoffrey addresses as Perro, and thereafter a disquieting sense of timelessness descends on the entire scene: ". . . had not this incident occurred, was it not now, as it were, occurring an hour or two ago. . . ." He falls deeper into an illusory state, during which the "normal" and the "supernormal" are interchangeable. The garden now appears not as "ruined," as it had earlier, but even seems to possess a chaotic "charm." Extending this revised impression, Geoffrey permits himself the perverse pleasure of *enjoying* the disordered state of his soul. Now totally confused by the demons, he surveys "a vision . . . which inadvertently blended at this moment . . . into a strangely subaqueous view of the plains and the volcanoes with a huge indigo sun . . . blazing south southeast. Or was it north northwest?" His watery view of the setting is the result of his return to his overriding element, water, by having submerged his consciousness in the tequila. The sun is "indigo" rather than yellow or gold or red because blue again denotes the watery element. He is unsure of its location (is it above or below him?) because he is "upside down," so to speak: the man of destruction in the ruined garden. "In this garden . . . there existed at the moment certain evidence of work left uncompleted: tools, unusual tools, a murderous machete, an oddly shaped fork, nakedly impaling the mind, with its twisted tines glittering in the sunlight. . . ." The "oddly shaped fork" is the magical *Shin,* now become destructive pitchfork.

Then he comes upon a new sign never seen in the garden before, which Lowry uses as a reference to Adam's eviction notice from God:

¿LE GUSTA ESTE JARDÍN?
¿QUE ES SUYO?
¡EVITE QUE SUS HIJOS LO DESTRUYAN!

You like this garden—which is yours? Don't let your children destroy it. Geoffrey reads the last part as "We evict those who destroy!" The Spanish punctuation serves also as a symbol of the reversed condition of the garden, with the tree of life now become the tree of death. Reacting to the sign, the Consul feels "a kind of colourless, cold, a white agony, an agony chill as that iced mescal drunk in the Hotel Canada [another ironic reversal of Yvonne's Canadian paradise] on the morning of Yvonne's departure." In other words, he is reexperiencing the agony of the first separation from the *Shekinah,* and perhaps, even further back than that, the archetypal isolation of Adam on being cut off from the tree of life. In the vicious cycle that characterizes his hell, Geoffrey drinks further of the devil in order to forget that his is a "dishonest vision of order."

The "subtle bouquet of pitch" merely reinforces illusions, however, and he is just about to take the path to Parián when he sights a figure "in some kind of mourning" (Yvonne as weeping Merope), which, for some reason, he does not comprehend, diverts his steps. Magnetized by the demons, however, he is inexorably drawn to the Farolito. But the sight of the barranca itself temporarily diverts him: "He had almost fallen into the barranca. . . . Ah the frightful cleft, the external horror of opposites! Thou mighty gulf, insatiate cormorant, deride me not, though I seem petulant to fall into thy chops. One was . . . always stumbling upon the damned thing . . . Tartarus and gigantic jakes." The *Kelipah,* as the end and bottom of creation, is God's jakes, or toilet, so to speak.

At this point, although the *neshama* (spirit) abhors the abyss, the *nefesh* (*mor*tal soul) finds itself seduced by it. In contrast to Hugh's wish to climb Mt. Popo, therefore, Geoffrey contemplates the possibility of climbing down into the barranca "by easy stages of course, and taking the occasional swig of tequila on the way, to visit the cloacal Prometheus who doubtless inhabited it." Samaël, the light-bringer (Prometheus) doomed to rule the abyss, is accurately identified by Lowry with the hind parts of man, for Cabbalists equate the backside of *Adam Kadmon* with the Devil, and part of the witches' Sabbath consisted of worshiping Satan's rump.

Nevertheless, in spite of his initial attraction to the pit, the Consul is not yet quite ready to face it. Preferring to speculate about the condition of his garden instead, he blunders into the English greenness of his neighbor's garden in the hope of locating momen-

tary salvation in memories of his past, which he sees as "the road
[that] would stretch out again in the Western Ocean of his soul,"
really a repetition of Hugh's desire to steer the world out of the
"Western Ocean of its misery." At that moment, however, he confronts the smug Mr. Quincey, who is in the process of watering his
perfect, symmetrical garden. Quincey is instantly materialized in
Geoffrey's mind as a type of Nobodaddy figure: ". . . I am God,
and even when God was much older than you are he was nevertheless up at this time and fighting it. . . ." In a comic confrontation
that parodies what might have passed between Adam and God after the Fall, Lowry has the Consul, debauched, tottering on his last
spiritual legs, attempting to engage the Puritanical, harsh, teetotal-
ing God of "Soda Springs," who waters and "sternly" moves on, in
neighborly conversation. The scene also serves as a humorous
counterpart to the tragically insurmountable breach between man
and God that makes up the crux of the plot.

The Consul, "not sorry to leave the fruit tree, to which he had
noticed clinging the sinister carapace of a seven-year locust, followed [Quincey] step by step." Leaving the tree in the midst of the
garden, which is already infected with the seven sins to come,
Geoffrey, as Adam, tries to placate "God," at the same time trying
to work out the Fall, in an exact Zoharistic interpretation, from
Adam's point of view: "What if his punishment really consisted
. . . in his having to *go on living there,* alone, of course—
suffering, unseen, cut off from God . . ." Suddenly "God" notices
that the Consul's fly is open and he becomes overtly disturbed,
which is a reflection of the Cabbalistic view that Adam's sin was
primarily sexual, for he had disobeyed God's commandment not to
lie face to face with Eve. Correspondingly, the confrontation between Quincey and Firmin assumes an embarrassingly sexual turn,
Quincey asking about Yvonne's return, and Geoffrey addressing
Quincey's cat as "Priapuss" (lechery) and "Oedipuss" (incest).

Although he almost instinctively reverts to his persona, William
Blackstone, for protection, the Consul momentarily forgets Blackstone's first name, wondering if it really wasn't "Abraham." This
slip is pregnant with allusions in light of the biblical character of
the foregoing scene; moreover, it can pertain to Geoffrey's own
identification with his mentor, Abraham Taskerson, who, in the
guise of the Cabbalist's Father Abraham, was, like Blackstone, an

outcast and an exile from his people, a man who had brought a new revelation in the form of the *Sefer Yetzirah.*

Quincey misunderstands when Geoffrey taps his own chest saying, ". . . the [American] Indians are in here. . . . Yes, just the final frontier of consciousness, that's all. . . . Genius will look after itself . . . ," for he is probably referring to his secret powers.

Jolted out of his one-sided dialogue with Mr. Quincey by the striking of a clock, Geoffrey checks his incorrect watch, which reads quarter to eleven (the path to be avoided) as the mournful air spirits hover about whispering, "alas, alas." Wings on a package of cigarettes called *Alas* become identified with the *Ofanim,* a class of angels who intercede in man's behalf.

Dr. Vigil enters the garden, and at his appearance "the hoses had suddenly failed as if by magic. . . ." Master of the fiery element, Vigil's presence alone is enough to still the water. Geoffrey is apprehensive about Vigil's "spying upon him," for he is coming toward him with "that accusing newspaper . . . *El Universal"* in his hands.

As light-bearer, Vigil can also see into the "universal" plan, and he uses this power in an effort to save the Consul. Misguided by his own deep guilt about the past, Geoffrey becomes frightened of the possible discovery of his role in the *Samaritan* case: " 'Firmin innocent, but bears guilt of world on shoulders' [he reads on the front of Vigil's newspaper]. . . . [The] creatures of his more immediate conscience . . . seemed silently to accompany that morning paper too. . . . 'You cannot lie to us. We know what you did last night.' "

The doctor, however, is conscious of Geoffrey's true greatness as the "God intoxicated," so that he "bow[s] to him profoundly from the waist; bow[s] once, twice, thrice, mutely yet tremendously assuring the Consul that after all no crime had been committed during the night so great he was still not worthy of respect." In his capacity as magician, Vigil wears "an immaculate blue suit" and repeats his earlier assertion: "I must comport myself here . . . like an apostle," for he is Geoffrey's last hope for salvation. In a gesture of sympathetic understanding "in the obscure language known only to major adepts in the Great Brotherhood of Alcohol," the doctor assures Geoffrey that he may drink in his presence without coming to harm. Lowry's terminology here indi-

cates that Vigil, also a drinker of light, but an apostle and healer
as well, is one of the more successful adepts and has been sent
back to earth to aid those initiates who, like the Consul, are in
difficulty.

When they walk back to the house together, Geoffrey is momentarily surrounded by "an amber glow" (*Tiphereth,* the sun, amber
colored in the material world), which, thanks to Vigil's presence,
protects him. This sudden illumination is matched by the one that
takes place within the Consul as he comes to terms with his strange
salvation in damnation, which, in spite of its promise of "ineluctable personal disaster . . . might even be found at the end to
contain a certain element of triumph." The natural world reacts to
Geoffrey's transfiguration by coming alive in a strangely elemental
fashion. The light emitted from *Tiphereth* (a metaphor for supersensual power) enables him to see and hear lizards, butterflies,
ants ". . . a continual sound of whistling, gnawing . . . even
trumpeting. . . ." Geoffrey wonders: "Where was his friend the
snake now?"—where the serpent is wisdom, as he momentarily
aligns himself with life in an attempt to save an insect from Quincey's demon-possessed cat. The insect, however, escapes on its
own, an emblem of "the human soul [escaping] from the jaws of
death . . . up, up, up, soaring over the trees . . . ," in anticipation of Yvonne's later release of the eagle.

The brief interlude in which the Consul is attracted to life
(motivated by the vision of nature's activity, or the Yetziratic
world) ends when he catches sight of Hugh and Yvonne in his garden. The snake, no longer symbol of wisdom, is transformed into
seducer as the Consul greets his brother with, "Hi there, Hugh,
you old snake in the grass!" Like the vision of heaven nearly attained earlier, in Geoffrey's dream of the Himalayas, the vision of
creation proves too overwhelming, and the Consul passes out in
the bathroom. When he comes to, he realizes that it is "only 12:15
in fact by his watch" (he is fifteen minutes ahead) and recalls having just "glimpsed the new moon with the old one in its arms
. . . illumined only by earthlight."

The image here, which Lowry takes from Coleridge, indicates
that Geoffrey has fallen back into the first stages of a trance, which
has put him back into touch with the celestial machinery by which
he will order the remainder of the day to suit his purpose. He be-

gins by preventing Hugh's departure (presumably so that his brother will protect and console Yvonne after his own death) and mentally cuts himself off from Vigil entirely by concluding at the last moment that "In the final analysis there was no one you could trust to drink with you to the bottom of the bowl." Nevertheless, in a parting display of confidence, he tells his potential mentor about the "sunflower [that] watches me and I know it hates me," an image incorporating his attitude toward Yvonne, earlier identified with sun and flowers, and the blinding gaze of God's sun. The Consul goes so far as to describe what he experiences when he drinks as the "thousand aspects of . . . infernal beauty . . . each with its peculiar tortures," to which Vigil replies in warning: ". . . sickness is not only in body but in that part [that] used to be called: soul."

In significantly faltering English, Vigil goes on to describe the nervous system in the mystical terms of Abbé de Villars as "a mesh . . . an eclectic systemë." The Consul corrects him: " 'You mean an electric system.' " Vigil responds by warning Geoffrey that too much drink cuts off the messages from the key centers to the brain. Spurred on by the doctor's description, Geoffrey conceives of the state of his soul as being that of a town

. . . ravaged and stricken in the black path of his excess [and he envies those] . . . who were truly alive, switches connected, nerves rigid only in real danger, and in nightmareless sleep now calm, not resting, yet poised. . . . Christ, how it heightened the torture ([while] . . . the others imagined he was enjoying himself enormously) to be aware of all this, while at the same time conscious, of the whole horrible disintegrating mechanism, the light now on, now off, now on too glaringly, now too dimly . . . plunged into darkness, where communication is lost, motion mere obstruction. . . .

Lowry uses this detailed description—which is figuratively of the remorse engendered by the choice of the left-hand path, the horror entailed in loss of potency (sexual and creative), the psychological and physical anarchy externalized in the symbol of the movie house where the "lights always fail"—to introduce an intimate glimpse of the black magician at work. Seated appropriately (the *Kelipah*/jakes again) in the bathroom, the Consul is "gazing at the . . . wall in an attitude like a grotesque parody of an old attitude in meditation." The Consul clairvoyantly sees and even partially manipulates the coming war. Like the medieval Cabbalistic Masters of the Holy Name, he knows more than "even the hierophants of science . . . [about the] fearful potencies of . . . unvintageable evil." Feeling himself "shattered by the very forces of the universe," he sees himself sitting "up in an organ loft somewhere playing, pulling out all the stops at random, and kingdoms divided and fell, and abominations dropped from the sky. . . ." As he wills his destructive fantasies, he is amused by the thought of his own influence:

> . . . who would ever have believed that some obscure man, sitting at the centre of the world in a bathroom, say, thinking solitary miserable thoughts, was authoring their doom, that, even while he was thinking, it was as if behind the scenes certain strings were being pulled, and whole continents burst into flame, and calamity moved nearer . . . and, without the Consul's knowing it, outside the sky had darkened.

On one level this observation is a prophecy of World War II, the impact of which only comes to the Consul as he himself is falling into the abyss. On the other hand, however, it sounds like Achad's type of Cabbalistic prediction in *Anatomy of the Body of God,* which ascribes to the mighty magician the power to utilize the left-hand pillar of severity in order to balance the earthly forces; that is, equilibrium must be maintained at all costs. So runs the occultist's justification for war, natural catastrophe, and death. In this aspect the Consul might be functioning as an agent of the cosmic plan in whose keeping lies the responsibility for maintaining equilibrium by using his own body and soul as a magnetic force and who, at the last moment, is required to sacrifice himself as well. Thus, Lowry speaks in Yeatsian tones of the events taking place in this scene as "The uncontrollable mystery on the bathroom floor," which would help to explain the deliberate, almost preformulated nature of Geoffrey's actions.

Lowry's principal question in the book at this point becomes clear: Can Geoffrey assume the guilt of the world on his shoulders, is he equipped to perform the Messianic descent; or has he merely become an engine of destruction for destruction's sake?

Geoffrey leaves the bathroom to find Yvonne, with whom he exchanges "a look of understanding," perhaps willing her to go along with his plans for the day. Vigil tries to convince him to accompany him to Guanajuato, his home town, which he describes as "the old golden jewel on the breast of our grandmother," another form of sanctuary, associated with "Mother" in Geoffrey's mind. But the doctor's faulty English and the Consul's deliberate misinterpretations result in a breakdown of communication, after which Geoffrey feels "a return of energy" (a renewal of confidence in the electromagnetic power he had resumed as a result of his bathroom magic). He, in turn, invites Vigil to accompany him to the Farolito in Parián, where he claims to have left his "favorite pipe" (light). But of course the doctor cannot go there because "Wheee, es un infierno. . . ."

At that moment the darkening sky and the sudden thunder of gunfire accompanied by the clock striking twelve (noon is the beginning of the occultist's day) all seem to seal the fate of the magician. "Twelve o'clock, and the Consul said to the doctor: 'Ah, that the dream of dark magician in his visioned cave, even while his hand . . . shakes in its last decay, were the true end of this so lovely world. Jesus. Do you know, compañero, I sometimes have the feeling that it's actually sinking, like Atlantis, beneath my feet. Down, down. . . .'" The doctor unavailingly pleads with him once more, "But . . . your esposa has come back," and then leaves reluctantly "in a shower of plaster" that falls from Geoffrey's decaying house.

The power of Vigil's goodness now absent from the house, Geoffrey endures another terrible insect vision upon returning to the bathroom: ". . . a scorpion was moving slowly towards him" —in an externalization of his own suicidal impulses— ". . . the whole insect world had somehow moved nearer and now was closing, rushing in upon him." His demonic familiars are now free to take over, and they mock him by assuming the voices of his guardian angels:

—Stop it, for God's sake, you fool. Watch your step. We can't help you any more.
—I would like the privilege of helping you, of your friendship. I would work you with. I do not care a damn for moneys anyway.
—What, is this you, Geoffrey? Don't you remember me? Your old friend, Abe? . . .

.  .  .  .  .  .  .  .  .  .

—My son, my son!
—My lover. Oh come to me again as once in May.

# Chapter Six

Hugh lies back on the porch daybed and assembles his past, present, and future. Lowry demonstrates Hugh's tendency to overdramatize himself and his restlessness and irresponsibility. He switches on the radio and hears only news about death and disaster until a jazz tune emerges from the chaos to remind him of his own musician's past. Giving up the guitar for the sea, Hugh had set out on the S.S. *Philoctetes,* leaving a sheaf of semi-plagiarized jazz tunes with his Jewish friend and publisher, Bolowski. Disillusioned and bored at sea, and spiritually beaten by the cruelty of his shipmates, Hugh had signed aboard another boat, the *Oedipus Tyrannus,* where he had truly learned about the hard and unromantic life of the sailor. Back in London, Hugh learned that Bolowski had cheated him, and giving up the music business, he had entered Cambridge as an ardent anti-Semite. During his further meditations about his university life, Hugh is interrupted by Geoffrey, whose face is covered with lather, but who is trembling too much to shave himself. Hugh shaves his brother, shares a drink with him, and reminisces aloud about Cambridge, where the Consul had previously built up a mad reputation. In a counterpoint to Hugh's private thoughts, the Consul banteringly reads some very strange classified ads from *El Universal.* Passing through Geoffrey's room, Hugh notices heaps of alchemical and Cabbalistic books, which even further whet his curiosity about his brother's activities. During their ensuing conversation, Geoffrey enumerates the names of the various demonic spirits. When he is shaved and they are both ready to leave, Geoffrey and Hugh are joined by Yvonne; the three set out toward the bus station. The Consul is in a jaunty mood until Laruelle appears before them and somehow manages to invite the trio to his home against their will. A dwarflike postman suddenly bears down upon them with a year-old post-card from Yvonne that pleads for Geoffrey's assurance that he still loves her. The card is an ironic reminder that it is too late.

Devoted essentially to Hugh's meditation as a counterpart to Geoffrey's contemplation on the bathroom floor, then tying the two together in a ritualistic meeting between the two half brothers, this chapter begins with Hugh's introspective rehearsal of his past and future accomplishments. Smoking a cigar Geoffrey had given him, he is put into a philosophical frame of mind. As he counts twenty-nine clouds passing overhead, he muses over his age (twenty-nine), his guilt, and the passage of time: "I have no excuse any longer to behave in this irresponsible fashion." He realizes that commitment must follow soon, for a man's life is short in comparison with the intensity of his task. Like Jacques and the Consul, he is brought to thoughts of Yvonne, for each man seeks the *Shekinah* in his own way. He recalls and reviews the deceitful manner in which he had set out to "do good." Even his "passion for helping Jews" had been associated with guilty self-aggrandizement.

He remembers having once freed a seagull (a parallel to Geoffrey's attempt to free the insect and Yvonne's freeing of the eagle), which had "soared away on angelic wings," a symbol of an early stage of his soul's longing for goodness. But "Not even the seagull was the answer of course. The seagull had been spoilt . . . by his dramatising it."

A man who desires action and worldly acclaim, Hugh is too egotistical to penetrate as deeply as his brother has into the cosmic mechanism. Silence, one of the primary requirements of the occult undertaking, is not part of his make-up. He is, rather, an example of the soul still in search of an identity—not as materialistic as Jacques, for example, but still not prepared to give up its attachment to the world. Hugh is ruled by *ruah,* the intermediate part of the soul, which can be drawn in either direction: ". . . I am without a place on earth . . . No home. A piece of driftwood on the Indian Ocean. Is India my home?" (another parallel to Geoffrey, who is convinced of his Indian origins—that is, committed to the mysteries). The radio suddenly comes alive "with a vengeance," in response to Hugh's lack of direction in his reflections, announcing flood, bankruptcy, disaster, misery, "While static rattled on eternally below—poltergeists of the ether. . . . Hugh inclined his ear to the pulse of the world. . . ."

Because he is "half" of Geoffrey, Hugh can tune in on the coming disaster perpetrated in part by his brother. But he stands for the healing influence, the preserver as opposed to the destroyer, which, when combined, make up the equilibrium on which the world rests. All occultists consider the ether to be a fifth element. More refined than the others, it contains all events of our world, past, present, future. It can be "tuned in" on by those who are sensitive to its presence. From it all the other elements are considered to emanate, so that in troubled times the magician might find it difficult to communicate through the ether due to the interfering "static" of air spirits.

In an attempt to relieve his melancholy spirit, Hugh turns the dial and thinks he hears "Joe Venuti's violin . . . the joyous little lark of discursive melody soaring in some remote summer of its own above all this abyssal fury." Music, and more specifically jazz, will represent for Hugh what the northern paradise represents for Yvonne and what the completion of his great work represents for the Consul: a form of earthly salvation. Hugh has given up his guitar, now a "soundless cave for spiders," because he had misused it in a way similar to his brother's misuse of wine. Like the magic liquor, the magic lyre is also a double-edged sword, functioning for good or evil in accordance with its master's predisposition. Hugh had begun his initiation because of it, for "it was largely owing to a guitar . . . that he had first gone to sea." But it was also because of a guitar that Hugh had become "the magician of commotions." In a sense, the instrument is his source of both trial and advancement with regard to the secret wisdom since it brings him into his first contact with Jews—a people soon to be identified as the bearers of this powerful wisdom when Geoffrey reveals Cabbalistic information to him.

Unlike his brother, whom Lowry draws as secretive and bookish, Hugh had been extroverted and unintellectual "without the dubious benefit of a degree." His first real failure had come as a result of his lack of faith in his own creative power and his dependency on others. Ashamed of his potential as a composer, ". . . it struck him, more than prophetically . . . that these songs alone . . . of the requisite thirty-two bars . . . locked in a secret drawer of his mind—might be insufficient to do the trick." By trying to follow in Geoffrey's footsteps (toting his music in the Consul's bag, wearing his clothes), Hugh has not developed a sense of personal identity in spite of his vast egotism. His music, the one medium between himself and his soul's development (the path of the *Sephiroth* also has thirty-two stages), remains "secret" as long as he is dishonest with himself. The drawers of his mind begin to unlock when he signs aboard the S.S. *Philoctetes* in order to find his own identity—the lost bow of Philoctetes, as it were. But even his assault on the initiatory sea turns out to be a self-deception in that he seeks "the promise of unlimited delight . . . an illusion, to say the least."

Capitalizing on the "mystery of his father's disappearance" to make himself newsworthy (leaving the investigation of the self entirely to God's mercy without assuming any accompanying responsibility results in little or no development regardless of the novice's mystical affiliations), Hugh had regarded himself as an archetype for the "shipless buccaneers everywhere, who found their lives under a sad curse of futility because they had not sailed with their elder brothers the seas of the last war." (Premature efforts on the part of beginners to emulate the more advanced "mariners" in their war against the elements are doomed to failure.) Members of Hugh's mysterious family who had come "as if springing out of the ground" in order to detain him were squelched by the Consul, who, with characteristic foresight, felt that the trial was a necessary lesson for the young hothead. Although he had been involved in his own activities at the time, Geoffrey had wired from the East: *"Consider Hugh's proposed trip best possible thing for him"*—for which Hugh had never forgiven him. He had significantly sailed on a Friday the thirteenth, "not knowing whether he voyaged east or west," a comment reflecting the chaotic nature of his search.

The voyage predictably turns out to be Hugh's version of *Kelipah,* as Oaxaca and Parián are for his brother. Tortured by malicious shipmates, he travels aboard a ship on which fore is aft and vice versa—another example of the topsy-turvy nature of hell. Hugh finds his spiritual level among the stewards, which Lowry may have meant as a double entendre characterizing Hugh's inner need to serve mankind. Hugh's experience leads him to conclude that "far above was perhaps another sea, where the soul ploughed its high invisible wake," a sign that he has begun to awaken to the awareness of the real "sea," or the training ground of the soul. With the awareness comes a second opportunity to prove himself, this time by boarding the *Oedipus Tyrannus:*

. . . foul and rusty . . . battered, ancient . . . perhaps even about to sink. And yet there was something youthful and beautiful about her, like an illusion that she will never die. . . . It was said she was capable of seven knots. . . . Ah, his brother Geoff, too, knew these seas, these pastures of experience, what would he have done?

The second voyage turns out to be a truer test of the soul's quality. His egotism curtailed, Hugh now realizes that the mariner's life "was dead serious. . . . [He] was horribly ashamed of ever having so exploited it." But the trial had barely begun, for on returning to land, he found himself cheated and abused by both his shipmates and his publisher, further stages of his "initiation." At that point in his life his thoughts had turned hopefully to his brother, but "Geoff, like some ghostly other self, was always in Rabat or Timbuctoo." *

And because it is now Hugh's turn to reciprocate, the Consul interrupts his protégé's meditations with a call for "help." Geoffrey, being too tremulous to shave himself, is assisted by Hugh in an oddly ritualistic scene: "The room was pervaded by some sweet heavy scent of Yvonne's . . . fragrant asses' milk soap lying in the basin." †

From here on the brothers' conversation assumes a thoroughly magical connotation. They begin by discussing the Consul's "shakes," which he calls the "wheels within wheels" (Ezekiel's vision). He can neither "stand still" nor "sit down," for he is whirling after the effects of his previous meditation, vertigo being a common sensation of black magicians. In this disoriented state he drinks a bottle of lotion for a "charm against galloping cockroaches . . . imaginary scorpions" and is sick as a result. In a reiteration of the Tower of Babel theme, Hugh turns on the faucets so that Yvonne would hear only "the usual bathroom babel."

Regaining control of the situation, the Consul wills a restorative and Hugh, "as if absentmindedly obeying the other's wordless instructions," goes to get the whiskey hidden in a cupboard, which the Consul telepathically points out to him. On his way through the room Hugh becomes fascinated by the titles of his brother's books, which he now sees for the first time. Geoffrey seems to have

* All theosophical disciplines, from Ouspensky to Cabbala to Yoga, emphasize the fact that the mentor never appears until the initiate has successfully passed many trials alone, proving himself independent.

† Equipment necessary for evocation of spirits mentioned in Agrippa's *Natural Magic* and in Abra-Melin's prescription for evoking the guardian angel.

judged him ready to receive the answer to his earlier question (to Yvonne: "Is Geoff a black magician?"), for he now permits Hugh to ponder the secret arcana on his bookshelves.* Hugh sees:

Dogme et Ritual de la Haute Magie, Serpent and Siva Worship in Central America . . . together with the rusty leather bindings and frayed edges of the numerous cabbalistic and alchemical books, though some of them looked fairly new, like the Goetia of the Lemegaton of Solomon the King, probably they were treasures, but the rest were a heterogeneous collection: Gogol, the Mahabharata, Blake, Tolstoy, Pontoppidan, the Upanishads, a Mermaid Marston, Bishop Berkeley, Duns Scotus, Spinoza, Vice Versa, Shakespeare, a complete Taskerson, All Quiet on the Western Front, the Clicking of Cuthbert, the Rig Veda—God knows, Peter Rabbit; "Everything is to be found in Peter Rabbit," † the Consul liked to say. . . .

Hugh returns from his foray into the supernatural with a tooth-mug and a razor and proceeds to shave Geoffrey as they relive past experiences at Cambridge in a scene very reminiscent of Joyce's opening chapter of *Ulysses*. Hugh recalls Geoffrey's weird reputation at school and repeats an old story in which the Consul is said to have ridden into college on a horse. The Consul claims that he is frightened of horses, to which Hugh replies, "A pretty ferocious horse too." The shaving ritual entails the binding together of many threads: the relationship between the brothers, in which Hugh (with his razor) is cutting away the Consul's defenses, entering his private domain, discovering his secret books, and disclosing his hidden past. But Hugh is also Lowry's "son that castrates the father" in anticipation of his appearance in the Consul's last hours as the sword-bearing adulterer who has cuckolded him.

Further, there is now a new direction to Hugh's own introspection, evoked by Geoffrey's presence, in which he discovers that "the experience of the sea . . . had invested one with the profound inner maladjustment of the sailor who can never be happy on land" (that is, the Cabbalist who has seen beyond *Malkuth*, or Ouspensky's hanged man of the tarot). He is even moved to reconsider his anti-Semitism of the past, now feeling that "only a

* Mrs. Lowry points out that many of the books listed here by Lowry actually lined the bookshelves of Achad's home, and that her husband spent time there in order to investigate them. He included some of his own books which were less esoteric, but of a related nature nevertheless.

† The rabbit is the Aztec symbol of drunkenness. It will reappear in Chapter Twelve.

Jew, with his rich endowment of premature suffering, could understand one's own suffering, one's isolation . . . ," a statement characteristic of the rationalizations of Christian Cabbalists that Lowry would have been subjected to in his reading of books like Mathers' translation of *Kabbala Denudata* and Lévi's treatises on magic.

In the meantime the ritual element builds in a dreamlike fashion until the sympathetic force between the two men causes them to sway "imperceptibly, as to another control . . ." Hugh is brought out of his introspection by the Consul, who seems to have been reading his thoughts all along and who asks, "Is that right?" as he points out a "poor exiled . . . tree outside . . . propped up with those crutches of cedar. . . . One of these days . . . it's going to collapse," in warning that he can no longer continue to prop up his younger brother because of his own impending collapse.

The entire scene evolves as a test of Hugh's preparedness for the secret knowledge and thus reads like the unconnected series of a rambling alcoholic. In this way, for example, Geoffrey informs Hugh of the "sunflower. . . . It stares into my room all day . . . . Stares. Fiercely. All day. Like God!" * In a covert attempt to pass on his secrets to his brother, Geoffrey offers him "a communal drink," whereupon he begins reading a cryptic, prophetic newspaper litany, from *El Universal,* as an accompaniment to the ritual:

"Kink [sic] unhappy in exile [i.e., Adam, Geoffrey himself]. . . . Eggs have been in a tree . . . for a hundred years. . . ." † And what would this mean, do you suppose? "And a white horse also." Apply at box seven [premonition of Yvonne's death] . . . Strange . . . Anti-alcoholic fish [reference to the possibility of salvation in Christ]. . . . Hullo . . . "grave objections" have been made to the immodest behavior of certain police chiefs in Quauhnahuac. "Grave objections to—" what's this?—"performing their private functions in public" [another warning from the "Universal" to beware of the destructive forces that are soon to be externalized in the form of the chiefs who are performing their private functions (cf. abyss as toilet theme) openly].

* *Kether,* the blinding light, manifested here in its harsh, judgmental aspect; the fiery-eyed Microprosopus.
† Cf. the Consul's search for eggs that morning; the continuation of the fertility theme, with eggs representing the secret of life, which can only be found on the Sephirotic tree.

Counterpointing Geoffrey's concern with the demons of the barranca, Hugh ruminates on the possibility of mountain climbing,
which he has come to associate with conquering the problem of
self-identity: "So now, as I approach the second half of my life,
unheralded, unsung, and without a guitar, I am going back to sea
again: perhaps these days of waiting are more like that droll descent, to be survived in order to repeat the climb."

Hugh has begun to understand the purpose of all the trials and
failures that form a necessary part of the last true voyage (to the
degree of developing an insight into Geoffrey's mission) as he contemplates his own approaching sacrifice. He indirectly likens his
own hard-won decision to that of the "actor in the Passion Play
[who] can get off his cross and go home to his hotel. . . . Yet in
life ascending or descending you were perpetually involved with
the mists, the cold and the overhangs, the treacherous rope and the
slippery belay; only, while the rope slipped there was sometimes
time to laugh." In a sense, Lowry is saying, it is easier for the universal Savior to follow the course of self-sacrifice than it is for the
fool, the former returning to his "hotel" (*Tiphereth*) immediately,
while the latter bungles his way up. Indirectly picking up the train
of his brother's intended political mission, Geoffrey launches a discussion of the fascist police with pretended disinterest. He tells
Hugh about the various chiefs and their functions in a detailed list
of his future accusers. Hugh helps the Consul into his clothes, returning the jacket he had worn that morning, which now contains
the telegram that will indirectly identify the Consul as a Jew and a
Bolshevist. The identities of the two brothers are thus merged.
Hugh is further enlightened about his brother's true condition. He
unconsciously hits on the occult metaphor of the snake (referring
to the Consul as being in the clutches of a boa constrictor) as wisdom become the snake as destroyer and finally comes to recognize
the Consul not as a deliberate black magician but as a "man of
abnormal strength and constitution and obscure ambition [who
cannot be reconciled to God] . . . but [one who is capable of
being] loved. . . ."

The Consul, for his part, is even brought to confess his most
guarded crime, the episode of the *Samaritan,* as he describes a picture of the heavily camouflaged gunboat—his engine of destruction. Going still further, he alludes to the Germans as a "queer

people" and quickly shifts the subject to his occult books. Lowry uses the entire *Samaritan* episode as an allegory of the conflict between good and evil forces during which Geoffrey had mishandled his power and for which Hugh is soon to compensate by giving his life at sea. Guardedly warning Hugh about the Germans (that is, the evil practical Cabbalists), the Consul now opens up his Cabbalistic library: * "But I see you're interested in my old books all of a sudden . . . Too bad . . . I left my Boehme in Paris." †

Having literally and figuratively left Böhme behind, Geoffrey no longer controls his life in accordance with the cosmic "order" and has thereby forfeited the mystical path for that of pure magic. Since Geoffrey intends his brother to carry on after his own fall, however, he now opens his hidden library consisting of: *A Treatise of Sulphur, written by Michall Sandivogius i.e., anagrammatically Divi Leschi Genus Amo; The Hermetical Triumph or the Victorious Philosophical Stone, a Treatise more compleat and more intelligible than any has been yet, concerning the Hermetical Magistery; The Secrets Revealed or an Open Entrance to the Sub-Palace of the King, containing the greatest Treasure in Chymistry never yet so plainly discovered, composed by a most famous Englishman styling himself Anonymous or Eyraeneus Philaletha Cosmopolita; The Musaeum Hermeticum; Sub-Mundanes, or the Elementaries of the Cabbala, reprinted from the text of the Abbé de Villars, Physio-Astro-Mystic, with an Illustrative Appendix from the work Demoniality, wherein is asserted that there are in existence on earth rational creatures besides men.*

Hugh, entranced by all this strange "Jewish knowledge" has "a sudden absurd vision of Mr. Bolowski [his publisher] in another life, in a caftan, with a long white beard, and skull cap, and passionate intent look, standing . . . reading a sheet of music in which the notes were Hebrew letters. . . ." And he sees Bolowski in an entirely new dimension with regard to his own life. Now the

---

* "[Geoffrey] . . . shows Hugh his alchemistic books, and we are for a moment . . . standing before the evidence of what is no less than the magical basis of the world . . . and Hitler was another pseudo black magician . . . a British general actually told me that the real reason why Hitler destroyed the Polish Jews was to prevent their cabbalistic knowledge being used against him. . . ." Lowry, *Letters.*

† "Boehme would support me when I speak of the passion for order even in the smallest things that exist in the universe. . . ." *Ibid.*

Jewish music publisher of the strange habits and mind changes is portrayed as a reincarnated Cabbalist who, by means of *notarikon,* has acted all the while as a kind of mentor and guide to Hugh, serving now to assist, now to frustrate, him. Geoffrey, in the meantime, has opened the arcana to a full inspection, and he begins to enumerate the different varieties of conjurable demons:

Erekia, the one who tears asunder; and they who shriek with a long drawn cry, Illirikum; Apelki, the misleaders or turners aside; and those who attack their prey by tremulous motion, Dresop; ah, and the distressful painbringing ones, Arekesoli; and one must not forget, either, Burasin, the destroyers by stifling smoky breath; nor Glesi, the one who glistens horribly like an insect; nor Effrigis. . . . all these at one time or another have visited my bed * [an open admission of the terrible price he has paid for consorting with these spirits].

Bringing these creatures even closer to the surface, he informs Hugh, who is "listening in a dream to the Consul's voice rambling on," that they are at work even at the moment, searching for "just such arcana as could be found behind them in his bookshelves." Geoffrey obliquely indicates that he himself is in danger from the "German" forces when suddenly the telephone rings again—a second warning, which, we later learn, comes from Vigil but remains unheeded. It beats "around the rooms like a trapped bird, then it stopped," preparing us for the image of the soul's final release in the guise of the freed bird of Chapter Eleven.

In direct connection with her personal symbol (the bird), Yvonne enters the scene immediately after the unheeded phone call. But she has changed her clothing for the trip from "yellow" (the merciful *Tiphereth*) to "red" and "white" (*Geburah*). Thus, she is "envious of the male—angel to him as he is bright or dark, yet unconscious destructive succubus of his ambitions. . . ."

The three leave the house together. Still intent on dropping wide hints about his own condition, Geoffrey discovers a scorpion on the wall as the three of them walk down the street and comments: " 'A curious bird is the scorpion. He cares not for priest nor for poor peon . . . It's really a beautiful creature. Leave him be. He'll only sting himself to death anyway.' The Consul swung his stick." In its nobler aspect, the scorpion is the occult reversed

---

* Lowry took this list directly from Mathers' *The Book of the Sacred Magic of Abra-Melin, The Mage.*

image of the eagle. Here Lowry is making the Consul present a rueful picture of his own suicidal struggle with its subsequent defeat of the nobler aspects of his purpose. In addition, there is a pointed reference to his coming display of indifference to the dying Indian, or "poor peon," both allusions implying some hidden connection concerning their mutual doom. In fact, the dead peon *is* the nobler side of the Consul.

. This time when they pass the advertisements Geoffrey notices to his "quiet delight" a new poster for an insecticide: "666." Even Hugh chuckles to himself, for as a result of his previous session in the Consul's room, he too is now aware of the symbolic number of judgment. Geoffrey (soon to be designated as a "spider") is amused and continues to play the fool by singing a mysterious little ditty about "Nemesis" and then adds "with heroism," "It's really an extraordinarily nice day to take a trip" (referring, of course, to his coming death). In a warning to maintain silence, the Consul is then confronted with a sign that reads: "No se permite fijar anuncios" (Post No Bills).

From this point on, to the close of the chapter, Lowry takes the reader into a world full of mysterious symbols and undisclosed Cabbalistic allusions. The trio passes a group of goats, associated here with Yvonne, which are thinking: *"Father is waiting for you though. Father has not forgotten,"* a dual warning that includes a reference to Geoffrey, who is soon to be merged with "Il Papa," and the father who resides in *Kether* and who awaits completion of Yvonne's mission.

Geoffrey, casting aside all caution, is delightedly giving away Cabbalistic secrets like ". . . [No] angel with six wings is ever transformed. . . . Thomas Burnet, author of Telluris Theoria Sacra entered Christs in . . . ," when he is suddenly overcome by a buzzing airplane that flies directly over his head with "a shattering and fearful tumult" (the demons whom he has alienated come to silence him).

As if in further retaliation for the Consul's loose tongue, Jacques, his most detested enemy, appears on the street. As the seducer, Jacques is described as a man seemingly occupied by "the essence of some guilty secret." Lowry appropriately depicts him as a man both "false" and "engaging" in keeping with his archetypal ancestor in the garden. As Jacques invites the trio into what will become for the Consul a literal "madhouse," still another interception arrives from the forces of preservation. A "grotesque little creature," a "pleasing animal advancing on all fours" who "yelps with triumph" upon spotting them, turns out to be not an animal at all, but the mailman, another one of those little earth gnomes who delight in helping men (cf. Concepta, the maid). He says to the Consul: ". . . a message por el señor, for your horse," meaning to say "house," but significantly mistaken in his choice of words, for Geoffrey's occult power is embodied in the horse symbol. Moreover, since the note turns out to be a belated plea from Yvonne, written *twelve* months before, which had "gone badly astray," it is now too late. Because this error in communication will eventually contribute to her death, the note acquires even greater irony when it reads: *"Darling, why did I leave? Why did you let me? Expect to arrive in the U.S. to-morrow. . . . Hope to find a word from you there waiting. Love Y."* In implementation of the finality of their parting, the postcard displays a mountain peak—symbol of Yvonne's yearnings—and a desert—symbol of Geoffrey's arid path. "The road turned a little corner in the distance and vanished" in a pictorial forecast of the permanent departure of the *Shekinah*.

# Chapter Seven*

As he climbs the tower of Jacques' house, the Consul becomes increasingly annoyed, until he recalls that he had recently vowed never to enter the house again. This disturbing thought leads him to further drinking. He and Yvonne gaze out over the landscape, she pleading for a second chance, and he hating her for her betrayal. He wanders around Laruelle's bedroom, trying to imagine the adulterous scene with Yvonne until he is faced with a temperance poster, which suddenly seems to depict his own life. He knows now that he is in hell. Turning toward the balcony, he thinks about the Farolito, the little cantina in Parián that, in spite of its depravity, or perhaps *because* of it, symbolizes his personal haven. Brought back to his present situation, he climbs to the roof and gazes out toward a golf course. Golf had been his forte once, but he no longer plays, and he now associates the sport with his own failure to conquer life's trials. There is some highly charged nervous conversation among Yvonne, Laruelle, and the Consul until Geoffrey and Jacques are finally left alone together. Laruelle attacks his friend for continuing to drink in spite of Yvonne's return; the argument builds until the Consul can no longer think clearly. He runs to the phone for help, but is so confused by now that he cannot remember Dr. Vigil's number. The phone book presents him with some outstandingly odd names, and his fear is increased to a point where he screams for "God" into the receiver, hangs it up the wrong way, and runs from the house. Having placed Yvonne's postcard under Jacques' pillow, and after finishing all the drinks in sight, Geoffrey walks down the street conversing with Jacques.

Time is displaced. Events of the morning seem to be repeated. The two men pass the Cortez Palace, where the Consul is frightened by the menacing Indians of the Rivera murals. They pass the Indian peon of the morning, whose horse bears the 7 brand. They enter the fair, where Geoffrey relates the picture panels on a carousel to his love for his wife; and then they go into a

* Lowry has made the significantly numbered Chapters Seven and Twelve the longest and most deeply symbolic.

café, where he drinks tequila. The argument begun in Laruelle's bedroom continues, with Jacques questioning Geoffrey's alcoholic mysticism and suffering. The Consul claims that he is learning how to conquer death and warns Jacques that this is only the beginning of his martyrdom. Suddenly the Consul realizes that he has really been talking to himself, and he staggers out of the café toward the bus terminal, singing a childhood tune that had been recalled by Laruelle in Chapter One, the "wibberlee, wobberlee WALK"—really a foreshadowing of his present drunken course. Diverted by the Ferris wheel, Geoffrey mechanically boards it and is turned upside down until all his possessions fall from his pockets. Some children return his things (including Hugh's telegram, which is still in his jacket pocket), but his passport is missing. With Yvonne and Hugh in sight, he continues making his way toward El Bosque, the bus terminal cantina owned by Señora Gregorio. In the gloomy bar, he locates this old half-English, half-Spanish confidante. Unaware that Yvonne has returned, Señora Gregorio gives motherly advice assuring him that he and Yvonne will someday be happy. As she shuffles off, leaving him with a full glass of tequila, a starving pariah dog enters the bar. The Consul is overwhelmed by sadness at the sight of the creature, but he suddenly begins to intone: "Yet this day, pichicho, shalt thou be with me in—" as the frightened dog hurries away. More miserable than ever, Geoffrey calls for the señora and barely resists crying on her ample bosom. Sensing his despair but unable to communicate adequately in English, she offers him her house, which is only a "shadow," and tells him that one cannot "drink of life." Geoffrey exits, only to back quickly out of sight when he spots Vigil in "impeccable" tennis clothes. The chapter ends with a reiteration of a newspaper headline that Geoffrey had applied to himself: "Es inevitable la muerte del Papa."

As Lowry himself attests, this chapter was written to be read on many levels: "There were the usual thicknesses and obliquities, stray cards from the tarot pack, and odd political and mystical chords . . . in this chapter. . . ." * The Consul is fixed on two planes of experience, the universal (the name of the newspaper that bears information about his fate) and the earthly. Jacques' invitation, therefore, proves an untimely and unwelcome intrusion on his plan. Noting his location in time and space as he had checked his watch at key moments previously, he finds that he is "On the side

* Lowry, *Letters*.

of the drunken madly revolving world hurtling at 1:20 P.M. toward Hercules' Butterfly . . ." perhaps not enough time for him to make the smooth transition to Parián.

Jacques' house encompasses the Consul's guilt and punishment, with its two towers (the blasted tower being the destruction of God's house, according to Achad) "as if camouflaged (almost like the *Samaritan,* in fact): blue, grey, purple, vermilion . . . [now only a] dull mauve." * Once easily mistaken for a symbol of life, perhaps for the tree of life itself, the house is actually a camouflaged symbol of the destruction of Geoffrey's marriage, for it had been Jacques who lured Yvonne there as the Zoharic seducer had lured Eve to sin. Like the tree of death, the house is a mockery of heaven with its spiral staircases on each side and "two bilious-looking angels" in front of "two nameless objects like marzipan cannonballs" on the left. The right hand side is unadorned, and the Consul notes that "this contrast was somehow obscurely appropriate to Jacques, as indeed was that between the angels and the cannonballs." Jacques, as betrayer, is another agent of the left-hand side. But as friend and adviser he qualifies as a type of "angel"—another indication that he is designed to represent the "average" Assiatic (*Assiah* = the world of matter) man who is composed partly of heaven, partly of hell.

As he is led up to the tower on the left, Geoffrey recalls too late that only a few weeks before he'd sworn never to enter Jacques' house again. Jacques and Geoffrey are now played off against each other in terms of the "world card" (pleasure, sensuality) of the tarot, which conflicts with "judgment" (ascetic, suffering), its counterpart. Having entered the tower, the Consul completes the breach between himself and his wife (the "lovers" card).

Hugh characteristically *climbs* to the roof for a better overall view of the scene, while Geoffrey sees "Far away . . . a green corner, the golf course, with little figures making their way round the side of the cliff, crawling . . . Golfing scorpions." Once again the green stands for the aspiration toward *Netzach* (Victory). The Consul, having been temporarily sidetracked from his own path, can now watch others like himself—"golfing scorpions," or Cabbalistic adepts in their attempts to win the contest. He is moved by

* According to Achad, blue = cohesive *Chesed;* gray = illuminating *Chokmah;* purple = pure *Yesod;* vermilion = radical *Geburah.*

the sight to remember Yvonne's postcard in his pocket because *Netzach,* as Venus, would remind him of their love, and for a moment he wishes "to say something tender to her . . . to turn her towards him, to kiss her." But because Venus is also a horned star, which reminds him of her betrayal, and because he is in the betrayer's very room, he cannot approach his wife, shame for his morning's impotence driving him to push her away even further. Although his attention is still focused on the stars, he thinks about but cannot articulate his position, "What do you think, Yvonne . . . with your astronomical mind . . . doesn't all that revolving and plunging up there somehow suggest to you the voyaging of un- seen planets, of unknown moons hurling backwards?" * So sensi- tive is she to his moods and thoughts that Yvonne responds to this unspoken question defensively: ". . . [Believe] me, I didn't want to be drawn into this. Let's make some excuse and get away as quickly as possible . . . Haven't you got any tenderness or love left for me at all?"

Again thinking rather than speaking to her outright, the Consul admits their irreparable estrangement, using the image of the weep- ing Merope to emphasize his isolation: "Yes, I do love you. . . . only that love seems so far away from me and so strange too, for it is as though I could almost hear it, a droning or a weeping, but far, far away, and a sad lost sound. . . ." But the droning, as the pro- jection of his thought, is really that of the "flying machines . . . belabouring him all over." The spies and agents of hell are at him still.

Now the airplane, a symbol associated in his mind with Yvonne's return, becomes the accuser of *Geburah* (Judgment), to which the Consul reacts with anger and suspicion: "Listen . . . are you starting to exhort me again about drinking?" And in his confusion, he cannot read the hopeful message of the postcard in his pocket. "It ought to have been a good omen. It could be the talisman of their immediate salvation now. . . . if only it had

* This metaphor for Geoffrey's own turbulent inner state, for which he partially blames his wife, can be traced to Ouspensky's *A New Model of the Universe* in the chapter dealing with sleep and dreams, in which he mentions that the sensation of hurling or flying backward is regarded by occultists as a phenomenon of black magic. This painful shock is actually experienced by the Consul when he is thrust backward and upside down on the infernal machine.

arrived yesterday or at the house this morning. . . . And how could he know whether it was a good omen or not without another drink?" Time and his recalcitrance have ruined their chances, especially since noon has passed and with it the aspirations toward redemption. Now bitter and lacking forgiveness, the Consul begins to dwell entirely on his own "abandonment, bereavement, as during this last year without Yvonne, he had never known in his life, unless it was when his mother died." But his desire to retaliate for the hurt sustained had begun with his stepmother so that he can no longer forgive, "Even though here was God's moment, the chance to agree, to produce the card, to change everything; or there was but a moment left . . . Too late."

The Consul has been confronted with the three important female aspects of his initiation, the good mother, *Binah;* the harsh stepmother, *Geburah;* and the personification of God's love, *Shekinah.* He is allotted a final moment during which he may reconcile himself to all three, saving not only his wife and himself but perhaps even the world. Yet he is so steeped in the abyss that he "disengages" himself from Yvonne in order to enter the room where he had been betrayed.

Lack of forgiveness, overweening self-love as well as self-hate, vindictiveness—all personified at one time or another as his demonic familiars—draw Geoffrey away from love back to the scene of the crime committed against him. The room becomes a personally relevant chamber of horrors containing no liquor but hung about with pictures of "harpies . . . among broken bottles of tequila," laden with "poltergeist-stacked" books, all a mirror of his own hopelessness. The demonic forces cause the room to come alive with a grotesque parody of the Consul's and Yvonne's coming deaths as presented in "Los Borrachones," a prohibitionist poster depicting the misery of the alcoholic.

Down, headlong into hades, selfish and florid-faced, into a tumult of fire-spangled fiends . . . shrieking among falling bottles and emblems of broken hopes, plunged the drunkards; up, up, flying palely, selflessly into the light toward heaven, soaring sublimely . . . shielded themselves by angels with abnegating wings, shot the sober. . . . A few lone females on the upgrade were sheltered by angels only. It seemed to him these females were casting half-jealous glances downward after their plummeting husbands, some of whose faces betrayed the most unmistakable relief. The Consul laughed, a trifle shak-

ily. . . . [Had] anyone ever given a good reason why good and
evil should not be thus simply delimited? * . . . One part of the
Consul continued to laugh, in spite of himself, and all this evidence
of lost wild talents. . . .

When he calls up to Hugh, he learns that his brother has focused
Jacques' binoculars on Parián (Jacques as guide through hell
again). This immediately clarifies for him the meaning and extent
of "Los Borrachones": "It was that he was in hell himself." He
now feels "curiously calm" as he thinks of his planned jaunt to the
Farolito, "The Lighthouse, the lighthouse that invites the storm,
and lights it." Merely the thought of going there "filled him with an
almost healing love . . . for it was part of the calm, the greatest
longing he had ever known."

Lowry means this reflection as a preparation for the last journey
into the farthest recesses of the *Kelipah,* the abyss at the center of
the earth that, in Geoffrey's intoxicated state, appears miragelike
to appease his thirst with the promise of light—the Farolito being
the path out of hell. In addition, the lighthouse that invites the
storm is also an alchemical allegory for the etheric or divine fluid.
Geoffrey envisions the scene of his judgment as follows:

The Farolito! It was a strange place, a place really of the late night
and early dawn, which as a rule . . . did not open till four o'clock
in the morning. But to-day being the holiday for the dead, it would
not close.† At first it had appeared to him tiny. Only after he had
grown to know it well had he discovered . . . that it was really
composed of numerous little rooms, each smaller and darker than the
last, opening into another, the last and darkest of all being no larger
than a cell. These rooms struck him as spots where diabolical plots
must be hatched . . . here, as when Saturn was in Capricorn, life

* Acquainted as he was with the Egyptian and Tibetan *Books of the
Dead,* Lowry may have drawn much that is connected with this scene from
theosophically influenced "Egyptian" alchemy. Cf. the following description
of a drawing on the walls of a crypt in Thebes: "representing the flight of
the worthy upward toward heaven, while the wicked are being cast by
means of pitchforks into eternal fire." Further, Jacques wears a scarab ring
and drinks El Nilo water and is closely identified with the tarot—an Egyptian invention. Thus, the Consul's experience in Chapter Seven is also analogous to the symbolic death journey of the Egyptian mysteries, with Jacques
enacting the role of the priest.

† On the Day of Atonement, the Cabbalist indulges in a full twenty-four
hours of ritual prayer, cleansing, and fasting as a symbol of death and rebirth, for on that day the gates of heaven and hell remain open for judgment. The Day of the Dead represents a similar opportunity for the Consul.

reached bottom.* But here also great wheeling thoughts hovered in the brain. . . . He saw it all now, the enormous drop on one side of the cantina into the barranca that suggested Kubla Khan . . . the beggars . . . one of whom one night . . . had taken him for the Christ, and falling down on his knees before him, had pinned . . . under his coat lapel two medallions, joined to a tiny worked bleeding heart like a pincushion, portraying the Virgin of Guadalupe. . . . He saw all this, feeling the atmosphere of the cantina enclosing him already with its certainty of sorrow and evil, and with its certainty of something else too, that escaped him. But he knew: it was peace. He saw the dawn again, watched with lonely anguish from that open door, in the violet-shaded light, a slow bomb bursting over the Sierra Madre—*Sonnenaufgang*—the oxen harnessed to their carts with wooden disc wheels patiently waiting outside for their drivers, in the sharp cool pure air of heaven. The Consul's longing was so great his soul was locked with the essence of the place as he stood and he was gripped by thoughts like those of the mariner who, sighting the faint beacon of Start Point after a long voyage, knows that he will embrace his wife.

The Consul's vision of the Farolito is, of course, the description of the seemingly endless little corridors of hell that must be traversed in order for the soul to come to the light. But these rooms were once cells in a monastery, an oblique clue to the religious significance of Geoffrey's longing. He feels that he must return there in order to sink to the lowest (Saturn in Capricorn) as a means for regaining the upward path (cf. Messiah in *Kelipah*). Yet the "great wheeling thoughts" hidden in the depths of the Farolito also recall Ezekiel's vision, the beginnings of a comprehension of the Aziluthic world, which is mysteriously tied to the world of matter (*Assiah*) by means of the sun (*Tiphereth*)—hence, the sunrise vision, emerging "in the violet-shaded light" (*Yesod* once again) of the new dawn of the soul drawn by the "oxen of the sun" harnessed to the wheels of Ezekiel's chariot, an emblem of the Cabbalistic ascent over Sierra Madre ("Mother Mountain," *Binah*), all the way to *Kether* itself, "sharp cool pure air of heaven." All this could presumably reveal itself to him once he is removed from the initial filth and corruption represented by the Farolito—that is, the false light of the material world.

The Consul does, in a sense, consider himself to be a kind of

* Saturn is astrologically responsible for epidemics, wars, and mass and personal misery.

alcoholic Christ whose "certainty of sorrow and evil" entitles him to the ultimate calm, which will descend only after the Day of the Dead has passed, which could also explain his continual wrist-watch checking throughout the day.

The simile of the mariner's final return to his home and the arms of his wife is another metaphor of the reunification of the soul with the *Shekinah* and ultimately with the First Cause, "Start Point." Corroborating this image is the immediate reversion to guilt over Yvonne:

Had he really forgotten her, he wondered. . . . [H]ow could one begin all over again, as though the Café Chagrin, the Farolito, had never been? . . . Could one be faithful to Yvonne and the Farolito both?—Christ, oh pharos of the world, how, and with what blind faith, could one find one's way back . . . from a place where even love could not penetrate, and save in the thickest flames there was no courage?

Again, as though in direct response, Yvonne, now recast as "one of the little Mayan idols" surrounding the room, "seemed to be weeping."

Geoffrey suddenly displays great insight into the nature of his suffering. In a final decision to renounce Yvonne and commit himself entirely to the Farolito and what it represents, Geoffrey "took the postcard he'd just received from Yvonne and slipped it under Jacques' pillow." He has evidently begun the contemplation required for his sevenfold journey, since his "reflections had not occupied seven minutes." Emerging from his lonely meditations, he comments rather ironically on his own decision, repeating, "Oh God . . . God that the dream of dark magician in his visioned cave . . . were the true end of this so lousy world . . ." as he had to Dr. Vigil on rejecting him, for he is still intent on renovating the world in some way, as reflected by his previous amusement at seeing the 666 advertisement announcing the judgment of which his machinations are a contributing part.

As he gazes over the countryside through binoculars, Geoffrey conceives a picture of the Sephirotic path as a golf course again:

It was as if they were standing on a lofty golf-tee somewhere. What a beautiful hole this would make. . . . The Golgotha Hole. High up, an eagle drove downwind in one. It had shown lack of imagination to build the local course back up there, remote from the barranca.

Golf = gouffre = gulf. Prometheus would retrieve lost balls.* And on that other side what strange fairways could be contrived, crossed by lone railway lines, humming with telegraph poles, glistening with crazy lies on embankments, over the hills and far away . . . the course plotted all over these plains, extending . . . through the jungle, to the Farolito, the nineteenth hole . . . The Case is Altered.

He has drawn a mental chart of the thirty-two potential paths of the Sephirotic tree in the form of a golf course with its eighteen holes. Covered with the elusive lines of communication that only serve to confuse the adept, it is reminiscent in its complexity of Frater Achad's mazes. The danger inherent in such an undertaking is the route through the jungle to the nineteenth hole—that is, the equivalent of the eleventh path, which, once crossed, "alters the case" of the initiate, who, having lost his innocence, falls into the sand trap (*Kelipah*) as a result.

Ironically at this moment, it is the earth-bound Jacques, standing "over by the angels," who claims he has "visions," as Geoffrey conducts the *real* search for his pre-Adamic self on the golf green:

. . . what on earth was he . . . continuing to look for out there on those plains . . . for some figment of himself . . . ? To climb, and then to see, . . . far below, resting near the pin on the green, his new Silver King, twinkling. . . . The Consul could no longer play golf: his few efforts of recent years had proved disastrous . . . Who holds the flag while I hole out in three? Who hunts my Zodiac Zone along the shore? And who, upon that last and final green, though I hole out in four, accepts my ten and three score?

Lowry equates golf with skill in accomplishing the various Sephirotic worlds, conquering obstacles, scoring accurate successes that are acknowledged by approval from above, guided and assisted by beneficent spirits who inhabit the zodiac zone (*Yetzirah*), where, by now, Scorpio, the Consul's constellation, is beginning its decline.

Injecting further self-irony into the conversation, the Consul explains that he has always admired Shelley, who "just let himself sink to the bottom of the sea—taking several books with him of course—and just stayed there, rather than admit he couldn't

---

* Prometheus, another robber of divine light destined for torment. Geoffrey implies that there is no salvation without hazard, that the "green" must include the barranca if winning the game is to prove a worthwhile effort—that is, conquer the abysses that cross each *Sephirah*.

swim." He is alluding to his own sinking under the weight of the heavy spirits with whom he can no longer cope, which are inscribed in the weighty unwritten Cabbalistic book he carries within himself. Impressed by Shelley's strange courage, the Consul compares his own sinking process:

No angels nor Yvonne nor Hugh could help him here. As for the demons, they were inside him as well as outside; quiet at the moment . . . he was nonetheless surrounded by them and occupied; they were in possession. The Consul looked at the sun. But he had lost the sun: it was not his sun. . . . [He] did not want to go anywhere near it, least of all, sit in its light, facing it. "Yet I shall face it." How?

Besieged by demons, he fears the light of truth, *Tiphereth*. He longs instead for the illusory light of the Farolito. Nevertheless, the moment dedicated to a thought of the sun is sufficiently positive to draw upon the beneficent, awaiting power of Dr. Vigil, who phones at that moment in order to offer still another chance for hope.

" 'He wants to know if you've changed your mind, if you and Yvonne will ride with him to Guanajuato after all . . . ,' " Jacques relays.

" 'How did he know I was here?' The Consul sat up, shaking a little again. . . ."

Torn between newly offered salvation and his predetermined path, the Consul is momentarily unnerved by the invitation from the "good fellow [who] seemed by now unreal to him." But he is soon restored to the "loathsome reality" of Yvonne's adultery by gazing at Jacques, now in the shower and washing quite openly before him (that is, the equivalent of being deterred from the guardian angel and drawn toward the seducer). Miserable to the point of weeping, the Consul distracts himself by looking over the volumes of books surrounding the room, "everything . . . from Les joyeuses bourgeoises de Windsor to Agrippa. . . . Yet in none of these books would one find one's own suffering." Thus Lowry repeats Geoffrey's rationale for defection from the great work: the intellectual discipline proves cold comfort in the face of the actual quest.

The Consul's alienation builds, extending to a fantasy that confuses sex with destruction, and as an externalization of his own negativity, the observation plane descends upon him once again:

". . . oh Jesus, yes, here, here, out of nowhere, she came whizzing . . . at the Consul, looking for him perhaps, zooming . . . Aaaaaaaah!"

Jacques, unaware of what is actually going on, significantly predicts "thunder," to which the Consul returns a frightened "No" and rushes to the phone in a panic "shaking all over" in his attempt to locate help.

A.B.C.G. . . . 666 . . . Erikson 34. He had the number, had forgotten it: the name Zuzugoitea . . . then Sanabria [the names of his murderers] came starting out of the book at him . . . forgotten the number 34, 35, 666 . . . he could not hear—could they hear? see? . . . "Who do you want . . . God!" he shouted, hanging up.

This scene is an almost allegorical portrayal of a magical ritual performed in desperation. The phone book takes the place of the *grimoire,* which contains the intricate numerical formulas necessary for evoking spirits. (*Goetia, or Lesser Keys of Solomon* is the name of such a book of demons that Lowry read.) In his confusion, Geoffrey forgets the correct formula—that there are 32, not 34 or 35 and certainly not 666, paths to salvation. At the height of his desperation (provoked by the uncontrollable clairvoyant vision of his murderers), he conjures by the Tetragrammaton itself, shouting "God" into the receiver, which he is characteristically holding "the wrong way up" all the time. Feeling that "He would need a drink to do this. . . . He . . . drank down all the drinks in sight. . . . [and] heard music. Suddenly about three hundred head of cattle, dead, frozen stiff . . . sprang on the slope before the house, were gone." The demons, at this point rejuvenated by his confused exhortations, come to life around him, embodying themselves in the books he picks up: *La Machine infernale,* which is actually a premonition of the Ferris wheel on which he is tossed upside down; the devilish reversal indicated by the appearance of Baudelaire's contention that the "gods . . . are the devil"—and they accompany him out the door. In harmony with his ineluctable course, he turns and assures both the devils and himself that the entire thing is "Absolutamente necesario." And leaving the house accompanied by Jacques—the world of material hopes and fantasies—he reads *No se puede vivir sin amar* on the wall as they turn into the Street of the Land of Fire. 666 (that is, toward judgment, or the transmuting fire that accompanies the apocalypse and the completion of the Agrippan alchemistic work).

Lowry now involves the reader even more deeply in Geoffrey's thoughts when it is made clear that Jacques is another of the Consul's alter egos, another creation of his own in the manner of the Golem, who, created to reflect the wishes of its master, suddenly turns against him, becoming the mirror of his master's destructive powers:

. . . how all-permeating [the Consul's] influence had been, an influence that showed even in [Jacques'] choice of books, his work. . . . Was it not much as though he, the Consul, from afar, had willed it, for obscure purposes of his own? . . . Was it not almost as though the Consul had tricked him into dishonour and misery, willed, even, his betrayal of him?

Soon Geoffrey falls into another temporary condition of time displacement and disorientation in which he relives the events of the morning. *"Eggs!"* calls the "jovial proprietor of the abarrotes," and "Mesca*lito*," once again calls the man with the wooden plank —parallels to the Consul's conflicting desires for life and inebriation. He is still being followed by the man in dark glasses, "who seemed familiar, and to whom the Consul motioned. . . ." This stranger is, of course, the Consul's "familiar," for magicians are capable of creating doubles to act as familiars, other selves, so to speak, who are capable of moving undetected from one body to the next. But they must be careful lest they lose their identity between trips.

Geoffrey and Jacques stop to look at the Rivera murals in Cortez Palace, which depict

. . . Tlahuicans who had died for this valley in which he lived. . . . As he looked it was as though these figures were gathering silently together. Now they had become one figure, one immense malevolent creature staring back at him. Suddenly this creature appeared to start forward, then make a violent motion. It . . . was telling him to go away.

In still another forewarning of his fate, the ancient savage inhabitants of Mexico portrayed on the walls, who are to return to life on the Day of the Dead in the form of the fascist accusers, are, in this sense, visible only to the Consul, who had previously declared his acquaintance with the ominous "handwriting on the wall."

Because part of the adept's mission is the conquest of duality, of good and evil both, Geoffrey maintains a continual struggle between himself and the outer worlds that seek to perpetuate their power. He tries to transcend them, depending on mescal for support. Nevertheless, he is followed by a constant procession of representatives from both sides: the demons, spies, airplanes, police, and animals of the dark powers; and—on the side of light—Vigil, garden keepers, sunflower, Hugh, Yvonne, and now the singing Indian rider who appears as the direct antithesis to the menacing Indians of the mural. The man is described as

a fine-featured Indian of the poorer class, dressed in soiled white loose clothes. . . . singing gaily to himself. But he nodded to them courteously. . . . He seemed about to speak, reining in his little horse . . . upon whose rump was branded the number seven. . . . But the man did not speak and . . . he suddenly waved his hand and galloped away, singing.

The Indian is an embodiment of hope, life, love, and kindness who appeals to the Consul for a moment as he will once again later before his death by the roadside. But Geoffrey is too conscious of his isolated and amoral mission to concede to the seductive power of earthly goodness (which, according to Ouspensky, does not assure man's redemption) in spite of a momentary softening: "The Consul felt a pang. Ah, to have a horse, and gallop away, singing, away to someone you loved . . . into the heart of all the simplicity and peace in the world; was not that like the opportunity afforded man by life itself? Of course not." Shaken out of his illusion, Geoffrey touches on the truth of the matter, for the Indian is actually riding to his death. The Consul identifies instead with the horse, who, "Weary of liberty . . . suffered himself to be saddled and bridled, and was ridden to death for his pains." Yet it is the horse too (supernatural power unleashed) that destroys Yvonne as soon as it is unbridled and set free by him.

Heading toward the fair, he sees the warning headlines once again: "Es inevitable la muerte del Papa. The Consul started . . . an instant, he had thought the headlines referred to himself." Now insulated by the numerous drinks at Jacques', Geoffrey is able to read the astral messages that surround him; he sees the underlying correspondences in all things. The carousel pictures painted on an "inner wheel that was . . . attached to the top of the central revolving pillar" become still another representation of the spectacle of life, portraying scenes ranging from a mermaid singing to sailors to what appears to be "Medea sacrificing her children" but is actually a "group of monkeys," to "a panel showing lovers, a man and a woman reclining by a river. Though childish and crude it had about it a somnambulistic quality and something too of truth, of the pathos of love."

The wheel of life depicts the animal, the earthy, the fantastic, as well as Eden, all of which the Consul dimly experiences as a kind of Jungian memory trace, and he is again suddenly drawn back toward Yvonne as a result, wanting "to raise his head, and shout for joy, like the horseman: she is here! Wake up, she has come back again!" The return of the *Shekinah* should inaugurate celebration, the Indian being a symbol of what Geoffrey *should* feel on such an occasion. By denying his message, Geoffrey denies the life of the Indian, who is subsequently killed by the sinister forces turned loose by the Consul himself in his meditation on the bathroom floor. On a mystical level, the Indian is really his guardian angel (as Juan Cerillo is to Hugh). According to Abramelin, if he is disobeyed, this benign figure is transformed into an engine of destruction; therefore, it is the Indian's horse that turns wild.

The Consul is momentarily overwhelmed by a

desire to find her immediately . . . to put a stop to this senseless trip. . . . to reverse their doom . . . Raise your head, Geoffrey Firmin, breathe your prayer of thankfulness, act before it is too late [advises his guardian]. . . . The desire passed. At the same time, as though a cloud had come over the sun, the aspect of the fair had completely altered for him.

Alternating throughout the book from light to darkness, he is again impressed by the prevailing tragedy of *Malkuth,* which, in its ignorance of heaven is "awful and tragic, distant . . . an obscure region of death" that cannot be faced without a drink. As he orders a tequila at an open café, he feels the "fire . . . run down his spine like lightning striking a tree which thereupon miraculously blossoms": the energizing of the mystical nervous system by divine fluid as described by Abbé de Villars. He tells Jacques "dreamily" that "if I ever start to drink mescal again, I'm afraid, yes, that would be the end." Laruelle is moved to awe at this revelation, murmuring, "Name of a name of God," a precisely appropriate commentary on his friend's power to draw upon the Tetragrammaton. "I am afraid of you . . . Old Bean." *

Lowry now has an emotional exchange between the Consul and Jacques, during which Geoffrey says, "You are interfering with my great battle. . . . Against death," interspersed with another reminder that *Las Manos de Orlac* begins at 6:30 (the approximate time of his own battle against the "murderer's hands"). Jacques is forced to concede somewhat, admitting that Geoffrey sees "more clearly" when drinking and suffering. But he then confronts the Consul with the fact that in spite of his clairvoyance, he is blind to this life, to "the things so important to us despised sober people. . . . your inability to see them . . . turns them into the instruments of the disaster you have created yourself," to which the Consul responds by blasphemously offering himself as the Host in the form of a "devilled scorpion" during this sacramental drinking rite. Ignoring the taunt, Jacques continues: "I admit the efficacy of your tequila—but do you realize that while you're battling against death . . . while what is mystical in you is being released . . . while you're enjoying all this, do you realise [the allowances made by] the world which has to cope with you . . . ?"

Sunk in a tequila-induced lethargy, the Consul only half listens, for he is simultaneously considering the Ferris wheel as *"the wheel of the law, rolling"* through "the emerald pathos of the trees." He is still, therefore, immersed in vague Sephirotic speculations about the missed opportunities offered by the turning wheel. These thoughts are immediately projected outward when he hears a voice on a radio somewhere singing, "Samaritana . . . then [it] went dead"—a reminder of his transgression as captain of the *Samaritan* and a foreshadowing of his un-Samaritan-like behavior on the approaching bus trip. Meanwhile, Jacques has been continuing his harangue:

"And you forget what you exclude from this, shall we say, feeling of omniscience. And at night . . . or between drink and drink, which is a sort of night, what you have excluded, as if it resented that exclusion, returns—"

"I'll say it returns. . . . There are other minor deliriums too,

* See Appendix D for reference to "Bean" man.

*meteora,* which you can pick out of the air before your eyes, like gnats. . . . But d.t.'s are only the beginning, the music round the portal of the Qliphoth, the overture, conducted by the God of Flies . . . You deny the greatness of my battle? Even if I win. And I shall certainly win, if I want to," the Consul added, aware of a man near them . . . nailing a board to a tree.

Lowry combines the garden notice here both with the motif of the man with the plank who shouts "Mescalito" and with Geoffrey's self-identification with the Messiah.

The Consul concludes the argument, therefore, by making a point-blank confession of his singlehanded intention to conquer the *Kelipah,* and thereby eliminate death, noting that he is as yet merely on the threshold of the abyss.* But he is immediately lurched out of his dialogue with Laruelle when he realizes that "M. Laruelle wasn't there at all; he had been talking to himself."

Leaving the café, "His steps teetered to the left, he could not make them incline to the right," which is still another sign of his heightening confusion; the direction he takes is not his choice but rather the irresistible magnetism of the left-hand path, which, once embarked upon, assumes control of the magician. Likening himself to Faustus, he checks his watch once again, fearful that it may be past the appointed time for his scheduled trip; but he is relieved to find that it is not yet two. In fact, "It was already the longest day in his entire experience, a lifetime. . . ." On his way to El Bosque, the cantina run by Señora Gregorio, he passes the British Consulate, "where the lion and the unicorn on the faded blue shield regarded him mournfully. . . . But we are still at your service, in spite of all, they seemed to say." These symbols of the British Empire are also the symbols of the heavenly empire, which represent strength and virtue bounded by blue, *Chesed,* or mercy.

The Consul is then struck by a "coincidence" as he approaches the Ferris wheel, the "Infernal Machine," † for he had just glanced at the book by Cocteau, and it is as though he is being "drawn inexorably" to the spot where he can see this "huge evil

---

* Death exists only in the world of *Assiah* because it is isolated from the other branches of the tree. Geoffrey is therefore proving by his admission that he wishes to conquer death, which, in the Cabbalistic sense, means that he is intent on restoring *Malkuth* to the tree.

† ". . . the wheel of the law, the wheel of Buddha. It is even eternity, the symbol of the Everlasting Return." Lowry, *Letters.*

spirit, screaming in its lonely hell, its limbs writhing, smiting the air like flails of paddlewheels. Obscured by a tree, he hadn't seen it before." (That is, he had not come to grips with the wheel of karma because it had been hidden behind the tree of life. Now prepared to "conquer" death, he is "inexorably" drawn to try it out.) In a trance, he boards the wheel and finds himself "alone, in a little confession box," merged in actuality with the tormented figures of Prometheus and Ixion. Hanging over the earth in reverse,* he can see the "666" advertisement as "999." †

Obliquely he was aware that he was without physical fear of death [magicians experience "physical" death while still in the body in preparation for final dissolution; hence, the importance of the instructions in the Books of the Dead] . . . perhaps this had been his main idea. . . . It was . . . unnecessary suffering. . . . though it was symbolic. . . . [He experienced] the sensation of falling . . . unlike anything, beyond experience. . . . ah, my God! [Adam's fall; a prelude to his own final fall in Chapter Twelve.] Everything was falling out of his pockets, was being wrested from him, torn away. . . . [He] was being emptied out [kenosis]. . . . What did it matter? . . . There was a kind of fierce delight in this final acceptance. Let everything go! Everything particularly that . . . gave . . . identity to that frightful bloody nightmare . . . that went by the name of Geoffrey Firmin, late of His Majesty's Navy, later still of His Majesty's Consular Service. . . .

As a representative of His Majesty (that is, God), Geoffrey had been a positive "force for good" at one time, but this concession of his identity reflects the final phase of his ordeal, in which he has entirely divested himself of all possible assistance. Instead of his passport, the necessary identification required to pass the "guardians of the threshold," he now carries Hugh's incriminating telegram in his pocket. He has spun out his identity on the wheel, and he finds it is now "seven minutes past two."

But the horrors are not yet over, for the Consul is now faced with a replica of himself in the form of a

---

* ". . . an individual who has experienced the four-dimensional vision, on . . . re-entering three-dimensional consciousness, sees things *upside down*. . . . To him in this higher wisdom virtue and vice are equivalents, for both are illusions when compared to reality. . . ." Fuller, *The Secret Wisdom of the Qabalah*. Cf. also the hanged man of the tarot.

† "At Judgment Day although there be 999 who condemn a man, he shall be saved if one shall plead for him." Westcott, *Numbers*.

madman wearing, in the manner of a lifebelt, an old bicycle tire. With a nervous movement he continually shifted the injured tread round his neck. . . . [He] took off the tire and flung it far ahead of him. . . . Picking up the tire he flung it far ahead again, repeating this process, to the irreducible logic of which he appeared eternally committed, until out of sight.

Lowry is drawing the earthly correspondence of Geoffrey's own mad, whirling path down to the *Kelipah,* the worn tire set in motion by the madman being the illusory wheel of life in *Malkuth.* Firmin is faced by a further ominous correspondence when he sees a man trying to climb a slippery pole who, like himself on a spiritual plane, is "neither near enough to the top nor the bottom to be certain of reaching either in comfort" and a turtle dying "in two parallel streams of blood"—the image to be recapitulated in the form of the dying Indian. Avoiding these demonic manifestations, the Consul makes his desperate way to the "magic wood" cantina located significantly at the "terminal." The entry to the deepest stages of matter is dirty, draped in black, the bar, "which, facing east, became progressively darker as the sun, to those who noticed such things, climbed higher into the sky. . . ." As a black magician who is sinking fast, the Consul picks the perfect refuge from sunlight. However, the consoling darkness bears with it the residential demons who continue to taunt him with hints of the death to come: " 'Geoffrey Firmin, this is what it is like to die, just this and no more, an awakening from a dream in a dark place, in which . . . are present the means of escape from yet another nightmare. But the choice is up to you. You are not invited to use those means of escape; it is left up to your judgment. . . .' " *

Here the Consul is among familiars like Señora Gregorio, a kind of sympathetic witch, among her barrels of mysterious concoctions, who dispenses fatalistically tinged advice. This is the realm of *Geburah,* the site of the "dark mother" whose hair is "dyed red" and who offers mescal "in a queer, chanting half-bantering tone," smiling slyly. Jolting him back into the timelessness of these

---

* Lowry's description is derived from the Tibetan *Book of the Dead,* which infiltrated theosophical teachings about the afterlife. After death the soul crosses to the astral world, where it has the choice of remaining there, climbing higher, or reincarnating. In cases where the soul is still troubled by its earthly life, it will "haunt" the area in which it once lived. See also excerpts from Lowry's unfinished manuscript *Ghostkeeper,* in Appendix E.

souls in purgatory, she resumes a conversation begun "weeks before" when "Yvonne had abandoned him for the seventh time that
evening."

Señora Gregorio is a projection of Firmin's lost mother, who, although Yvonne is only some feet away at the moment, is anachro-
nistically informing him that he cannot have both his wife with her
offer of love and *all things,* that is, as Böhme would say, the initiate must not hope for any fulfillment here on earth, all things
being valued oppositely in heaven. " 'So it is. If your mind is occupied with all things, then you never lose your mind. Your minds,
your life—your everything in it. . . . Life changes, you know,
you can never drink of it.' " "All things" are the universe, eternity,
things *outside* the immediate self. The magician must lose his
mind, so to speak, before he can find it. He cannot, as Geoffrey is
trying to do at the moment, hold on to both lives at once. He cannot *drink* the life or the answers to it that he is seeking by physically imbibing it.

For a moment Señora Gregorio's observation seems to take root
in Geoffrey's mind when he finds himself alone facing the "over-
flowing cup" of tequila, now transformed into life itself, which
"suddenly within reach, had lost all meaning."

A starving pariah dog [the embodiment of his own thirst] . . .
looked up at the Consul with beady, gentle eyes. . . . [It] began to
bow and scrape before him. Ah, the ingress of the animal kingdom!
Earlier it had been the insects; now . . . these animals, these people
without ideas.* . . . then wanting to say something kind, added,
. . . "For God sees how timid and beautiful you really are, and the
thoughts of hope that go with you like little white birds—"
The Consul stood up and suddenly declaimed to the dog: "Yet
this day, pichicho, shalt thou be with me in—"

As Lowry claimed, the Consul's suffering is only exacerbated by
his compassion for other creatures. In this scene, piteously addressing his own mongrelized soul, the Consul again visualizes his
death; but soon after he is gripped by the terror of his prediction
and calls for Señora Gregorio, who is suddenly transformed into
his own mother: "Now he found himself struggling with his tears,
that he wanted to embrace Señora Gregorio, to cry like a child, to

* According to occult theories of metempsychosis, "people without ideas"
are reincarnated as animals.

hide his face on her bosom." She, on the other hand, repeats: "Life changes. . . . You can never drink of it. I think I see you with your esposa again soon. I see you laughing together in some kernice [*sic*] place where you laugh." In broken English she ambiguously confuses "live" with "laugh," but for Lowry both were combined in essence as "cosmic laughter"—or the humorous acceptance of the burden of living; the "(ker-)nice" place is, of course, the promise of Eden once again. But Señora Gregorio's house turns out to be "only a shadow" (the dark mother being death), and therefore, her vision of Geoffrey and Yvonne's paradise can only apply after they have died. Because *Binah* represents the female, passive/negative principle of the deity, she can only offer him death as a final consolation: "I have no house, only a shadow. But whenever you are in need of a shadow, my shadow is yours." In direct contrast to this scene, just as he leaves her cantina of darkness, Geoffrey nearly falls over Dr. Vigil (the masculine positive symbol of sunlight, healing, and life, who has offered Geoffrey a home, not merely a shadow, by inviting him to Guanajuato), but "the Consul drew back, fearful now of Vigil. . . ."

"Es inevitable la muerte del Papa."

The Consul's stopover at El Bosque—the dark wood—was the second stage of his loss of identity, of his total commitment to death. Therefore, when he sees Vigil now, he *must* avoid him, for he has abjured the light entirely and his death is now "inevitable."

# Chapter Eight

Hugh, Yvonne, and Geoffrey are on the bus to the bull-
fights in Tomalín. The bus driver harbors some pigeons in his
shirt; the general mood is gay. Along the route, they pass
another garden (where a man in a devil's mask sits out the
fiesta), the barranca, and a café from which emerges still another passenger—a "pelado," or one who preys on the poor.
The road grows rougher until they find themselves in volcanic
earth territory. Some of the jolly boys leave the bus, and the
gaiety begins to dwindle. Hugh's mind is cluttered with political issues and guilt about avoiding the Battle of the Ebro. The
driver suddenly stops the bus without warning, for there is a
man lying on the detour road before them. It is the very same
Indian they had all seen before, his horse still at his side. He
has been beaten, but not completely robbed, for some silver
coins still lie under his loose collar. The passengers and bus
driver spend a long time deliberating, but no one does anything to help the dying man for fear of becoming involved
with the military police. Yvonne, repelled by the sight of blood,
remains in the bus. The police finally arrive, and when Hugh
tries to intervene, there is a small scuffle. Geoffrey pulls him
onto the bus, away from the scene, and the driver starts off
quickly. Hugh is shaken with self-disgust. The other people
on the bus are merely resigned to authority. But the pelado has
stolen the dying man's silver and appears to be proud of his
accomplishment. They arrive at Tomalín in a cloud of dust
and head for the bullfight arena as the vultures float overhead.

This chapter, originally a separately created short story,* was
incorporated into the novel as a device for further character portrayal. More important, however, are its moral and political implications, the central theme of the dying Indian being symbolic of

* First published as "Under the Volcano" in special Lowry issue of *Prairie
Schooner*, Winter 1963–1964.

the murder of Mexico by the fascists, a contemporary repetition of the Spanish Conquest. Although reflected through Hugh's consciousness, for the Consul's obscure purposes this chapter is another manifestation of Geoffrey's own predetermined death, whereas for Hugh it provides another testing ground for the sincerity of his approaching sacrifice. Yvonne, least investigated of the protagonists up to this point, becomes more real on this bus trip, emerging as a character with her own weaknesses and fears, which prepare us for her long meditation in the following chapter.

Its setting strongly influenced by the imagery of Burnet's *The Sacred Theory of the Earth,* this chapter is Lowry's pessimistic appraisal of the future of mankind, which begins and ends on the road "Downhill . . ." The bus trip begins with still another repetition of the *Orlac* theme, now illustrated by posters that "showed a murderer's hands, laced with blood," which prepares us for the murder, central to this section, and the Pilate-like response of the Consul. But it is also interlarded with positive religious symbols like the "little secret ambassadors of peace, of love, two beautiful white tame pigeons" carried in the bus driver's bosom "to keep them warm," and doves in a garden.

This time Hugh reads the garden sign correctly—"Do you like this garden . . . that is yours? See to it that your children do not destroy it!" Occupying this garden, however, is "the devil himself, with a huge dark red face and horns, fangs, and his tongue hanging out over his chin, and an expression of mingled evil, lechery, and terror. The devil . . . shambled . . . toward a church almost hidden by the trees." This "devil" is actually a masked peasant who has strayed away from the festivities for the dead, but on another level, the figure actually *becomes* the devil, who is sharing the garden with "doves and a small black goat"—symbols for Yvonne and the Consul. Characteristically, "the Consul . . . seemed calmly to have accepted the devil, while [Hugh and Yvonne] . . . exchanged a look of regret . . . ," ostensibly at missing the native celebration.

As the bus descends farther Hugh is permitted a glance into the ravine, where he sees garbage and "a dead dog," for he has been partially initiated into Geoffrey's world earlier that morning. But Yvonne tries bravely to concentrate on the "blue sky" above, and she "looked happy when Popocatepetl sprang into view" because, having been born in Hawaii, the mountain volcano is for her a spiritual symbol of home and security.*

Tension mounts, however, when a "pelado" (one who preys upon the poor) boards the bus. A drug addict, recognizable as a threat to the well-practiced eye of Geoffrey the alcohol addict (drugs being here indicative of magic power in the wrong hands), the man is a member of the fascist conspiracy. From the bus, the Consul also spots Vigil and Laruelle in a game of tennis: "M. Laruelle . . . tossed a ball high into the blue, smacked it down, but Vigil walked right past it, crossing to the other side." The two men are symbolically depicting the fate of the Consul, who now, like the ball tossed into the blue (*Chesed*), is no longer on Vigil's side.

Hugh is busy with thoughts of his own "pilgrimage," which for him has now become encompassed by the image of the "lonely platform" of the railway station where oil tanks line the embankment, "Their burnished silver lightning . . . playing hide-and-seek among the trees. . . . [where] to-night he himself would stand, with his pilgrim's bundle." The ambiguous "he" seems intended by Lowry to refer to both men, each making his own *last* pilgrimage in search of the elusive "silver lightning" path to God. Hugh tries to put himself and the others into a cheerful mood, "yet the naked realities of the situation, like the spokes of a wheel [wheel of life again], were blurred in motion toward unreal high events." Beneath the superficial event of the bus trip, Hugh senses, but does not identify, the "supernatural" significance of the occasion. Vaguely connecting it with his own quest, which he had traced along the railroad ties that morning, he now passes "the interminable narrow-gauge railway, where—though there were twenty-one other paths they might have taken!—they had ridden home. . . . And there were the telegraph poles refusing, forever, that final curve to the left, and striding straight ahead . . ." Lowry here is actually presenting Hugh's positively oriented restatement of the Consul's gloomy observation from Jacques' balcony, which had also compared the Sephirotic paths to the crisscross lines of a railway, all of which strive essentially straight ahead to

* According to Burnet, the presence of the volcano subdues and covers the abyss.

*Kether;* the telegraph poles "refuse" to curve left because the adept of the true path does not choose to recognize or concede to evil. Telephone poles, the interconnecting wires in the vast system, become identified with the entire problem of communication in the novel, as, for example, in the phone messages sent and not received, Hugh's telegram in his brother's pocket, Yvonne's letters gone astray; all of these are outward manifestations of the Consul's inner confusion. His messages from above are intercepted from below; hence the interminable static of his radio and the coming nightmare train vision in Chapter Ten.

When the downhill road grows worse, "Hugh's soul [jumps] between his teeth" because of his basic aversion to the abyss. The Consul, however, seems happy in his element as the bus "crashed into . . . a second series of deeper potholes:—'This is like driving *over* the moon,'" says Hugh. It is, in a sense, for the entire journey represents their collective attempt to climb beyond *Yesod* up into the higher spiritual spheres. But the Consul is familiar with those realms where most people are least comfortable, and he is calmly reciting magical formulas to himself: "A faint calm smile played about the Consul's lips which from time to time moved slightly, as if, in spite of the racket, the swaying and jolting . . . he were solving a chess problem, or reciting something to himself." More passengers (dressed in white and purple, and therefore meant by Lowry as pilgrims traveling along the middle pillar of the Sephirotic tree) enters the bus, some carrying poultry destined for sacrifice.

The bus soon enters volcanic fields, where there is "Nothing but pines, fircones, stones, black earth," which Lowry compares to the mysterious attractive power of destruction, especially with regard to Geoffrey, who resembles "people . . . always seen standing in the midst of the encroaching flood [of volcanic lava], delighted by it." Just then "Popocatepetl loomed, pyramidal, to their right, one side beautifully curved as a woman's breast, the other precipitous, jagged, ferocious," and the dead volcano assumes the dual aspects of God's countenance in the form of Microprosopus and Macroprosopus.

As they ride through the dead world, around them the individual souls in the bus become collectivized for security on this hazardous journey, each "pleased at last to have transferred one's responsibilities. . . ." But this proves to be a deceptive safety, for the bus (like life) makes a sudden "detour leftward too quickly," leading them to a road where "there was nothing to be seen, just the soft indigo carpet sparkling. . . ." The moral trial of each character continues: *Yesod,* being purple in its lower regions and shading toward indigo in the higher ones, is, according to occultists like Achad, a probationary sphere. The problem unveiled here is the choice between assisting a dying man who at first appears only to be lying "peacefully on his back with his arms stretched out toward [a] wayside cross" or minding one's own business. The critical moment occurs when they realize that the man has been set upon by bandits and is gravely wounded, but they do not act, so that their collective souls are embodied in the image of "A single bird [that] flew, high."

The Consul appropriately feels "terrible," probably more than any of the others, because his present spiritual position precludes sympathy. Yet his innate sense of human decency gets the better of him. As for the bus driver, a likable man, "what could he do, with his pigeons?" Each man considers his own soul first, each is unwilling to "lose his mind" in order to find himself—oddly enough only Geoffrey will have the crazy courage it takes to face the murderers in his own bungling fashion. But at the moment "time was moving at different speeds, the speed at which the man seemed dying contrasting oddly with the speed at which everybody was finding it impossible to make up their minds." Both brothers recognize the man's horse, standing over him, and the Indian reaches out supplicatingly to Hugh, murmuring, "Compañero." After a brief and ineffectual skirmish with the newly arrived fascist police, during which the man is left on the road, Hugh has a waking guilt vision of the horror of war, which he compares to "the creatures . . . in Geoff's dreams."

In the meantime, the entire scene is being covered by the moon dust of *Yesod,* the symbol of the collective Pharisee-like failure of the passengers to transcend themselves. And they resume their lethargy as the dust of the universe surrounds them, heralding the dissolution of the world. "Dust, dust, dust—it filtered through the windows, a soft invasion of dissolution, filling the vehicle," while evil, in the form of the pelado-Judas who has stolen the dead man's silver, has triumphed, leaving the Consul, Yvonne, and Hugh standing under the fiery gaze of Microprosopus, "again in the dust, dazzled by the whiteness, the blaze of the afternoon."

# Chapter Nine

At the arena in Tomalín, Yvonne, relaxed by a few drinks, is having a wonderful time. As the drinks wear off, however, the events become less colorful. She feels a storm hovering in the air overhead and notices that Hugh and the Consul seem gloomy. A bored bull is walking around the ring. Geoffrey wryly christens him "Nandi, vehicle of Siva." The bull is not only bored, but afraid, and he is literally dragged into the fight. This reminds Yvonne of her father, whose life had somehow resembled the Consul's, with its succession of schemes and failures and alcoholism. Recollection of her past brings Yvonne to her movie career and her own moral and spiritual past failures. At fifteen she had been a cowgirl star, expert horsewoman. She had married impulsively, leaving college in Hawaii in order to escape from a rigorous Scots uncle in whose charge she had been placed when her father had finally gone mad and died. Divorced, with one dead child still on her mind, she had tried Hollywood again. Nearly insane with loneliness after her comeback, Yvonne had fled to New York, where, in a 14th Street cinema, she had seen her life reenacted. According to the film, her personal salvation lay in a trip to Europe; and it was to be in Spain that she would marry Geoffrey. Brought back to the present, Yvonne experiences renewed hope in the possibility of making Hugh's dream shack a reality. But the ugly events in the bull ring constantly interfere with her vision of happiness. Before anyone realizes what is happening, Hugh jumps into the arena and begins to wrestle a bull. Geoffrey flies into a rage at this, while Yvonne sees it as an opportunity to broach the idea of a new start in Canada to the Consul. Temporarily in a state of shock, Geoffrey agrees, as Hugh conquers the bull amid much shouting and cheering. At the Consul's direction, the three of them walk silently toward another cantina after the event. Before they enter, however, they are faced with a strange sight. An old, lame Indian emerges from the doorway bearing a still older Indian on his back.

The arena bull ritual, seen through Yvonne's eyes, begins with sensuous gaiety and hope. Underlying the gaiety (imposed on the

scene by her few drinks from Hugh's habanero bottle), however, is
the seriousness of the ancient bullfight ritual as a representation of
the life and death struggle. By observing that there are "some responsive borrachos straying into the ring [who] prematurely
essayed to ride the bull. This was not playing the game: the bull
must be caught in a special way . . . and they were escorted off,
tottering . . . protesting . . . ," Yvonne is actually correlating
Geoffrey's mishandling of life, his premature efforts at winning
the game (cf. "golf") on the one hand, and Hugh's daring, somewhat immature romanticism on the other.

In the midst of the excitement she notices an airplane "droning
. . . in abyssal blue. Thunder was in the air though, at her back
somewhere, a tingle of electricity." Conscious of her mission,
Yvonne is aware of the hovering airplane (which brought her and,
in another aspect, which will carry her back up to the stars) that
seems to observe the double-leveled struggle going on below—the
life/death ritual incarnated in the bull and his contestants and the
life/death struggle between Geoffrey and Yvonne that is going on
in the stands.

Lowry's "abyssal blue" here is a paradoxical image considering
that blue is the color of heavenly mercy. But he is making an
ironic reference to the redeemer as the hanged man of the tarot,
who is both in heaven and dangling over the abyss at the same
time. The air is charged with expectancy of the electromagnetic
struggle for equilibrium that Cabbalists believe results from thun-
derstorms. From the occult point of view, however, this elemental
setting merely reflects the conflict between Yvonne's positive (electricity and air) concentration and Geoffrey's negative (water)
pull. Hugh (earth), by seeking to subdue the bull later, is actually
attempting to stabilize the elemental process and, with it, all their
lives.

Yvonne draws security from the visible presence of the volcanoes, "poor Ixta . . . [and] Popocatepetl . . . its summit brilliant against pitch-massed cloud banks." Then she has "the awful
sensation that, not Popocatepetl, but the old woman with the
dominoes that morning was looking over her shoulder." Under the
Consul's influence, she too is sensitive to specters of guilt and
premonitions of imminent danger, this one being a personification
of *Geburah,* the dark and dangerous aspect of *Binah.*

Immediately affected by this manifestation, the drink having worn off at this point, Yvonne now sees the arena in its ugly actuality. "The only happy people were the drunks"—another insight into the Consul's struggle against the banality of life without the mystical lens provided by alcohol. In fact, she reflects, the entire event is a gloomy bore; even the bull refuses to immerse himself in his role. Characteristically aware of the ritual's significance, as he has been aware of all ritualistic correspondences throughout the day, the Consul christens the bull "Nandi, . . . vehicle of Siva, from whose hair the River Ganges flows and who has also been identified with the Vedic storm god Vindra—known to the ancient Mexicans as Huracán." Continuing in his obsessive magical directives toward world destruction begun in the earlier bathroom scene, the Consul, under the guise of humor, has given his brother more information regarding cosmic secrets. Unlike Jacques, who never fully comprehends Geoffrey's cryptic references, Hugh seems more responsive—on an intellectual, witty basis, at least. There seems to be no indication that Hugh consciously shares in Geoffrey's plan when he says, "For Jesus sake, papa . . . thank you." This dialogue is a culmination of all the gathering references to Geoffrey as Pope, Tezcatlipoca, missing father, and master of Hugh's own initiation into life. The little exchange is soon to be repeated in the ring when the indecisive bull (Hugh) is goaded into activity by a dog (Geoffrey) and again when Hugh, now commissioned by the Consul as an agent of destruction, goes to sea against the fascists.

The bull next becomes identified with life itself, which is "drawn, lured, into events of which [it] has no real comprehension, by people with whom [it] wishes to be friendly, even to play, who entice [it] . . . because they really despise" it. Stimulated by Hugh's remark and partially hypnotized by the scene before her, Yvonne is urged into a meditation on her past, which begins, naturally, with the father she adores. Lowry indulges in some rather heavy-handed Freudianizing in this section, which is devoted to a kind of background identification between her incompetent, alcoholic father and the Consul.*

Yvonne regards the entire bullfight-lassoing as an extended met-

* In the original short story that became Chapter Eight, Geoffrey actually *is* Yvonne's father, and Hugh, her beau.

aphor of life, death, and resurrection in appropriate
fashion as she reflects on the failures of the men in he
neath this rather obvious musing, however, there lies als
parison between the bull ritual and the cycle of progress
feat encountered in the mystical initiation process, v
enumerated in precisely *ten* stages (cf. the *Sephiroth*): "the ͜por-
tant birth, the fair chance, the tentative, then assured, then half-
despairing circulations of the ring, an obstacle negotiated—a feat
improperly recognised—boredom, resignation, collapse: then another, more convulsive birth. . . ." All this crosses her mind as
she looks at the Consul, "who was sitting, meditative . . . apparently intent on the arena," because he is at this very moment un-
dergoing this very experience and has been devolving through
these stages since her appearance that morning.

Yvonne, a cowgirl movie star at fifteen,* has lived a life of illusory and actual terror, during which she "had been caught in a
ravine with two hundred stampeding horses," an event of "coincidental" relevance to the manner in which she is to die. Associated
with horses from the beginning, she has been related, in a way, to
both Hugh (cowboy) and Geoffrey (legendary man who rode a
horse into school) even before she has met them.† Because she
has already undergone her own initiatory trials in the form of an
alcoholic father, Hollywood, a broken marriage, and a dead child,
Yvonne's expert horsemanship is a symbol of her earned ability to
master most of her own destructive impulses. A gossip column ac-
count of her life is actually a disguised record of her spiritual progress: ". . . *though you may not think it now, Yvonne has been
submerged in burning lakes, suspended on precipices, ridden
horses down ravines* . . . ," all of which qualified her for her literal
and Cabbalistic place among the "stars," but not before she had
lived out the consequences of her rebellion against the discipline
entailed in her development (personified by her harsh, old Scots
uncle, Macintyre ‡), could she have earned her freedom. He dis-

* "Yvonne is something of me, for among other things I made a lot of
'Westerns' when I was a young girl and an actress." Margerie Bonner
Lowry, in a letter to the author.

† Lowry seems to have derived some of Yvonne's background from
Yvonne Orlac, the heroine of *Las Manos de Orlac*, who also played dam-
sels in distress at a theater.

‡ Cf. the white magician McCandless in *October Ferry to Gabriola*. See
Appendix E.

owned her when, *"discouraged in her University work, restless under Uncle Macintyre's strict regime, lonely, and longing for love and companionship.* . . . [she was persuaded] *beneath the Hawaiian moon"* to leave with Cliff Wright (actually "Wrong") and become his wife. Her rebellion against the strict regimen required for study of the stars (astronomy, in her case) and development of the soul is, like her major weakness, a sexual one—evidenced by the influence of the moon on her decision (*Yesod*).

In the end she walked alone down Virgil Avenue [her own trip through the *Kelipah*, perhaps] . . . the dark and accursed City of the Angels. . . . [She] walked or drove furiously through her anguish and all the red lights [*Geburah*], seeing, as might the Consul, the sign . . . "Informal Dancing . . ." turn "Infernal"—or "Notice to Destroy Weeds" become "Notice to Newlyweds." . . . [The] great pendulum on the giant clock swung ceaselessly. Too late!

Like Geoffrey now, Yvonne had also once despaired of ever leaving the *Kelipah* and finding *Chesed*. Now she feels that "through Jacques she had been mysteriously able to reach, in a sense to avail herself of . . . the Consul's innocence. . . ." As Eve, alienated from the father she adores but cannot understand, first of the primordial couple to lose her own innocence at the lure of the seducer, having met the Consul before at the same party, outdoors, in the form of Lilith ("Yvonne the Terrible"), Yvonne had come the long way to a recognition of the Consul as a "force for good." She had been led to that conclusion by Jacques and Hugh, both the Consul's alter egos. Her connection with them is and has been illusory, for they are really only Geoffrey's creations in a sense, willed in order to draw her to himself.

Her first divorce had symbolized the spiritual severance from the tree of life that Geoffrey is now experiencing. In her case, New York rather than Parián represented the lowest depths, with its secret path to salvation taking the form of a 14th Street cinema. She too had once wandered through the Consul's "territory" of Golgotha, peopled with cripples and hoodlums, followed by mysterious dark figures until she had come to the cinema where her own life and that of the heroine, also named Yvonne, linked together and gave her the answer to her soul searching: "Was she doomed to an endless succession of tragedies [in] . . . mysterious expiation for the obscure sins of others long since dead and damned. . . . *was* one doomed? . . . what was the use of a will if you had no faith. . . . in life itself. . . . [in] unselfish love—in the stars!"

Enlightened as to the meaning of her trials, even strengthened by them, Yvonne is prepared for the next stage of her life—the trip to Europe that brings her to Geoffrey for the first time. Having undergone her own form of initiation, it is now her turn to guide Geoffrey out of hell if she can. She is an archetypal figure—". . . her own destiny was buried in the distant past, and might for all she knew repeat itself in the future."

Her attention is now drawn back to the struggling bull, in the midst of the labyrinth of ropes, which is enacting the very meaning of her current plight: "Death, or a sort of death, just as it so often was in life; and now, once more, resurrection," for completion of the initiation into occult recognition of the universe is regarded as a death in life, while death and reincarnation provide further opportunity for struggle followed by enlightenment. As she catches a glimpse of a pair of lovers seated in the stands, the woman "in a dove-grey suit," * she thinks of the couple's future as "pure and untrammelled as a blue and peaceful lake," thereby incorporating *Chesed,* mercy, with *Yesod,* Achad's *Sephirah* of sexual purity and cohesiveness. And, in an ironic contrast with Geoffrey's upside-down paradise envisioned at the Farolito, she is gradually immersed in a vision of her own northern paradise, which is located near the "blue and cold" sea; neighbor to a tree "that bloomed twice in the year with white stars," the colors of which are principally yellow, white, blue, silver, green; and located in full view of the zodiac zone.

The original Eden is a Cabbalistic allegory of the combination of Sephirotic states externalized by the natural flora and fauna that flourished there. Geoffrey had referred to it tangentially as Atlantis, which, he mentioned to Jacques, might have been located in what is now Mexico. Perhaps the Consul had even come to Mexico originally in search of this lost paradise (that is, his equilibrium), as Yvonne now imagines it to lie in the north. In the midst of her ethereal musing, Hugh, the earthy cowboy, seems "an interloper, a

---

* *Chokmah* = illuminating, grey.

stranger, part of the scene below," who intrudes on her vision along with the sordid bull-ring activity counterpointing her thoughts.

The Consul, for his part, is disgusted with the bull, and he chants little jingles like: "See the old unhappy bull . . . in the plaza beautiful. . . . [Waiting] with seven wild surmises, for the rope which tantalises" (life's sevenfold trials). Yvonne is distracted by the man in the dark glasses, "or had she imagined it?" In a receptive visionary state at this point, Yvonne might be sensitive to the appearance of Geoffrey's familiars. Geoffrey, of course, avoids answering her question about the man and comments instead on the deceptive passivity of the bull (life): "Next time you meet him you might not recognize him as an enemy at all." (Reincarnation does permit development and provides man with another chance.) Hugh calls this bull an ox, to which Geoffrey adds, in another covert reference to himself as the world fool, "An oxymoron . . . Wisely foolish."

In the ring great confusion follows about who will ride the bull when suddenly, "something extraordinary had happened, something ridiculous, yet with earth-shattering abruptness—"

"It was Hugh" riding the bull, much to the rage and disgust of his brother: " 'Good Christ, the bloody fool!' " Hugh, as seen by Yvonne, "looked serious. . . . All his thoughts now were bringing that miserable bull to its knees." She feels that "Hugh's mind [is] rigid with concentration upon defeat of the bull." * Hugh has momentarily assumed the magical power himself and is fixing their fate as he unwittingly brings about corresponding elemental changes in nature: ". . . there were black clouds climbing the sky from the northeast, a temporary ominous darkness that lent a sense of evening, thunder sounded in the mountains, a single grumble, metallic, and a gust of wind raced through the trees, bending them. . . . Hugh's impossible yet somehow splendid performance in the midst of it all. . . ." The wrestling of the bull here is a spiritual

---

* Geoffrey's unappeasable rage at Hugh's action is more understandable in light of Lowry's awareness of Jung's interpretation of the bull sacrifice: "The Mithraic sacrifice is essentially a self-sacrifice, since the bull is a world bull. . . . [It is] a motif that corresponds to Christ carrying the cross . . . representations of the sacrificial act . . . recall the crucifixion between two thieves, one of whom is raised up to Paradise while the other goes down to hell." Jung, *Psyche and Symbol.*

equivalent of the Jewish Cabbalists' interpretation of Jacob's
wrestling with the angel as a conquest of his own spiritual deficien-
cies.

The Consul, who sees completely into the esoteric nature of
the bull's ordeal, and Hugh's attempt to conquer the destructive
force, relates it to his own approaching role as scapegoat and,
perhaps, even foresees the long-run consequences resulting in the
deaths of both his wife and his brother. Geoffrey, "pale, without
his dark glasses [for he is seeing the real horror unleashed on the
others because of his own purposeful isolation], was looking at
her piteously; he was sweating, his whole frame was trembling.
'No . . . No . . . *No!*' he added, almost hysterically." Then in
the midst of his terror, she appeals to him, " 'Geoffrey darling . . .
what are you afraid of? Why don't we go away, now, tomorrow,
today . . . ?' "

"No . . ." he answers, still trapped in his nightmare insight
into their true fate. But, at that moment, this knowledge is so unbearable that Geoffrey permits himself to entertain the illusion that
"a spirit of intercession and tenderness hovered over them" (the
wings of the *Shekinah*). " 'Why not. Let's for Jesus Christ's sweet
sake get away. A thousand, a million miles away. . . . Away
from all this. Christ, from this.' " There is a double meaning to this
statement in which he seems to be agreeing with Yvonne's plan to
flee to Canada and also a weary accession to death, to which
Yvonne innocently returns: " 'It could be like a rebirth.' " And the
guardian spirit does actually seem to promise a mystical rebirth in
*Tiphereth,* which is illustrated by the image of the "golden moon."
Touched by the immediate need for decision, for they are "like
prisoners who do not have much time to talk," Yvonne chooses
the right-hand or heavenly path, and once again the image of the
"train that wandered through an evening land of fields beside . . .
an arm of the Pacific" recurs. The implicit tragedy of this scene is
conveyed by the juxtaposition of the love struggle with that of the
bull's agony; for Geoffrey's train is that which delivers the corpse,
and his circuitous means of regaining paradise is incompatible with
Yvonne's. The bullfight at an end, Yvonne continues to "plead
hurriedly," as she unconsciously realizes that her chance is over
with Hugh's conquest, for the power of the spirit evoked is transmitted to Hugh, who, in his zeal to save Geoffrey and Yvonne, has,

as Geoffrey seems to have willed, unwittingly released its destructive potential as well.

Of course the dream of paradise is quickly dispelled by the Consul, who "was finishing the habanero." He then relates a rather cynical fable about the Bishop of Tasmania (mentioned previously with regard to his own Cabbalistic book) that is designed to inform Yvonne that her hope for his salvation is a mirage: " 'The Bishop of Tasmania . . . or somebody dying of thirst [consoled for a time by "the distant prospect of Cradle Mountain"—that is, Yvonne's childish misunderstanding of the true facts] . . . saw this water . . . Unfortunately it turned out to be sunlight blazing on myriads of broken bottles' " (an allusion to the reality of his mad thirst, which is punished even further by the sun-created mirage—that is, Yvonne as an unwitting agent of his agony).

Bright sunlight "fell too on another little silver lake glittering cool, fresh, and inviting before them, Yvonne had neither seen on the way, nor remembered [as if Geoffrey had spitefully willed it by telling his little story]. . . . The lake was a broken green houseroof . . . only weeds lived in the greenhouse" (that is, shattered *Netzach,* Venus; hope for their love broken among the Consul's bottled mirages). Nevertheless, Yvonne deliberately maintains the hope of her fantasied home "tiny, in the distance, a haven and a beacon against the trees, from the sea." Her little lighthouse is the directing beam of faith that leads the adept unharmed along the Sephirotic tree, directly opposed to the false light of hell that lures mariners into its depths.*

" 'Forward to the Salón Ofélia,' cried the Consul," in an ironic parallel to the insistent, annoying "figure of a woman having hysterics, jerking like a puppet and banging her fists upon the ground," that crops up in Yvonne's mind at that moment—she, of course, being identified with Ophelia, and Geoffrey with Hamlet. Once aroused, the elements rumble with activity, and the air is filled with omens as the approaching tragedy draws nearer: "A hot thundery wind launched itself at them . . . and somewhere a bell beat out wild tripthongs," announcing their triple death. "Their shadows

* This pervasive theme is central to the Cabbala. *Book Bahir* of the Jewish school identifies *Kether* as pure light, whereas Christian Cabbalists begin to assimilate it at first with such concepts as that of the Paraclete, and theosophists, with divine "fluid."

. . . [which] slid down white thirsty walls of houses [caught on]
. . . the turning wrenched wheel of a boy's bicycle" (the wheel of
life stopped). Obviously all three are now making their way through
scenery reflecting the Consul's surrender of identity, his inability
by now even to *wish* for salvation. The last stage of the trial can be
recognized when the adept no longer evinces hope. The bull ring,
with its dust, dirt, wind, and arid earth, has only served to enhance
Geoffrey's thirst. The ring (center for life's struggle as the carousel
had been the center for life's hopes) now reverts to the image of
the "spoked shadow of the wheel, enormous, insolent, swept
away."

Three pilgrims, none of them really contented at this moment,
they stop before the tavern called Todos Contentos y Yo También
("Everyone Happy and Me Too"), from which emerges "an old
lame Indian . . . carrying on his back . . . another poor Indian, yet older and more decrepit than himself. . . . [Trembling]
in every limb under this weight of the past, he carried both their
burdens." The old man's trembling immediately identifies him with
the Consul, personified here as Adam-Christ (*Adam Kadmon*),
the bearer of man's burdens and guilt. In addition, there is an elliptical reference to the sacrifice inherent in *Gilgul,* the situation in
which stronger souls bear weaker ones through life.

# Chapter Ten

Hugh and Yvonne are swimming in a stream outside the Salón Ofélia. In spite of his fear of its effects, Geoffrey is drinking mescal at the bar as he recalls a nightmarish experience. He relives the event in detail, beginning with his early-morning watch at a small-town train station in the United States. He visualizes the drunkenly perceived setting in all its Baudelairean ugliness—distorted flowers, lamp poles made of live snakes, and a tavern where all the customers seem to be madmen. The recollection ends with a reminder of the "corpse that will be transported by express." He watches the swimmers for a while, drinks more mescal, and converses with Cervantes, the owner of the restaurant. Cervantes produces a fierce fighting cock from under the counter and then takes Geoffrey to a private back room, where he displays a statue of the Madonna and a set of books concerning the city of Tlaxcala. The Consul prays to the Virgin for help but at the last moment changes his prayer into a cry for destruction. Outside, Hugh and Yvonne are humorously discussing the possibility of climbing Mount Popocatepetl as they change their clothes. They all gather at a table, where Geoffrey makes bawdy puns on the menu items. For a moment Yvonne and he exchange a happy glance, and he is moved to recall their engagement in Granada. This tender moment is short-lived, however, for his guilty addiction to alcohol brings him back to the harsh facts of their separation. He finds himself in the bathroom once again; Cervantes offers him a stone, a lemonade bottle half full of mescal, and a Tlaxcalan travel folder. He reads the folder carefully as Hugh and Yvonne indulge in a recapitulation of the events surrounding the dying peon. By now totally intoxicated, Geoffrey emerges with new-found enthusiasm for the glories of Tlaxcala, and he demands that they immediately set out for the "white" city with its "stricken in years trees." He is received coldly by Yvonne, who is at the point of tears. Geoffrey responds to her by channeling his frustrated hostility into an outburst against Hugh, which includes a frenzied enumeration of the elements. Thunder sounds outside as the tension grows between them. Geoffrey, no longer capable of discriminating between his thoughts and his spoken words, launches into a dissertation on the esoteric nature of fire, mescal, ancient Indian rituals, and legends that, to his surprise, has not been uttered by him at all. Suddenly, all the suppressed emotions erupt, and the two brothers find themselves involved in a heated political argument, which eventually results in personal attack. Geoffrey accuses Hugh and Yvonne of betraying him and makes a mockery of his brother's political humanism and his wife's sanctimonious disapproval of his alcoholism. Blending Othello and Firmin, Geoffrey spits out a long attack on lechery and stumbles out the door. Once outside, he finally decides to head for Parián.

Lowry's central theme at this stage in his novel is the newly introduced Tlaxcala refrain,* surrounded by a repetition of such other familiar motifs as train, volcano, and Virgin. It is now also that the Consul starts the fatal round of mescal drinking, enacting the final transgression that will culminate in his death.

Largely involving Lowry's method of beginning and closing with the same theme (in this case, a description of the Kelipathic experience and a return to it), this chapter is particularly dense with recurring images that the reader will now find familiar. The opening statement, an "absentmindedly" given order of "Mescal" on the part of the Consul, coincides with Hugh and Yvonne's second swim of the day, this time in the "calm pool" of the Salón Ofélia, which resumes the bathing and soul-cleansing theme. Geoffrey bathes his soul in drink hoping that he will regain his lost innocence: ". . . it was not merely that he shouldn't have, not merely that, no, it was more as if he had lost or missed something. . . . as if, more, he were waiting for something, and then again, not waiting."

Turning this thought around in his mind, Geoffrey associates "waiting" with another inner monologue of great complexity. Waiting, on the one hand, for the final ritual sacrifice to take place, he recalls another situation in which he had inadvertently stumbled into the *Kelipah* while awaiting the arrival of a "fair-haired angel" on a "Suspension Bridge" (that is, between *Sephiroth*). He had been "in that state of being where Baudelaire's angel indeed wakes,

---

* "Tlaxcala is probably the only capital in the world where black magic is still a working proposition. . . ." Lowry, *Letters*.

desiring to meet trains perhaps, but to meet no trains that stop, for in the angel's mind are no trains that stop. . . ." Recognizing his suspended state over the abyss, Geoffrey (himself the dark Baude-lairean angel), in search of the "Virginian" angel Lee Maitland, is reliving another previously attempted-and-failed contact with the spirits of light. The setting for this vision is again that of the *Kelipah,* during which the train becomes established as a dual motif—bearer of corpses in its evil aspect, the express can also act as a bearer of souls to their fitting destinations:

The railway lines went into the far distance uphill. . . . To the right of the level-crossing . . . stood a tree . . . frozen. . . . then the coal companies. . . . *Daemon's Coal* . . . Rows of dead lamps [i.e., lightless] like erect snakes poised to strike. . . . [The] terrible trains appeared . . . the frightful spouting and spindling of black smoke, a sourceless towering pillar . . . downhill . . . with one light burn-ing against the morning . . . a single useless strange eye, red-gold. . . . Which was north, west? . . . [The] flowers were on the wrong end of the stalks (and he on the wrong side of the tracks). . . . What had he lost?

Beginning with the reference to the "frozen tree," Lowry is mak-ing a frenzied portrayal of the upside-down world of the *Kelipah,* where, in their misguided stumbling in search of their guardian "angels," black magicians wander about in the land of the tree of death, with its unlit lamps, snakes, the pillar of severity, the red eye of *Geburah,* the demonic flowers of the garden *after* the Fall, the land of no direction peopled by idiots, exiles, gravediggers, where water is contaminated by sulfur and cannot be drunk (cf. also the "metallic" taste of mescal). "But that battle against death had been won," leaving him to look forward only to the final battle which will be fought within the next hour. The Consul is, however, temporarily revived (deluded) by the mescal and erases the mem-ory of that past unsuccessful attempt to emerge from the abyss— "How sensible! For it was the right, the sole drink to have under the circumstances. . . . [He was] well able to cope with anything that might come his way. But for this slight continual twitching and hopping . . . as of innumerable sand fleas. . . . The only thing wrong with him was that he was too hot." The flies around "the portals of the Qliphoth" and the fire that emerges from the victim's own body indicate that the profoundest tortures of *Gai-hinnom* are about to be endured. The great waterfall now becomes

for him "suggestive of some agonised ultimate sweat" in contrast
to the preritual cleansing now experienced by Hugh and Yvonne,
who are also preparing (though unknowingly) to take part in the
mystery. The entire concatenation of events in this chapter is, in
fact, intended as a prologue to the Eleusinian mystery rites that
form the model for Chapter Eleven, including the drinking of the
sacred wine, with its disorienting effect, and the symbolic search.

The Consul now associates his route with the sulfurous depths
of the "Oakville" train depot, which now merges also with
Oaxaca, both having, among other things in common, "hydro-
electric power . . . in the air." (Etheric fluid is a combination of
refined fire and water of the astral plane, which occultists often
compare, in its powerful influence on human life, to electricity.)
"Parián was an even greater mystery. . . . One met people going
there; few, now he thought about it, ever coming back." (The other
hells have been only outer layers of the *Kelipah,* the true center of
hell being lodged under the volcano, from which no one ever returns.) Merely the thought of Parián seems to evoke its spies:
"The Consul started. Near him lurked some hooded photogra-
phers . . ." who seem to be taking pictures of Hugh and Yvonne
at the falls, now identified by Geoffrey with Niagara's "Cave of the
Winds"—a theme picked up again and transmuted from "sweet"
love to the toilet of stone to which the Consul repairs for further
meditation later.

There were, in fact rainbows.* Though without them the mescal . . .
would have already invested the place with magic. . . . But now the
mescal struck a discord . . . to which the drifting mists all seemed
to be dancing. . . . It was a phantom dance of souls, baffled by these
deceptive blends, yet still seeking permanence in the midst of what
was only perpetually evanescent, or eternally lost. Or it was a dance
of the seeker and his goal, here pursuing still the gay colours he did
not know he had assumed, there striving to identify the finer scene
of which he might never realise he was already a part . . .

With the aid of the magic liquor, Geoffrey can see directly into
the astral plane, gazing at the individual souls enmeshed in an
eternal dance along the different Sephirotic paths; he is like Faust
at the moment of his vision of the earth spirit when he sees souls

---

* Cf. the rainbow that appears after the flood as a covenant between God
and Noah.

on various stages on an evanescent ladder. In the allusion to the "seeker and his goal," Lowry is pointing to the initiate in his travels along the tree, who becomes unified with symbolic color (degree) along the way. The awful aspect of this scene is that Geoffrey, seeing his own plight in the mist, is doomed to seek beyond, without ever realizing that he is, by the very experience of life itself, already there.

In an effort to escape from this painful recognition, the Consul enters the dark shadows of the bar, where he sees the fighting cock (Cabbalistic symbol of death and atonement) owned by the barman, Cervantes, who calls it "Un bruto." * The Consul despises the cockfight as he had Hugh's role in the bullfight earlier, seeing it "as some hideously mismanaged act of intercourse," relating his own impotence of the morning to his final impotence in the face of death.

Hearing the roar of "eternity" in the background, the Consul contemplates the significance of the mescal, without which

. . . he had forgotten eternity, forgotten their world's voyage, that the earth was a ship, lashed by the Horn's tail, doomed never to make her Valparaiso. Or that it was like a golf ball, launched at Hercules' Butterfly, wildly hooked by a giant out of an asylum window in hell [himself]. Or that it was a bus, making its erratic journey to Tomalín and nothing.

Having declared previously that mescal would be his end, he now equates his own doom with that of the world embodied in the ship of the soul set out on its mysterious voyage on the sea of wisdom that is lashed by Leviathan; the soul, like a golf ball tracing its course along the hazardous green, falling into the "Golgotha Hole," the bus, a collective soul heading interminably downhill— all these images correspond to his path of destruction. Dazed by the drink, he hears "above the roar . . . the voice of Yvonne . . . dear . . . shortly to be lost.

"Why lost? . . . The voices were as if confused now with the blinding torrent of sunlight . . . turning the scarlet flowers along the path into flaming swords." Earlier that morning it had been he, with Yvonne at his side, who had beheaded the scarlet flowers along his path, as later Hugh was to identify the Consul with the

* Later, Geoffrey envisions Hugh as the slaughterer and says, "Et tu Bruto!"

little flowers growing along the tracks of the railway that are destroyed by the terrible "sun" (train).

Now that the Consul realizes that he is about to lose the *Shekinah* forever, the collective images of blinding sunlight, swords, and red, the color of justice, merge into the figure of the queen of swords of the tarot in her merciless capacity as judge (soon to be transformed as the figure of the Virgin in the back room of the bar, whose candle diffuses "a ruby shimmer" and to whom he prays for destruction). In addition to the roar of eternity here, he is again haunted by the roaring voices of the mourning women of Kashmir (his lost mother), who cry, "Borrrrraaacho." This again brings him to the roaring corpse-bearing train association, which manifests itself in a passing thought: "What is man but a little soul holding up a corpse?" The journey he hopes to make with the assistance of the mescal consists of the loosening of the soul from the material body. To accomplish this "by express" is a euphemistic representation of the lightning-fast ascent of the mystic to *Tiphereth,* which involves a sacrifice of his earthly life.

From the moment of the first sip of mescal to the end of the book, the Consul continues in a visionary state. Because there are no boundaries of time or space in this state of superconsciousness, the Cabbalist is aware of all things at all times on many planes beyond that of earth. If he is not himself in control of this state that approximates madness, he is subject to great danger. Lowry probed these states of consciousness, deriving many of their characteristics from Dunne's *Experiment With Time* and William James' *Varieties of Religious Experience.*

All parts of the chapter now converge into an enormous analogy to the climactic journey. Even Hugh and Yvonne's joking intention to climb Mount Popo becomes a counterpart of the refrain:

"—what do you think, Yvonne, if sometime we climb . . . Popo. . . ."
"Good heavens . . . ! Haven't you had enough exercise for one—"
"—might be a good idea to harden your muscles first, try a few small peaks" [the opposite of the Consul's intention to "climb," all at once, to the extremes of consciousness].
They were joking. But the Consul was not joking.

Cervantes, wearing "a black shade over one eye," is another of the "quaking ruined creatures," mirror image of Geoffrey himself.

He wishes, for some obscure reason, to show the Consul his room, where the statue of the Virgin with its candle becomes transformed in Geoffrey's mind into "the Virgin for those who have nobody. . . . And for mariners on the sea," a beacon, that is, to straying adepts pointed out by Vigil the night before. The Consul prays * before her:

"Nothing is altered [but compare "The Case is Altered" theme] and in spite of God's mercy I am still alone. Though my suffering seems senseless I am still in agony. There is no explanation of my life. . . . Please let Yvonne have her dream . . . of a new life with me. . . . Please let me make her happy, deliver me from this dreadful tyranny of self. I have sunk low. Let me sink lower still, that I may know the truth. Teach me to love again, to love life. . . . Give me back my purity, the knowledge of the Mysteries, that I have betrayed and lost. . . . [Then he suddenly reverses his plea.] Destroy the world!" he cried in his heart.

Although he begins with a genuine desire for life and love, the demons soon overcome him, and he cries out to the spirit of *Geburah* rather than to the merciful Virgin for assistance in his destruction of himself and the world.

Cervantes then displays a history of Tlaxcala in ten volumes, which he shuts immediately, claiming to be an "insignificant man" who merely obeys his grandfather and does not read such books. For the Consul, however, Tlaxcala becomes synonymous with the recouping of his power, the ten closed volumes corresponding to the knowledge inherent in the ten *Sephiroth*. Determined to force every situation now to the heart of his intention, namely the speedy culmination of the day, he becomes more overtly aggressive, taking over the dinner, which he considers to be "the supper at Emmaeus" as he blasphemously begins a bawdy interpretation of the menu. His self-control begins to weaken, and he allows his anger to come forward so that he finishes with another inverted reference to himself as the betrayed Christ: "What about it, Hugh—do you want to wait for the fish that dies?"

Catching Yvonne's eye, Geoffrey has still another mescal-induced train vision, this one an emblem of his fast-disappearing chance for salvation. It is the Granada train he sees, "waltzing from Algeciras over the plains of Andalusia, . . . the old number

* According to E. M. Butler, before entering hell the magician must enter a church and pray.

seven train . . . through the gardens, gardens, gardens everywhere, up, up, to . . . the extreme summit of the hill; here they
plighted their troth . . ." This upward-climbing train now becomes a symbol of the high point of his spiritual life, during which
he had achieved successful union with the *Shekinah,* in contrast to
the chaotic train vision of his first encounter with her in Oakville,
when she departed on the hell-bound express. But again, he had
not been able to hold on to her, ruining his chance by following the
mirage of the broken bottles, which he characterizes now as "a
babel of glasses—towering . . . built to the sky, then falling
. . . falling downhill from the Generalife Gardens. . . ." The
Tower of Babel here symbolizes Geoffrey's confusion of identity.
"How indeed could he hope to find himself, to begin again when
. . . perhaps, in one of those lost or broken bottles, . . . lay,
forever, the solitary clue to his identity? * . . . There was something in fact almost beautiful about the frightful extremity of that
condition the Consul now found himself in," and in his unremitting
descent into matter and away from spirit, he finds himself once
again in the bathroom. But this time it is the gray stone tomb-
"sanctuary" of the *Kelipah,* to be surpassed only by the filthy
mingitorio of Chapter Twelve.
    " 'It is what I deserve . . . It is what I am.' . . . Why was he
here? Why was he always more or less, here? . . . Perhaps this
was the eternity that he'd been making so much fuss about. . . ."
The stone toilet symbolizes the end, the lowest plane that can be
reached on the route downward from the gardens at the summit of
the hill. As the conversation between Hugh and Yvonne remains
an audible counterpoint to his own nihilistic contemplation, the
Consul merges his identity with that of the Indian (perhaps even
permanently here in preparation for his similar death), now the
subject of their discussion, which is filled with humorous double
entendre regarding the horse on whose "rump" is branded a 7 just
as Geoffrey himself is offered "a stone" on which to "clean" his
rump. Cervantes, in making this offer, is ironically yet unwittingly
committing the equivalent blunder of offering a stone to Sisyphus,
or eternity to a man who longs to lose it.
    Mysteriously, the Consul finds himself possessed of more mescal

----

* See Lowry's short story "The Bravest Boat" in *Hear Us O Lord* . . .
for the theme of identity lost and found in a bottled message.

and a "railway and bus time table" together with a "tourist folder"
—the initiatory wine together with a map outlining the magical
terrain of Tlaxcala.* Tlaxcala is characterized by the folder's far
from fluent English as a state "said to be like Granada [the scene
of the Consul's first positive step toward spiritual development]
. . . *said to be like Granada, said to be like Granada*. . . .
covered by stricken in years trees . . . a garden clothed by many
beautiful flowers. . . . emotional majesty, *emotional majesty*.
. . . in the middle . . . is a wood . . . in order to make easier
the rest days to walkers." This description covers the magical
path, with its tree, its garden, its centrally located forest, its old
church with "a secret passage, *secret passage*. On the right side of
the entrance is erected a majestic tower, which is rated as the only
one through America [contrast the right-hand majestic tower of
God with Geoffrey's fallen tower of broken bottles or Jacques'
blasted tower]. . . . The portico of the church [consecrated to
Virgin Mary] is of beautiful and severe appearance" (Mary as
*Binah* and *Geburah*).

The travel folder now describes the sanctuary of the church,
which is entirely the reverse of the Consul's "stone sanctuary." Its
"white and embellished steeples . . . [are] trimmed with sacred
archangels . . . and the epithet of Virgin Mary statues," which is
a reference to the curse inflicted on the world by the Consul in his
prayer to the Virgin—all this being really an elaborate parable of
the Consul's own previous condition of innocence as reflected by
his fascination with the inherent beauty and whiteness of Tlaxcala,
while his flaw is mirrored by this unintentionally worded "epithet."
He is reliving not only the history of his own initiation but that of
civilization as well, as Hugh continues discussing the fascist incur-
sion, which, in Geoffrey's mescal state, becomes synonymous with
the Spanish Conquest.

In his stone sanctuary, the Consul is correspondingly seated "In
said ruins [where] could be still appreciated the stone blocks
where were offered the sacrifices to their Gods." His identification
with the martyred initiates and political victims is now complete,

---

* Although Mrs. Lowry claims that her husband did not imitate Joyce's
method, that he considered it too conscious and intellectual, this Cave of
the Winds sequence is strikingly similar to the Bloom outhouse scene in
*Ulysses*. See Lowry, *Letters*.

and the demons once again resume their onslaught as they had in the previous bathroom sequence. " 'I'm watching you . . . You can't escape me. . . . I can see you.' "

Tlaxcala, like the reversed *Sephiroth,* now suddenly becomes the embodiment of the city of night, the *Kelipah,* all the voices blending in a cacophony of confused identities: " '—but oh my God, this city—the noise! the chaos! If I could only get out! If I only knew where you could get to!' " Then comes the elliptical answer to his panic-stricken search for the secret passage, the way out:

### MATLALCUEYATL

This mountain are still the ruins of the shrine dedicated to the God of Waters, Tlaloc, which vestiges are almost lost, therefore, are no longer visited by tourists, and it is referred that on this place, young Xicohtencatl harangued his soldiers, telling them to fight the conquerors to the limit, dying if necessary.

The Consul is to cleanse his soul, he feels, by sacrificing himself to the hands of the new conquerors of Mexico in Parián, also a place not visited by "tourists" but only by those committed to death. The final arrangements for this sacrifice are located on the railway timetable, which lists the schedule for the trip to Tlaxcala, the "Mexico–Vera Cruz Railroad," which leaves significantly at 7:30 —a half-hour after his death that evening—and arrives at 12:00 —the completion of the twelve stages of the initiation. Now pleased with the thought of returning to this white city (*Kether*), as a reward for his martyrdom, the Consul envisions

a white beautiful cathedral city toward which [his] soul yearned and which indeed in many respects was like Granada; only it appeared to him . . . perfectly empty. That was the queerest thing about it, and at the same time the most beautiful. . . . The white sanctuary . . . rose up before them: white towers and a white clock and no one there. While the clock itself was timeless.

When Geoffrey excitedly carries his mescal-induced vision of eternal salvation back to Yvonne, she receives him so coldly that he becomes enraged and filled with a sudden hatred for Hugh. "The Consul had not been away very long . . . no more than seven minutes all told . . . ," actually time enough for the mescal confusion of heaven and hell to take place. With the rage against Hugh, who, by overcoming the world bull, has assumed power in his own right, the Consul sees his brother "advancing [with a ra-

zor] as if to decapitate him. Then the vision darkened and Hugh
. . . was bearing down upon an ox: now he had changed the
razor for a sword. He thrust forward the sword to bring the ox to
its knees . . ." Then, in a display of his own enormous power of
destruction in comparison with what he considers Hugh's paltry
masculine pose, the Consul begins enumerating the elements in an
alphabetical torrent, thereby carelessly calling down the power of
the Tetragrammaton and endangering them all with the inevitable
response of nature: "Thunder suddenly sprang again outside with
a clap and bang, slithering." *

Wildly lashing out at everyone around him, Geoffrey ignores
Hugh's attempt to explain his communist affiliation, which, for
Geoffrey, is after all no more than an excuse to meddle in his
affairs and share his wife. Frantically questioning Cervantes about
Tlaxcala with its "stricken in years trees," its "sanctuary," and so
on, Geoffrey finally turns on the other two: " '. . . what's wrong
with my plan? What's wrong with all you people? Aren't you going
to Vera Cruz after all, Hugh? . . . the true cross . . . This is
the last time we'll be seeing you, old fellow. For all I know . . .' "
He has now angered the elements still further by giving out secret
knowledge and calling on them so thoughtlessly, and a second rap
of "Thunder, single, exploded in midair just outside the door.
. . ." Reflecting the elemental tumult outside, Cervantes lights
their cigarettes with a warning: " '. . . when three friends take
fire with the same match, the last die before the other two.' "

" 'Feurstick,' said Hugh, shielding yet another light for the Consul" as he fulfills the prophecy in the act. Suddenly the Consul
launches into a brilliant stream-of-consciousness treatise on the
nature of the sacred fire.† Infuriated by the lost opportunity of

---

* "My friend [Frater Achad] told me that a black magician who fell into
the abyss was in the unenviable position of having all the elements in the
universe against him. This is what accounts (though I had by this time
arrived at the same conclusion myself . . .) for the recital of all the elements in chapter X written long before the atom bomb." Lowry, unpublished letter to Clenens Ten Holder, March 21, 1951.

† The purpose of this apparently unrelated section becomes clearer in
the context proposed by theosophists: "The vision of . . . the unknown
God, on entering . . . an unbalanced body . . . becomes the Anti-Logos.
True, in both cases the fire brought down from heaven is identically the
same fire, but according to the medium it inhabits it, illumines or blinds."
Fuller, *The Secret Wisdom of the Qabalah*. Jewish Cabbalists main-

visiting Tlaxcala, for "they had missed the bus back . . . the bus
that was going to take them home to Tlaxcala . . . ," he proceeds to call down the destructive fire that will consume them all:

And the Consul was talking about the Indo-Aryans, the Iranians and
the sacred fire, Agni, called down from heaven, with his firesticks,
by the priest. He was talking of soma . . . the nectar of immortality,
praised in one whole book of the Rig Veda—*bhang*, which was, perhaps, much the same thing as mescal itself. . . . In any event the
Consul . . . was talking about the sacred fire, the sacrificial fire, of
the stone soma press, the sacrifices of cakes and oxen and horses, the
priest chanting from the Veda, how the drinking rites, simple at
first, became more and more complicated as time went on, the ritual
having to be carried out with meticulous care, since one slip—*tee
hee!*—would render the sacrifice invalid [hence his own previous
preoccupation with the exact number of mescals drunk and his own
meticulously kept record of the "drink situation"]. Soma, bhang,
mescal, ah yes, mescal. . . . He was talking of the immolation of
wives . . . the widow of a childless man might contract a Levirate
marriage with her brother-in-law. . . . The Consul was talking, like
Sir Thomas Browne, of Archimedes, Moses, Achilles. . . . of Jesus
Christ, or rather of Yus Asaf who, according to the Kashmiri legend,
*was* Christ . . . who had . . . wandered to Kashmir in search of
the lost tribes of Israel [cf. William Blackstone and the Consul's own
search for "what he had lost"], and died there, in Srinagar—
    But there was a slight mistake. The Consul was not talking. . . .
The Consul had not uttered a single word. It was all an illusion, a
whirling cerebral chaos, out of which, at last, at long last, at this
very instant, emerged, rounded and complete, order.

The Consul comes out of this dialogue with himself for a moment; his long dissertation on the efficacy of mescal as magic fire
has only served to bring down the fire that will disclose the truth
and give him the necessary daring to divorce himself from his
wife's offer of earthly salvation. Having now assumed the spirits of
the heroes enumerated by calling upon them, the Consul is prepared for the next step and so restores order to the chaos that has
apparently resulted from Yvonne's interference, Hugh's presence,
and his own indecisiveness. In retrieving the forgotten formula
"like that little bit in seven flats on the black keys"—that is, recol-
lecting the black-magical formula, a necessary preliminary for the

tain the idea that evil is the fire of wrath lodged in God's left hand, which
is always tempered by his mercy, but in its measureless outbreak from
mercy becomes the radically evil world of Satan.

descent—he can now reject Hugh's sanctimonious disapproval of the afternoon's events, which turn out to be in perfect harmony with the Consul's cosmic plans, after all.

" '. . . [Before] we pass judgement on the thief—if thief he were—we would have to ask ourselves: what were his connections with other thieves, ties of family, his place in time . . . his relation to the external world, and to the consequences leading to the act . . .' " Although this is ostensibly a commentary on the pelado's activities, Geoffrey's sudden *non sequitur* outburst is a logical derivative of his long, silent fire discourse—the thief, of course, representing himself in the role of Prometheus, thief of the sacred fire (mescal), which he now begins to order with open abandon. Having identified himself finally as a black magician though still not communicating his message successfully to Hugh, who takes it all literally, he goes on to discuss his role as martyr under the guise of describing the dying Indian: " 'Why should we have done anything to save his life? Hadn't he a right to die, if he wanted to? . . . Why should anybody interfere with anybody? Why should anybody have interfered with the Tlaxcalans, for example, who were perfectly happy by their own stricken in years trees . . . ' " (why interfere with a man's mission even if it entails death, even if it is that of the black magician, who is adapted to the struggle within the Sephirotic abyss?). Extending his argument, Geoffrey recriminates with Hugh about the condition of the world itself: " 'Ah, you people with ideas! . . . Can't you see there's a sort of determinism about the fate of nations? They all seem to get what they deserve in the long run.' " Lowry is reproducing here Frater Achad's view of world affairs occultly expounded in *The Anatomy of the Body of God*.

. "A gust of wind moaned round the house with an eerie sound. . . ." The element of air, container of cosmic secrets, resounds with Geoffrey's disclosure as the thunder had responded to the enumeration of the elements. Then, finally coming to the point of his harangue, he compares the state of his own soul to the "foreign countries" that so concern Hugh, blaming Yvonne for disturbing his alcoholic peace: " 'For all you know it's only the knowledge that it most certainly is too late that keeps me alive at all . . . You're all the same . . . trying to interfere with other people's lives . . . all because you haven't got the wisdom and the simplicity and the courage, yes, the courage. . . . For that matter, both your souls stink!' "

Openly avowing that his purpose in remaining alive at all depends on his own foreknowledge of his approaching death, the Consul berates them for their weakness of soul (*nefesh,* the bodily soul, particularly with regard to physical desires, is weakest) and proclaims his own courage (*neshama,* the immortal soul, which accounts for spiritual development). Then placing her part of the sin on Yvonne's shoulders, he excoriates her for her infidelity and childlessness, for one of the most important blessings of *Malkuth* is fertility. As he shouts at them both, now merging with Othello and all outraged husbands in his anger, "A glass, fortunately empty, fell to the floor and was smashed." * From this point on, the negative power set loose begins to take effect, and at the moment of his open denial of Yvonne's "non-alcoholic Paradise" and his announced choice of Tlaxcala (that is, black magic and hell), he is returned immediately to *Gai-hinnom,* back

. . . where Baudelaire's angel indeed wakes. . . . He was in a room, and suddenly in this room, matter was disjunct: a doorknob was standing a little way out from the door. A curtain floated in by itself, unfastened, unattached to anything [the formless world that constitutes the descent into the abyss]. The idea struck him it had come to strangle him. . . . "Hell," he finished absurdly. . . . He produced a twenty-peso note and laid it on the table.†

"I like it. . . . I love hell. I can't wait to get back there. In fact I'm running, I'm almost back there already."

He was running too, in spite of his limp, calling back to them crazily, and the queer thing was, he wasn't quite serious, running toward the forest, which was growing darker and darker, tumultuous above—a rush of air swept out of it, and the weeping pepper tree roared.

The ultimate commitment to hell, being made under the effects of the stolen sacred "fire" in the form of mescal, is irrevocable; the power of the Consul's statements now becomes so great that they become deeds. The resolution to "fly into the earth" is made here (cf. "mescal . . . I'm afraid, yes, that would be the end. . . ."). He is running in a frenzied ecstatic state (much as the victims of

* The breaking of the vessels in the *Zohar* is equal to the beginning of sin in the material world.

† According to Achad, the number 20 stands for both *Tiphereth* and will, and the fire of last judgment and regeneration.

Aztec sacrifice or the followers of Sabbatai Zevi might) to his own annihilation. He "isn't quite serious," for he is the world fool with his staff (the tarot club), who limps foolishly into the depths of the garden now transformed as sacred wood; the spirits of the air rushing out to draw him further, as a tree weeps and roars—the tree of life in its tragic aspect. Animated nature responds here in the manner of the land that had shaken and wept at the death of Christ.

". . . [He] would take the path to Parián, to the Farolito."

"Before him the volcanoes, precipitous, seemed to have drawn nearer. They towered up over the jungle, into the lowering sky— massive interests moving up in the background." All nature moves in closer, and the volcanoes, in "drawing nearer," serve to bring heaven and earth together in a great crisis (Lowry's prevision of World War II),* for such is the effect of the redeemer who, upon sacrificing his life, will unify *Kether* with *Malkuth*. In a sense, Geoffrey has begun the initial figurative ascent; he has restored a type of lost integrity by admitting the truth about himself and his quest to Yvonne and Hugh. Assuming the form of the nihilistic mystic, Geoffrey

. . . descends into the abyss in which the freedom of living things is born; he passes through all the embodiments and forms that come his way, committing himself to none, and not content with rejecting and abrogating all values and laws, he tramples them underfoot and desecrates them, in order to attain the elixir of Life . . . [no wonder that] such mysticism should [be] regarded as demonic possession.†

* Lowry, *Letters.*
† Scholem, "Religious Authority and Mysticism."

# Chapter Eleven

The sun is setting. Yvonne and Hugh are searching through the forest for the Consul. They take the longer but easier path to Parián, hoping that they will find Geoffrey at the Farolito. Yvonne experiences an obscure feeling of dread, which she associates with the strangeness of the heavens and the homeless whippoorwill. She comes across a small eagle in a cage, which she releases on a sudden impulse. They then stop at two restaurants and pubs along the route, where Yvonne tastes mescal for the first time. She begins to hallucinate images of the Consul until she finds a menu on the back of which Geoffrey has signed a bill for three drinks. Below this he has written a poem surrounded by some mysterious symbolic drawings. Interpreting the last line (which refers to fleeing "north") as a clue to the Consul's intentions, Yvonne hurries out into the forest in the direction of the Farolito. Hugh, in the meantime, has bought an old guitar and a light from the proprietor of the restaurant. As they make their way through the forest amid threatening flashes of lightning and crackling thunder, Hugh sings revolutionary songs, accompanying himself on the guitar. Suddenly, it begins to rain very heavily. Yvonne is vaguely conscious of danger, but she is unprepared for the sight of a runaway horse that comes charging at her through the brush. She trips and falls as the horse, bearing the "7" brand, tramples her to death. As she dies she has a vision of the stars, a momentary insight into the entire celestial mechanism. She even thinks she sees the Consul on the horse, until the image gives way to the scene of her burning Canadian dream house. As the "burning dream" recedes, Yvonne feels herself ascending toward the Pleiades.

On one plane, this chapter is devoted to a portrayal of Yvonne's final ascent to *Tiphereth,* or the *Shekinah* returning to its source (thus climaxing the "father is waiting" theme introduced earlier), as a result of Geoffrey's unleashed force, which will be personified in the horse and storm metaphors dominating the climax of the novel. On another level, it also represents a final reconciliation of opposites, effected by Yvonne's release of the eagle and her sacrificial death in the storm. Lowry's most mysterious and ethereal chapter has not been placed haphazardly, for

The number eleven is . . . so peculiar that it stands forth in a positively unique manner. This ominous number has been held significant of the Eleven Paths of Darkness in contrast with the Ten Paths of Splendor. We gather that the Eleventh Path is one of great difficulty and refers to a high initiation resulting from that purity of affection which leads to Beatific Vision . . . of all advanced Mystica. . . .*

From the ending of Chapter Ten on to the close of the book, Lowry combined elements from the Eleusinian mysteries † and the tarot into the preestablished Cabbalistic framework in the fusion of mythologies common to theosophical writers.

Sunset. Eddies of green and orange birds scattered aloft with ever wider circles like rings on water.‡ [The setting sun represents the opening of the trial journey through darkness, the imagery of promise contained in the ever wider circlings aloft.] . . . And their path became straight, leading on through the roar of the water. . . . The storm . . . must have been travelling in a circle: the real onset was yet to come [Geoffrey's path throughout the day had been circling around the Farolito until now]. . . . [The] sun had gone down at their back slightly to their left . . . where a red blaze fanned out into the sky . . . [the direction and color of *Geburah*, here the *final* judgment, all other difficulties during the day having by now become preliminaries].

Yvonne refuses to "abandon" Geoffrey *this* time, for the *Shekinah* remains with the initiate until the end. They pass the "chassis of abandoned American cars § [which] bridged the stream which they kept always to their left." Hints of the death and rebirth theme recur, particularly as they are reflected in the setting, which is extremely important:

* Colville, *Kabbalah.*
† "On the surface Hugh and Yvonne are simply searching for the Consul, but such a search would have added meaning to anyone who knows anything of the Eleusinian mysteries." Lowry, *Letters.* See Appendix D for details.
‡ Green represents *Netzach;* orange, *Hod;* both are repeated at the end of the chapter when Yvonne is herself carried beyond the Assiatic and Yetziratic worlds to *Beriah.*
§ Cf. the reference in Chapter One to the abandoned Ford; events come full circle now as Yvonne and Geoffrey reverse roles and she searches for him.

The clouds, no longer red, had become a peculiar luminous blue-white . . . illumined by moon rather than sunlight [*Geburah* counterbalanced by *Chesed*]. . . .
Birds were sailing up there, ascending higher and higher. Infernal bird of Prometheus!
They were vultures . . . defiling themselves with blood and filth, but who were yet capable of rising, like this, above the storms . . . [soon to be captured in the image of Geoffrey's soul as the freed bird]. On their left, through the trees beyond the stream appeared low hills . . . they were purple and sad. [The low purple hills of *Yesod* are depicted as being situated to the left and appear sad because the adept is yet to complete the descent. The volcanoes, in their legendary aspect, are like Geoffrey and Yvonne in that they seem to be a pair of lovers who are united only to be parted by death in which they are once again reunited. At this stage all paths are open and Yvonne must make swift choices.] . . . They had reached the limit of the clearing, where the path divided in two. Yvonne hesitated. Pointing to the left . . . another aged arrow on a tree repeated: *a la Cascada* [to the stream of life]. But a similar arrow on another tree pointed away from the stream down a path to their right: *a Parián* [now situated on the *right* because it is the path she should follow if she is to save the Consul].
Yvonne knew where she was now, but the two alternatives, the two paths, stretched out before her on either side like the arms . . . of a man being crucified.

The crucified man Yvonne sees is Geoffrey as *Adam Kadmon* and as the Indian at the wayside.

"If they chose the path to their right they would reach Parián much sooner. On the other hand, the main path would bring them to the same place finally. . . . They chose the main path. . . ." Since the difficult path is really open to Geoffrey only, their decision to take the longer and presumably less hazardous path is predetermined and results, in part, in the tragedy that befalls them. "And it was as though one's spirit were being swept on by the swift current with the uprooted trees . . . towards that final drop." The dangerous passage over the abyss between worlds cannot be avoided even by selecting the "main" or less difficult path, for all initiatory paths lead through the underworld, to which they too are committed by virtue of their association with the Consul. The images of the barranca and the reversed tree indicate that they cannot avoid following Geoffrey to hell.

. . . [Yvonne] became conscious she was laughing unnaturally to herself; at the same time she felt, crazily, as if something within her

were smouldering, had taken fire. . . . She had stumbled over . . .
a wooden cage . . . in which crouched a large bird. . . . The cage
was set between the cantina and . . . two trees embracing one another. . . . The intertwined roots of the two tree lovers [again
metaphors of her own soul's longing to join with Geoffrey's] flowed
over the ground towards the stream, ecstatically seeking it. [But she
is immediately forced into recollection of the hostile environment].
. . . In the taller trees beyond there was a cracking. . . . a sense of
black conspiracy . . . among these trees, suddenly through which
. . . lightning flew. . . . There the bird was still, a long-winged dark
furious shape, a little world of fierce despairs and dreams. . . . With
hurried quivering hands Yvonne began to unfasten the cage. The bird
fluttered out of it and alighted at her feet, hesitated, took flight to
the roof . . . then abruptly flew off through the dusk, not to the
nearest tree . . . but up—she was right, it knew it was free—up
soaring . . . into the deep dark blue pure sky above, in which at
that moment appeared one star. . . . She felt only an inexplicable
secret triumph and relief . . . and then, stealing over her, the sense
of utter heartbreak and loss.

The freeing of the eagle now corresponds to her innate understanding of Geoffrey's need for freedom. All the "conspiratorial"
elements attempt to hinder her, but in her great moment of mystical empathy she knows what she must do and is aware of the painful loss her action will entail. By allowing the creature of "fierce
despairs and dreams" (the Consul's soul) to escape from its cage,
she is helping him to soar out of the *Kelipah* into the pure blue
(*Chesed*), for which he has been striving. By these means the
scorpion is now transformed into the eagle, a symbol of the endur-
ance of light and of far-ranging vision.

Moving closer to the barranca, Yvonne and Hugh detect "a
smell of decay. . . . [And] the path was steeper. . . . They
were climbing . . . Yvonne could see the sky. But she couldn't
get her bearings. The Mexican sky had become strange and to-
night the stars found for her a message even lonelier than that remembered one of the poor nestless whip-poor-will." Yvonne herself is compared to the whippoorwill, which she regards as a
symbol of "love" and "wisdom"—perhaps the *Shekinah,* homeless
now, having given up her place in the soul of man, wandering until
she is finally drawn back home to the stars, which themselves seem
to say: "Why are we here . . . in the wrong place . . . so far
away from home? From what home? When had not she, Yvonne,
*come* home?" Nevertheless she is immediately reassured when

once again the heavens resume their familiar aspect as she feels "her mood of detachment [from earth] returning."

Gradually she prepares to rejoin the stars as Geoffrey at the same moment prepares for his descent—"Scorpio setting . . . 'As Scorpio sets in the southwest, the Pleiades are rising in the northeast.' " She speculates on the nature of the great wheel of life and death in an elaborate metaphor of initiatory death and rebirth not unlike that of Ezekiel's vision:

And the earth itself still turning on its axis and revolving around that sun, the sun revolving around the luminous wheel of this galaxy, the countless unmeasured jewelled wheels of countless unmeasured galaxies, turning, turning, majestically, into infinity, into eternity, through all of which all life ran on. . . . Scorpio setting . . . And rising, Yvonne thought, unseen behind the volcanoes, those whose culmination was at midnight to-night as Aquarius set. . . .

Yvonne watches the setting moon, "dead child of the earth!— with a strange hungry supplication. . . . [as] lightning blazed white and jagged in the northeast [and] thunder spoke. . . ." The setting moon indicates Geoffrey's downward path, as he makes his way farther into the volcano accompanied by the lightning and storm of the newly awakened Huracán. The horrors of the Consul's trial are reflected for Yvonne in the mirror of nature:

The path growing steeper inclined still further to their right [as the Consul moves farther away from her the terrain grows increasingly dangerous]. . . . It grew so dark it was surprising not to find the blackest night in the world beyond.
Yet the sight that met their eyes . . . was terrifying. The massed black clouds were still mounting. . . . bodiless black birds. . . . Snowstorms. . . . [The] whole precipitous bulk of Popocatepetl seemed to be coming toward them . . . [a] curious melancholy light shone [on] one little rebellious hilltop. . . . swarming with people visible only as their candle flames.

Yvonne and Hugh are entering the astral world, symbolized by the terrifying chaos swarming around and atop the volcanoes. Here where the animal and elemental worlds meet, where the dead souls on the hilltop cemetery attempt to make their way back up to the celestial spheres, is the world of the abyss. "But suddenly it was as if a heliograph of lightning were stammering messages across the wild landscape. . . ." and the cries of lamentation are overwhelmed by the ensuing "titanic roar" of thunder, which scatters mourning souls, candle flames still gleaming, down to earth once again.

Yvonne and Hugh then stop at a wayside cantina called El Petate the Impostor, and then on to the Hotel-Restaurant *El Popo*, where she sees "false" Consuls all over the place. It is located "at the edge of the jungle, giving the place something of the withdrawn, waiting character that pertains to a border at night, and a border of sorts there was . . . where the ravine, bridged away to the right. . . ." This place does, in fact, turn out to be a border between two worlds for Yvonne, who drinks her first mescal here and enters fully into Geoffrey's enchanted world, where she sees the results of his magic everywhere as her soul merges with his—"On the porch . . . the Consul sat dining quietly. . . . But only Yvonne had seen him. . . . [The] Consul sat frowning in a corner. . . . But none save Yvonne had noticed him. . . . Yet . . . the Consul was disappearing round every corner, and going out of every door. . . . [The] Consul . . . pushed his chair back and came forward, bowing, to meet them."

Now close enough to Geoffrey's world even to hear the "demonic orchestras," they hear music "which sounded like absolutely nothing on earth . . . an abysmal mechanic force out of control that was running itself to death"—the music of disorder that is heard in the *Kelipah,* being the cacophonous reversal of the music of the spheres.

The garden is "overgrown with flowers" (unnaturally vivid in their scarlet brightness) and weeds, inhabited by angry screeching birds—all the reverse of the pastoral setting of the morning, about which Hugh remarks: "Well . . . this is somewhat different from Cervecería Quauhnahuac."

"The sky was so blue, wasn't it?" Yvonne now sees that the nature of their journey has changed. She suddenly decides to take the dangerous forest path through the darkness, ignoring Hugh's recommendation to phone Geoffrey at the Farolito—probably because she implicitly senses the total breakdown in communication that the Consul is now experiencing with regard to the external world. Perhaps she can now communicate with him by sharing in the ritual drink. At her order of "Mescal," she feels that, "the air was so full of electricity it trembled. . . . [And as the drink takes

effect] No: she knew he was not here." Once again she becomes
conscious of the transmuting fire at work within her:

[She] was laughing unnaturally to herself [cf. the comic seriousness
with which Geoffrey has plunged into the dark forest under the
effects of the mescal], something within her was . . . on fire. . . .
But no, it was not herself that was on fire. It was the house of her
spirit. . . . It was . . . the Pleiades. . . . It was the Consul who had
been the first to notice it.

Yvonne is now entirely consumed by Geoffrey's magic, which provides her too with a kind of prescience, a vision of her doom. Because fire is the most refined of the elements, this burning house is
representative of the purification of the soul, or house of the spirit.
At last, she understands what the Consul had been alone in seeing
—that their complete and final departure is actually a kind of ultimate salvation. She thus becomes "overwhelmed by a sudden wave
through her whole being of desperate love and tenderness for the
Consul." * For just a moment, she can see her "house" calmly
now, as it will be after the fire, until Hugh's arrival jolts her back
into "reality."

Hugh too is treading his way back to self-recognition, for he
carries "a long battered key-shaped canvas case" and an "electric
torch." The case contains a guitar, his lost "key" to identity, and
the light, with which he now searches after truth.

Yvonne receives still another cryptic message from Geoffrey
when she finds a menu bearing "a design like a small wheel round
the inside of which was written 'Lotería Nacional Para La Bene-
ficencia Pública,' making another circular frame, within which appeared . . . a happy mother caressing her child"—a reminder of
the wheel of life, with its uncertain promise and a repeated taunt at
Yvonne's deliberate avoidance of her function in life. The lottery
and the detailed menu are like a symbolic chart outlining the
Eleusinian mystery feast and fertility rite, the left side of which is
"taken up by a full-length lithographic portrait of a smiling young
woman. . . . [who] held up a block of ten lottery tickets, on each
of which a cowgirl was riding a bucking horse and (as if these ten
minute figures were Yvonne's own reduplicated and half-forgotten

---

* Cf. Geoffrey's wave of love reaction at the carousel in Chapter Seven,
when he too realizes that his death is his only hope for salvation.

selves waving good-bye to herself) waving her hand"—a warning that the search will culminate in death, which, in her case, is to be associated with the destructive power of the horse, *Chavajah*. It is almost as if the Consul has written instructions for this very purpose: "At top left was written *Recknung*" (Judgment), a bill for three different drinks in a series of thirties, each for thirty cents. Below the bill she can make out parts of a poem interlarded with "scratchy drawings of a club, a wheel, even a long black box like a coffin." *

The cryptic poem discloses that the Consul was a magician who had been attempting rather unsuccessfully to climb out of the abyss into which he had inadvertently fallen. The unforgiving demons of the *Gai-hinnom* regard him only in this light and ignore his inner predilection for goodness, upward striving, as encompassed in the image of fleeing "north," which closes the poem. Yvonne becomes obsessed with the phrase and interprets his message correctly, for she seems to realize now that his intention is to seek the swiftest path upward, namely, death. "Outside the wind was blowing with an odd shrillness. . . . The clock . . . said twelve to seven: 'Who once fled north.' "

Deep in her mescal vision, and followed by lightning and thunder, with "Pegasus [pounding] up the sky unseen" overhead, she comes across "a ruined Grecian temple . . . with two tall slender pillars [severity and mercy] . . . now two beams of windy light . . . two telegraph poles." Through mescal, Yvonne has seen beyond material manifestation into the true nature of communication through light, here the "electric" power inherent in the occultist's tree of life. The message of danger perceived, she stops "abruptly, her hands clenched so tightly her fingers hurt, saying: 'We ought to hurry, it must be almost seven. . . .' " Closer to full enlightenment, for she realizes that she must reach Geoffrey before the seventh and last degree, she now confronts a hallucinatory projection of her own fate in the "imagined" figure of "the fixedly smiling woman with the lottery tickets" who beckoned "her on at the end of the path."

This image is followed by "a sharp pistol-like report" and "a lightning flash bright as day," which discloses the "sad useless arrow" pointing to Parián. The shots are those that will kill

* See Appendix D for details of Eleusinian mystery symbols.

Geoffrey; the lightning flash is the course of his final spiritual effort to emerge from the *Kelipah* to *Tiphereth* as his corporeal self is thrust into the barranca. Immediately, the purifying rain begins to fall "and a sweet cleanly smell rose from the woods," in contrast to the smell of decay before.*

A wind like an express train [the express that now, in fact, does carry the Consul's corpse] swept through the forest; just ahead lightning struck through the trees with a savage tearing and roar of thunder that shook the earth . . . some distortion of celestial privacy, a shattering insanity in heaven, a form of disgrace forbidden mortals to observe too closely. . . .

The unleashed forces that Yvonne has begun to investigate and understand (for she has by now herself taken part in unleashing the caged eagle) now return for vengeance: "In the slackening thunder something was approaching. . . . It was an animal of some sort . . . and now as the lightning crashed again and the thunder subsided she heard a protracted neigh becoming a scream almost human in its panic." Geoffrey is now manifested as the destructive power that he has unleashed in the form of a horse.

The next moment . . . she saw, by a brilliant flash of lightning, the riderless horse. . . . [She] saw its every detail, . . . even the number seven branded on its rump. Again trying to rise, she heard herself scream as the animal turned towards her and upon her. The sky was a sheet of white flame . . . [the naked power of *Kether*, which once viewed, spells inevitable death].

Racing past the lower *Sephiroth* she sees once again the great wheel of the zodiac "while the sun [*Tiphereth*] stood, burning and spinning and glittering in the centre." Then she sees the souls of others as they journey "over the sea" in the form of butterflies, and she hears her own name being called from

far away and she remembered, they were in a dark wood, she heard the wind and the rain . . . the tremours of lightning shuddering through the heavens [she is experiencing the forces of the elements

* The theosophical interpretation of the lightning and thunderstorm indicates a restoration of equilibrium—that is, the positive electricity from above joining with the negative electricity from the earth. Therefore, the martyr is drawn up to the higher planes of existence when his death, by drawing down the storm, acts to fuse the male (positive) with the female (negative) principle. This also substantiates the necessity for Yvonne's immediate death after he is shot.

and the "sinking" sensation common to the mystical experience, and
finally the terror] . . . the horse, rearing, poised over her, petrified
in midair, a statue, somebody was sitting on the statue . . . it was
the Consul. . . .*

Then she actually experiences the fiery transfiguration heretofore
only a fantasy. The "tree was burning . . . the walls with their
millwheel reflections of sunlight on water were burning . . .
Geoffrey's . . . book was burning . . . whirling up from the fire
they were scattered, burning . . . and now it was growing darker.
. . ." As the book of secret wisdom finally burns, Yvonne's agony
is over; the initiation process has come to an end; she dies along
with its secrets.†

. . . [The] pleasure boats that had ferried song upstream sailed home
silently over the dark waters of Eridanus.‡ . . . And leaving the
burning dream Yvonne felt herself suddenly gathered upwards and
borne towards the stars, through eddies of stars scattering aloft with
ever wider circles like rings on water, among which now appeared,
. . . towards Orion, the Pleiades . . .

In a letter to the *Vancouver Sun,* Lowry attempted to explain
the universal significance of the Pleiades, which relates to his use
of this image in *Volcano:*

The Egyptians, the Aztecs, the Japanese all worshipped them. And
the Festival of All Hallows, All Saints Day, the Mexican Day of the
Dead, etc., are all associated with the culmination of the Pleiades.§

* The sexual overtones of Yvonne's death also add to its validity as an
equilibrating process, for the Cabbalists believe that this cosmic mystery
is inherent in the nature of the sex act on the microcosmic plane.
† Her death is also associated very closely with a certain Aztec ritual
sacrifice described by Spence, whose book, *The Myths of Mexico and Peru,*
Lowry read: "As the first day of the fifty-third year dawned, the people
narrowly observed the Pleiades, for if they passed the zenith time would
proceed and the world would be respited. The gods were placated or re-
freshed by the slaughter of the human victim on whose still living breast
a fire of wood was kindled . . . the heart and body being consumed by
the flames . . . As the planets of hope crossed the zenith loud acclamations
resounded from the people . . . the domestic hearths . . . were rekindled
from the sacred fire which had consumed the sacrifice. Mankind was safe
for another period."
‡ Cf. Lowry, *Letters;* and "Nor is it without reason that the river
Eridanus is said . . . to pass through those celestial abodes; for this indicates
the prolific flow of spirit which accedes spontaneously from the occult
energy of [the initiation]." Atwood, *Hermetic Philosophy and Alchemy.*
§ Not included in Lowry, *Letters.*

# Chapter Twelve

An hour earlier than Chapter Eleven, the Consul is drinking mescal in the empty Farolito. His mind, flooded with supernatural sights and sounds, darts in and out of the external reality of his surroundings. "A Few Fleas," the son of the proprietor, absentmindedly serves him, reads a comic book, and swipes a dead scorpion from the calendar. The Consul surveys Parián at his leisure. He sees the headquarters of the military police, the dungeon, the ragged platoons, a corporal writing by lamplight. What first appears as a hideous visceral monster turns out to be a policeman leading a horse. Geoffrey returns to the bar to be greeted by Diosdado, the barman, who hands him a package of Yvonne's letters. The Consul, carrying still another drink, takes the letters to one of the cubicle-like back rooms. There he once again meets the ubiquitous old domino-playing woman who had been present at Yvonne's homecoming that morning. Yvonne's letters are filled with desperate pleas for him to reconsider his ways, assurances of her love, and confessions of great suffering. She speaks of his lost soul, which wanders in darkness, and offers him light and hope instead. The Consul stops reading, leaves the old woman sitting at the table, and wanders toward the door of the cantina. His thoughts of Yvonne are interrupted by the soft voice of a young girl, who lures him back to her room. He is surprised to find that it is not the room of a typical prostitute; with its Kashmiri sword and student's bookcases, it even resembles his own college digs. During the lovemaking that follows, his mental anguish is analogized by the memory of Oaxaca, where he had gone after Yvonne's departure. His sexual insecurity is manifested in his obsessive recollection of the night without alcohol spent in Oaxaca. Finally, repentant and fearful lest he may have contracted syphilis, Geoffrey leaves the girl. In the bathroom, he is confronted by a pimp, who sits surrounded by filth and advertisements for the cure of venereal diseases. The little man seems to be demanding payment for his services, for he keeps inquiring about the Consul's satisfaction with "María."

Geoffrey returns to the bar with mixed feelings of false light-heartedness and deep despair. As he gazes out the door, his attention is drawn back to the horse he had seen before. Upon closer examination, he sees that it is the beast belonging to the dying Indian of the afternoon. As he investigates further, he is approached by a suspicious policeman. Though he tries to joke his way out of the policeman's angry questioning, the Consul finds himself in still greater difficulty. Before he can tell just what is taking place, he is accused of being a Bolshevist, a deserter, an American, and a Jew. The policeman then points out another policeman, to whom he refers as the Chief of Municipality. Still another man, a civilian, is pointed out to him as the Chief of Gardens; while the immediate accuser informs the Consul that he is himself the Chief of Rostrums. A storm threatens outside as the bar grows crowded. By now the Consul is entirely disoriented, for the chiefs have been plying him with mescal. He longs for Yvonne to come to his rescue now: the seriousness of the situation is finally becoming apparent. Now the prohibitionist poster in Jacques' room comes back to mind. He sees it as a forewarning, a symbol of his own degradation and ensuing fall, and he realizes that he is still only at the opening of the abyss that awaits him. Sanabria, the Chief of Gardens, is obviously the highest authority. Geoffrey sees himself as he once was in the person of this polished but cruel figure. Leaving Geoffrey in the company of the unctuous pimp, a drunken English sailor who claims that "Mozart writ the Bible," and Weber, the American fascist who had been at the hotel that morning, the policemen go to the phone. The chaotic conversations of these "macabre people" are interlarded with scraps of Yvonne's letters, as the radio, also gone mad, emits a hysterical catechism. At this point, an old fiddler sidles up to the Consul and whispers a warning. The warning is repeated by an old woman, who also informs him of the police-man's murderous intentions. Nevertheless, the Consul remains. When the chiefs return from their phone conversation, they begin to search the Consul's pockets. They find Hugh's tele-gram and accuse him of being an anarchist and a Jew. Geoffrey claims to be William Blackstone, and as the threats grow louder and more insistent, he begins to fight back. Demanding that they return his letters, he finds that he is suddenly defending all the poor and downtrodden of the earth in his own person. He even swings a machete a few times—or thinks he does—as the vision of a crowing cock flaps before his eyes. As he rushes out of the Farolito and heads toward the horse, the Chief of Rostrums shoots him three times. As he dies, the bells ring and the rain falls. He can barely make out the face of the old fiddler, now offering the Consul his hand, as he himself had not done for the dying peon. He hears music and again finds himself in the meadows of Kashmir. There is a vision of his attempt to climb Popocatepetl without success. Finally, he feels strong hands lifting him and has a surge of hope for salvation until he realizes that he is being lifted only to be thrust down into the barranca. In the short space of his fall, he lives through the coming destruction of war in a vision of hurtling bodies and villages—the whole world exploding in volcanic eruption. A dead dog is thrown down after him into the abyss. A terse epilogue that reads

¿LE GUSTA ESTE JARDIN?
¿QUE ES SUYO?
¡EVITE QUE SUS HIJOS LO DESTRUYAN!

closes the book.

By far the densest and most varied in its symbolism, the last chapter of the novel is written in the form of a cosmic nightmare. Juxtaposing bits of scenery from black magic and Aztec ritual with Cabbala, Lowry leads up to the Consul's death with a graduated horror, somewhat in the manner of the slowly revolving wheel of the infernal machine, which climaxes in a rather ambiguous re-enactment of the fall. The entire chapter is set within the framework of a carefully prescribed witches' Sabbath consisting of three major events: (1) orgiastic drinking and eating on the part of the assembly, (2) sexual intercourse with an evil succubus in the shape of a woman, and (3) the cock crow that prefaces the human sacrifice and dissolves the enchantment. Almost every name and character appearing in the Farolito has been prepared for in a previous reference. Each speech, including the inner monologues, and the reading of Yvonne's recovered letters are ritually significant as either a blessing, curse, exhortation, warning, or accusation.

When the Consul first enters the Farolito, it is deserted. His own actions will determine what is to happen in this void, *Bohu* (void) being one of the earlier stages of hell. Ordering mescal, the Consul is apparently determined to carry out his solitary mission to "drink to the bottom of the bowl." As he gazes into the mirror behind the bar,* ". . . his face silently glared at him, with stern, familiar

* Magicians in the tradition of Paracelsus and Agrippa make "magic mirrors" of their souls, which reflect both the black and the white traits that dominate their actions. This permits them to judge the direction of their course.

foreboding." He is haunted still by perpetual noise, "the ticking of his watch, his heart, his conscience, a clock. . . . of rushing water, of subterranean collapse . . . voices that seemed to be wailing from a distance distressfully: 'Borracho, Borrachón . . .' " ("Drunk, Great Drunkard"). The ticking represents both the shortness of his life and the awaiting dripping abyss, while the mourning cry with its allusion to the mystical nature of his intoxication suggests the Zoharistic image of the Messiah who weeps in sympathy with a great suffering soul. The lamentations recall Yvonne to his mind, and afraid he will yield to her look, reflected by his own "white" reflection in the mirror, ". . . he shut out all thought of Yvonne. . . . [and] drank two swift mescals. . . . In one corner of the room sat a white rabbit eating an ear of Indian corn. . . . [nibbling] at the purple and black stops with an air of detachment. . . ." The rabbit (Aztec god of drink) is a projection of Geoffrey himself, who is also "nibbling" away at his chances for conquering the first "stops" of the triune worlds *Yesod* (*Beriah*, purple), *Tiphereth* (*Yetzirah*, yellow-corn), and *Binah* (*Aziluth*, black).

Surrounded by the bottles of magical ichor, the Consul begins to lose track of his sense of time, as evidenced by the advertisement for the previous day's Red Cross Ball to which "a scorpion clung." He experiences "icy relief"—one of the torments emanating from the victim's own body, soon to be combined with fire—and feels "safe here; this was the place he loved—sanctuary, the paradise of his despair." Now that he is finally settled in hell, the Consul's view of paradise is in direct opposition to Yvonne's. The scorpion is, of course, an emblem of himself who had *yesterday* clung to the hope of rescue—that is, the Red Cross Ball, which is synonymous with Dr. Vigil—but who had by now stung himself to death.

The demonic little son of the Farolito's proprietor, "A Few Fleas," is human counterpart to the little gnats that guard the "portals of the Qliphoth." He is reading a comic book that is actually an ironic concretization of his own and his father's personality: Son of the Devil. Lowry's touch of irony here duplicates the Consul's own mirror gazing and provides an insight into the Chinese-box quality of the entire chapter. Geoffrey calls the boy's attention to the scorpion, and the fellow "brushed it off with a vexed gesture: it was dead." Interspersing the words of the comic book, which consist of a call for help, the Consul becomes aware of the fact that he too will be easily "brushed off" soon, his drunkenness to be regarded as a form of death by the police. "Save me, thought the Consul vaguely . . . help: but maybe the scorpion, not wanting to be saved, had stung itself to death." The scorpion's suicidal sting is a reference to Geoffrey's own "agenbite," or prick of conscience, which has driven him personally to assume the conglomerate guilt of mankind. Faltering between life and death, newly aware of the dire choice he has made in coming to this place,

. . . he approached the open window on his right. It was almost a sheer drop to the bottom of the ravine. What a dark, melancholy place! . . . It was a tremendous, an awful way down to the bottom. But it struck him he was not afraid to fall either. He traced mentally the barranca's circuitous abysmal path back through the country, through shattered mines, to his own garden. . . .

The Farolito being the gateway to the center of the *Kelipah,* the Consul can peer down into the abyss to prepare himself for the descent. Increasingly committed as the chapter continues, he finds that he has no actual physical fear of the drop (cf. his prayer in Chapter Ten, exhorting the Virgin to help him sink even lower). Because the Consul's journey is symbolic as well, Lowry's reference to the circuitous path corresponds to the alchemical metaphor of the spiritual mines that are sealed in under the earth (matter) until they are opened by the successful alchemist. Naturally, the desired result of such a course is the repossession of the original "garden," with all its metaphorical connotations. In mapping out the setting of his own death as he had outlined it for Yvonne on the menu, Geoffrey notes that "Popocatepetl . . . appeared almost right overhead, the barranca, the Farolito, directly beneath it. Under the volcano!" (Volcano here is symbolic of the destruction of earth—the Cabbalistic sign for the earth being $\triangle$, two interlacing triangles representing the microcosm and macrocosm ✡ .)

The police, as guardians of hell, are quartered in a "ruined monastery or waterworks" where neither religious nor alcoholic thirst can be assuaged. Time is fixed on "a clock pointing to 6." Because 7 is the number of release, hell's clock does not move be-

yond 6. A corporal sits endlessly writing something in a copper-
plate handwriting.* A man in a dungeon seems to be gesticulating
at the Consul, perhaps in warning, perhaps pleading for help.

In spite of these sinister premonitions the Consul rationalizes

that it was necessary to remain. . . . He knew there was another
reason yet couldn't place his finger on it. . . . It seemed indeed then
as though he must stay here for [Yvonne's] sake, not because she
would *follow* him here—no, she had gone, he'd let her go finally
now . . . obviously she would return home and his mind could not
travel beyond that point—but [he must remain] for something else.

In the final stage, cut off entirely from the *Shekinah*, which is soon
to reascend to the seventh heaven, the redeemer must repay the
debt of mankind with his life, hence the Consul's concern with the
proper change on the bar and his hasty pocketing of the coins he
will require on entering the depths of Tartarus. To fool the little
demon behind the bar, as well as to divert himself from the awful
truth of this position, he shams an expression of self-disgust at
being "Abandoned by his friends, as they by him, [knowing] that
nothing but the crushing look of a creditor lives round that corner. . . . Why am I here . . . what have I done . . . why have
I been brought so low. . . ."

The place begins to fill with the damned and wretched, legless
beggars, thieves, and with the help of the mescal the Consul can
now see beneath the exterior and into the true evil in which he is
immersed manifested as "animals resembling geese, but large as
camels, and skinless men, without heads, upon stilts, whose animated entrails jerked along the ground . . . issuing out of the
forest path the way he had come." The vision fades and is replaced
by its external correspondence, "a policeman . . . leading a
horse," the creature that is to kill Yvonne.

The face of a beggar "was slowly changing to Señora Gregorio's,
and now in turn to his mother's face, upon which appeared an expression of infinite pity and supplication." This is *Binah*, who appears in various guises during this chapter: as Yvonne's letters, for
example, and the old woman with the dominoes. To propitiate her,
Geoffrey responds to her supplication by calmly reciting the already familiar demonic preludes to the climactic trial awaiting

---

* Cf. the scrivener of the morning, or recording angel, now transformed
into angel of death who is permanently engraving the names of his victims.

him: ". . . daemonic orchestras . . . his own name being continually repeated by imaginary parties . . . strumming . . . slamming . . . battling with insolent archfiends . . . terrible music . . . [and to obtain the sustenance with which to confront these horrors] he returned to the bar."

Diosdado (ironically named the God-given), one of his three accusers, has appropriated the Consul's favorite pipe, thereby depriving him of his last personal symbol of light. The proprietor taunts him with references to his drunkenness ". . . and his look, the insult, the implied extent of his downfall, penetrated the Consul." Carrying the torment a stage further, Diosdado exposes the package of Yvonne's lost letters, now obviously too late to help Geoffrey, yet early enough in the course of the evening to hurt him. *"Where are the letters Geoffrey Firmin the letters the letters she wrote till her heart broke?* Here were the letters, here and nowhere else: these were the letters and this the Consul knew immediately. . . ." He had had to return to hell in order to regain his lost knowledge of the mysteries that were contained in these letters, Lowry's insistent repetition of the word indicating that these are also, perhaps, the mystical letters comprising the all-powerful Tetragrammaton. Then, in a sentimental lapse of silence, the Consul draws a map of Spain in liquor on the bar, explaining to Diosdado that this was where he had met his wife. By drawing this map of Granada (symbolic meeting place between the Consul and his *Shekinah*), he will be suspected of being a Jew (and therefore aligned with the white antifascist magicians) and a spy in hell. He is, therefore, to be persecuted, much as the Cabbalists who practiced their beliefs in southern Spain were four centuries before.

Removing the letters to one of the little glass-encased cells, he

was not really surprised to find the old Tarascan woman of . . . this morning. Her tequila, surrounded by dominoes, was set before her on the round table. Her chicken pecked among them. The Consul wondered if . . . [it was] just necessary for her to have dominoes wherever she happened to be? Her stick with the claw handle hung, as though alive, on the edge of the table. . . .

The dark mother is manifested here as a type of witch or medium casting her dominoes of fate (*notarikon*). Accompanied by her familiars and living talismans, she will soon become the physical medium for Yvonne's pleading voice.

The Consul moved to her. . . . "Do you remember to-morrow?" he
read. . . . [The] words sank like stones in his mind.—It was a fact
that he was losing touch with his situation . . . it was after six in
the evening, yet whether it was being in . . . the presence of the
old woman . . . he seemed back in the early morning again: it was
almost as if he were yet another kind of drunkard, in different circumstances, in another country, to whom something quite different
was happening. . . .

Again time is shifted wildly, as in all mystical experiences, and,
merging with the souls of every other drunkard in the world at this
moment, the Consul encounters "his accusing eyes in another mirror [reminding him of a tale told to a bartender] . . . at too great
length, [of a] burning house" (a premonition of Yvonne's dying
vision). The Consul, worried about something he knows he must
recite, finds that he has forgotten the proper formula and can only
"gibber" nonsensically. As he looks into the black depths of his
guilty soul through the mirror, the Consul shakes "in impotent terror at himself, the beards and eyes [that] form in the curtains
. . . the eternal ghostly policeman outside," for total self-
exposure is an essential, often frightening stage in the initiation
process. He is unable to comprehend Yvonne's desperate message,
" 'Do you remember tomorrow?' " which includes all past, present,
and future and is, or has been, or will be their "wedding anniver-
sary." She calls to him as one "lost at sea" until, finally reading
into the words, Geoffrey discovers their message "his own lostness,
his own fruitless selfish ruin. . . . '[It] is as though you were
away at war and I were waiting . . . but no war could have this
power to so chill and terrify my heart. I send you all my love
. . . and all my thoughts and prayers.' " Yvonne is unable to accompany him while he is engaged in his "war" against the elements; she can only send assurances of her loyalty by means of
messengers. Therefore,

. . . the old woman with the dominoes was trying to attract his
attention, opening her mouth and pointing into it: now she was
subtly moving round the table nearer him.—"Surely you must have
thought a great deal of *us*, of what we built together. . . . What is
a lost soul? It is one that has turned from its true path and is groping in the darkness of remembered ways. . . . You are walking on
the edge of an abyss where I may not follow."

The plea for turning back from the *Kelipah* comes too late and is therefore all the more poignant in its urgency. Yvonne here states quite pointedly that Geoffrey is a lost soul who is mistakenly groping in the darkness for his exoneration, which she sees as residing only in the reconstruction of his life. The *Shekinah* cannot descend below *Malkuth* with him.

He posted himself at the door again, as sometimes before in the deceptive violet dawn [deceptive as his transient longing for Yvonne and as deceptive as the violet light of *Yesod*, the dawning cosmic consciousness that can lead a man either to heaven or to hell]. . . . He wanted Yvonne at this moment . . . wanted more than ever to be forgiven and to forgive. . . . Miserably he wanted Yvonne and did not want her.

His suffering is only exacerbated by the occasional longing for life and fertility that he must overcome entirely in order to fulfill his mission. Once again, however, the impulse is subdued, when upon renouncing Yvonne (positive sex), he is taken by a prostitute (the succubus, or sex in its negative aspect) through the corridors of hell to her room significantly located near the toilet, "out of whose evil-smelling gloom broke a sinister chuckle. . . ."

Then it struck him that some reckless murderous power was drawing him on, forcing him, while he yet remained passionately aware of the all too possible consequences . . . leading him irresistibly out into the garden—lightning-filled at this moment, it reminded him queerly of his own house, and also of El Popo, where earlier he had thought of going, only this was . . . the obverse of it. . . .

At this point, Geoffrey is led to commit one of the profoundest Cabbalistic offenses: the expense of seed (life force) in an adulterous encounter. In his case the sin is even more serious in light of his impotence with his own wife.

The room contains "a single blue electric bulb" (cf. the electric bulb under which he read Yvonne's messages; the blue bulb in this case is the Kelipathic obverse of the *Sephirah Chesed*). The whore's room is actually his student room at Cambridge—"a bookcase in a familiar place. . . . In one corner, incongruously, stood a gigantic sabre. Kashmir! He imagined he'd seen the word, then it had gone. . . . [The open book on a shelf is] a Spanish history of British India. The bed was . . . covered . . . with bloodstains. . . . [The] floor was red flagstone. . . ." The province of the queen of swords of the tarot is equivalent to the Cabbalistic realm of *Geburah,* home of the female destroyer, here indicated by the red-covered floor and the bloodstains. The book is open to *his* history and background (a Briton born in India), hence his familiarity with the surrounding objects, which represent his past. Capable of simulating Yvonne's form, the prostitute-demon assumes her face: "Lightning silhouetted against the window a face, for a moment curiously like Yvonne's. . . . Her body was Yvonne's too . . . electricity crackled under his fingers running over her. . . ." Because she is really only a creature of the air, "her body was nothing, an abstraction merely. . . ." The nihilistic sexual encounter serves only to compound the guilty horror even further by reviving memories of

the horror of waking up in the morning in Oaxaca * . . . [with its] vulture sitting in the washbasin . . . the cold shower bath back on the left . . . (. . . God is it possible to suffer more than this, out of this suffering something must be born, and what would be born was his own death) for ah, how alike are the groans of love to those of the dying. . . .

As a Cabbalist, Geoffrey knows that this sexual transgression, a confirmation of physical death, is the immediate prologue to his soul's annihilation. He has been powerless to write the letters that would have saved him from this act, which he equates with "a calamity he was now penetrating." Borne back by each succeeding wave of passion to his anguished "thirst that was not thirst . . . was death, death, and death again . . . ," he remembers the carafe of water in the hotel in Oaxaca, which "was too heavy, like his burden of sorrow—*'you cannot drink of it. . . .'* " † But somehow then he had found a bottle of wine "marked with someone else's room number"—for the role of Messiah is not designated to be his. The "blessed ichor" rushes through his chest like "boiling ice . . . or . . . a bar of red hot iron . . . for the conscience that rages underneath anew and is bursting one's heart burns so fiercely with the fires of hell a bar of red hot iron is as a mere chill

* "[Oaxaca] was as much a place of the dead as a place of punishment." Spence, *The Myths of Mexico and Peru.*

† Señora Gregorio/mother's refrain reminding him that he is capable of bearing neither the great burden of the world nor the blessing of life.

to it. . . ." In hell, even the antidote for suffering turns to poison. He had rushed to the cantina El Infierno then, where he could feel safe among "the beggars, the early workers, the dirty prostitutes, the pimps, the debris and detritus of the streets and the bottom of the earth." Geoffrey is inexorably driven to return to hell, while the true Messiah must be strong enough to *pass through* it only.

Life is once again allegorized by the figures of a man and a woman lying near a river, this time projected on "a calendar behind the bed [as a] picture of Canada [Yvonne's spirit continues to penetrate the depths until the very last moment when the Chief of Rostrums takes away her letters]. . . . This calendar was set to the future, for next month . . . where would he be then?" The fact that there is no time on the astral plane of existence allows for many possible answers to this question. The calendar, however, is still another reminder of the still-present opportunity for reunion with the *Shekinah* in paradise near the river Eridanus. Each vision of potential salvation is succeeded by a demonic taunt that lures the Consul further into damnation.

"Thunder blew the door open, the face of M. Laruelle faded in the door," and the devil as seducer assumes the face of the betrayer, just as the whore has assumed his wife's features, and thereby provides Geoffrey with a rationale for his own adultery.

As an indication of how far he has fallen into the lowest stages of matter, he is overcome by

a stench [which] clapped yellow hands over his face [yellow here the opposite sphere of *Tiphereth*, and as the reversal of the sphere of Redeemer would be the sphere of the Accusers] . . . he heard his voices again, hissing and shrieking and yammering at him: "Now you've done it. . . . Even we can help you no longer . . . Just the same you might as well make the most of it now, the night's still young . . ."

The nature of the Kelipathic demons, the "Zourmiel," is to promote disharmony. They continually work, even against each other, in order to confound their victims. The pimp in the toilet is a living embodiment of the Consul's own sexual depravity and is also yet another manifestation of the devil as seducer. Appearing amid advertisements for Dr. Vigil's cure for venereal disease and 666, the pimp, who leads Geoffrey further toward destruction, is contrasted with Vigil, who had been his only remaining guide toward salvation. "His versatile companion of this morning and last night might have been informing him ironically that all was not yet lost—unfortunately, by now he would be on his way to Guanajuato."

Turning from the thought of his last refuge, the Consul involves himself with the hierophant of the *Kelipah,* the hideous, filthy pimp whose offer consists of the contracting of syphilis. The man is sitting on a befouled floor (the bottom of the world of matter), on which the Consul sees once again "a dead scorpion; a sparkle of phosphorescence and it had gone, or had never been there," a figure of his own total surrender of identity. When he asks the man for the time, he gets an ambiguous reply: " 'Sick . . . half past sick by the cock.' " Earlier, Cervantes had answered, " 'half past tree by the cock,' " a pun with many meanings. The tree, for example, is the Sephirotic tree, which, at that point, he had only "half-passed," not yet having been completely committed to hell before the end of Chapter Ten. However, the sexual transgression that seals his decision renders him "sick"—morally, and probably, as he already imagines, physically as well. The cock also refers to the ritual animal that announces the Consul's death: He "remembered the strange Indian belief prevailing that a cock would crow over a drowned body. . . . shrilly seven times!"

Death and paradise now become linked in his mind. He could not, he feels,

return [to Canada] . . . to build . . . somewhere there, a new life with Yvonne. . . . The hope of any new life together . . . could scarcely survive. . . . [The reasons] were without quite secure basis as yet, but for another purpose that eluded him they had to remain unassailable. All solutions now came up against their great Chinese wall. . . . He laughed . . . feeling a strange release, almost a sense of attainment. . . . It was as if, out of an ultimate contamination he had derived strength.

Still battling for the identity of her son's soul, the voice of his mother pleads. " 'Alas,' a voice seemed to be saying also in his ear, 'my poor little child, you do not feel any of these things really, only lost, only homeless.' " Because he has been deceived by the lure of evil masquerading as courage, the Consul now begins to allow his life to seep out slowly until (on the last page) it leaves him entirely, for such is the illusory sense of strength experienced by the initiate preceding his fall. Yvonne's observation about

Geoffrey's lost soul is repeated now in the protective mother's supplicatory reference to his "homelessness." This last communication from his "guardian angel" brings him to investigate the presence of the horse: "Something familiar about the beast made him walk over." Having been drawn to the horse, he is suddenly enlightened: "Unbidden, an explanation of this afternoon's events came to the Consul," for as he identifies himself, even unwittingly, with the force for good, he derives a clear and honest perspective of the situation: "The police . . . or rather not the real police . . . were at the bottom . . . of the whole business. . . . As if out of some correspondence between the subnormal world itself and the abnormally suspicious delirious one within him the truth had sprung—. . . ."

Because the Consul is now stranded somewhere between the worlds above and below, he can see that the police, whom he fears "worse than death," are really the archdemons of the world of lies, a discovery that changes the nature of his ensuing actions entirely. Heretofore immersed in suffering and debauchery for its own sake, selfishly seeking causes for evil and thereby sinking even deeper into it, the Consul is momentarily permitted a glance into "the truth [which] had sprung—sprung like a shadow however . . .", perhaps not deeply enough for him to reassess his perilous course, which is growing more dangerous with every passing second. The suspicious policeman interrupts his thoughts by asking him what he wants there, to which the Consul replies: "I learn that the world goes round so I'm waiting here for my house to pass by." Just "to glance at him was to feel that mankind was on the point of being saved immediately."

Now that he has decided to become "involved," the Consul assumes the part of the "homeless" world fool who has been set on the precarious wheel of life in order to await the proper "house" of his spirit. Nevertheless, it is already too late for him to save the world, for "the Consul was aware [of] something that bade him escape at his peril. . . . But the Consul felt neither serious nor like escaping."

The sergeant pushes him toward the Farolito as lightning appears in the east, "a towering thunderhead." The east here is the pillar of mercy communicating further warning. The chief of the accusers, "a tall slim man in well-cut American tweeds with a hard

sombre face and long beautiful hands. . . . who looked pure-
bred Castilian, seemed familiar. . . ." And so he should, for he is
the Consul's younger self, the cruel persecutor of the S.S. *Samaritan* now returned to accuse himself. The policeman, on the other
hand, is the embodiment of Geoffrey's alcoholic obsession:
" 'Drink. Drink a all you ah want to have. We have been looking
for you. . . . You have murdered a man and escaped through
seven states. . . .[You] desert your ship at Vera Cruz?' " This is
an allegorical revelation of the Consul as a murderer of the German officers but also as a murderer of the "man" in himself, deserter of the *"true"* cross" (carrying a false burden of guilt instead),
who has escaped through the seven lower states of initiation and is
now to be taken through the final three *Sephiroth* of the *Kelipah.*

The policeman continues his interrogation: " '. . . hey, what's
your names?' " The ungrammatical plural here is Lowry's allusion
to the holy name, with its twelve powerful permutations and to the
Consul's fusion of identities with William Blackstone. Geoffrey's
new accuser, the Chief of Municipality, is the clairvoyantly perceived Zuzugoitea of the phone book.* " 'What ah are you for?'
And he repeated the catechism of the first policeman. . . ." A
demonic "catechism" is being conducted here in order to determine Geoffrey's motives and alliances, which, in a sense, he is even
at this point not quite sure about. His beard proves an object of
suspicion to the police, who ask:

"You are Juden?" . . .
"No. Just Blackstone. . . . Jews are seldom very borracho." †
". . . That man is Jefe de Jardineros." And there was a certain awe
in his tone. "I am chief too, I am Chief of Rostrums. . . ."
"And I—" began the Consul.
"Am perfecta*men*te borracho," finished the first policeman. . . .

The Consul is given a roll call of the archfiends participating in the
trial: Satan himself; the silent judge, Chief of the Gardens, who
evicts those who destroy; prosecuting attorney, the Chief of Rostrums; governor of the various cities of the *Kelipah,* the Chief of
Municipality. Geoffrey is not permitted to defend himself, for he is

---

* "Zuzugoitea" is Lowry's pun on Goetia, a catalog listing demons.
† Jewish practical Cabbalists were more dependent on charms and number
mysticism, while their Christian counterparts like Agrippa or Faustus depended on drugs and potions.

regarded by them as being *perfectly* (that is, mystically) drunk and, therefore, totally in their power.

And who were these people, really? Chief of what Rostrums, Chief of what Municipality, above all, Chief of what Gardens? . . . Albeit the Consul was prompted by a shadowy prescience he already had concerning the claimants to these titular pretensions. . . . Doubtless he'd seen them here before . . . but certainly never at such close quarters as this. . . . He gathered . . . that the respected Chief of Gardens . . . might be even "higher" than the Inspector General himself. . . . [The] Chief of Gardens might have been the image of himself when, lean, bronzed, serious, beardless. . . .

The Consul had known hell before, but never as deeply as now, when he recognizes that the projected image of himself has come back to act as his most powerful accuser, a witness to his misapplied power. Unrelenting in their questioning, the chiefs are interested in Geoffrey's version of the afternoon's events in order to determine his loyalty. As he begins to answer, "Thunder growled outside the Farolito. He sat down. It was an order. Everything was growing very chaotic." Nature mirrors the chaos of the procedure, in which diabolical force is strengthened by the Consul's increasingly drunken state induced by the innumerable mescals supplied by the chiefs.

Drinkers come in from the graveyards (the dead and the damned joining the assembly) "dressed in long black cloaks streaked with luminous paint to represent skeletons." Soldiers with "bugles and green lariats" move around ominously in the back room and are the militant archfiends of the *Kelipah,* "dilapidated" because they stand for defeat and confusion, the reverse of the *Sephirah Netzach* (Victory). Geoffrey learns that the Chief of Gardens is Fructuoso Sanabria, which, literally translated, means Fruitful Saint of the Yawning Path—or Saint of the Abyss, to whom ". . . he sent a mute appeal for help . . . : he was answered by an implacable, an almost final look. For the first time the Consul scented the tangibility of his danger." The immediacy of his physical death begins to penetrate, especially when the accusers go to a telephone ". . . and the curious thing about this telephone was that it seemed to be working properly." Ironically, the telephone, a supposedly direct line to God that did not work for the Consul before, now freely flows with the communication

between the devils and the "higher up." The implementation of his
fall requires the cooperation between above and below, as it did
with Adam. In Cabbalistic terms, this is a reflection of his own unbalanced state.

Suddenly realizing that he is an exile even in hell, "with a slow
burning pain of apprehension, [he] felt again how lonely he was.
. . . [He'd] half hoped all along Yvonne would come to rescue
him, knew, now, it was too late, she would not come." Here, at
last, is the final awareness of his irrevocable separation from God's
*Shekinah.* "[And] ah, those burning draughts in loneliness, he
would miss them, wherever he was going, they were perhaps the
happiest things his life had known! . . ." The worst part of his
separation from God is, paradoxically, that which has brought him
to this pass—the thirst for and overindulgence in heavenly knowledge. At long last he passively resigns himself, giving up the life-
and-death struggle that had been raging in him all that day. "Instead, leaning his elbows on the bar, he buried his face in his
hands."

During one of the intermittent reprieves from the confounding
accusers, the meaning of his great drunkenness is disclosed to him:

Mightn't [Los Borrachones] have another meaning . . . unintentional
as its humour, beyond the symbolically obvious? He saw those people
like spirits appearing to grow more free, more separate, their distinctive noble faces more distinctive, more noble, the higher they ascended into the light; [Yvonne being among these souls who extricate
themselves from matter] those florid people resembling huddled
fiends, becoming more like each other, more joined together, more
as one fiend, the further down they hurled into the darkness. . . .
When he had striven upwards, as at the beginning with Yvonne, had
not the "features" of life seemed to grow more clear, more animated,
friends and enemies more identifiable . . . the sense of his own reality, more *separate* from himself? And had it not turned out that the
further down he sank, the more those features had tended to dis-
semble, to cloy and clutter, to become finally little better than
ghastly caricatures of his dissimulating inner and outer self, or of
his struggle, if struggle there were still? Yes, but had he desired it,
willed it, the very material world, illusory though that was, might
have been a confederate, pointing the wise way. Here would have
been no devolving through failing unreal voices and forms of dissolution . . . to a death more dead than death itself, but an infinite evolving and extension of boundaries, in which the spirit was an entity,
perfect and whole [this is an occultist's description of the contrast

between black and white magicians; the successful redeemer of mankind descends into the world of the shells in order to rise to selflessness while the black magician is only drawn into profounder depths of chaos and egotism]: ah, who knows why man, however beset his chance by lies, has been offered love? Yet it had to be faced, down, down he had gone, down till—it was not the bottom even now, he realised. It was not the end quite yet. It was as if his fall had been broken by a narrow ledge, a ledge from which he could neither climb up nor down, on which he lay bloody and half stunned, while far below him the abyss yawned, waiting.

Here is Lowry's open disclosure that the Consul has diverged from the right-hand path by not having allowed himself to love or to be loved, that he has failed the test of spiritual strength provided the magician by the material world; and he sees that his alcoholic mysticism has limited rather than expanded his boundaries. Instead of achieving an extension of spirit (fire = the element of expansion), he is facing the watery abyss (water = the element of contraction).

[As] he lay he was surrounded in delirium by these phantoms of himself, the policemen, Fructuoso Sanabria, . . . the luminous skeletons, even the rabbit in the corner and the ash and sputum on the filthy floor—did not each correspond, in a way he couldn't understand yet obscurely recognised to be some faction of his being? And he saw dimly too how Yvonne's arrival, the snake in the garden, his quarrel with Laruelle and later with Hugh and Yvonne, the infernal machine, the encounter with Señora Gregorio, the finding of the letters [that is, the *seven* degrees of his trial] . . . how all the events of the day indeed had been as indifferent tufts of grass he had half-heartedly clutched at or stones loosed on his downward flight, which were still showering on him from above [opportunities and catastrophes ignored alike, now all subsumed in the metaphor of a doomed mountain climber]. . . .

His "blue package of cigarettes with the wings on them" remind him that "there was nowhere to fly to. And it was as if a black dog had settled on his back, pressing him to his seat." The cigarettes are the last angelic emblem of *Chesed* (blue), whose brand name, "Alas" ("Wings"), indicates that he can no longer rise on the wings of the *Ofanim* toward *Chesed,* for he is paralyzed by the hound of hell.

The two police chiefs "were still waiting by the telephone, perhaps for the right number" (the proper magical formula for disposing of the intruder). Another half-hearted thought of escape crosses Geoffrey's mind, but he is simultaneously overwhelmed by thirst and a mass of babbling fiends that prevent him from leaving. The pimp continues his unctuous pawing, claiming kinship with the English in an attempt to insinuate himself into the Consul's good graces. A sailor "from the county of Pope" claims that "Mozart was the man what writ the Bible." Mozart being a Freemason, this refrain is in the nature of a secret message. The Pope reference brings us back to the Consul's premonition of his death at seeing the news of the Pope's expected demise. The drunken English sailor, is, of course, another phantom self who provides the Consul with the subject matter for his dying message in addition to the purpose for his sacrifice, namely, " 'Man, here on earth, shall be equal. And let there be tranquility. . . . Peace on earth. . . .' " The same American fascist of the morning appears spouting the same violence—also a mirror of the Consul's own destructive impulses toward the world and mankind. The vicious American and the drunken ineffectual English sailor both articulate the Consul's struggle in the form of a maddening fugue. And all the while "The Consul was drinking with these macabre people inextricably."

Fearful of Zuzugoitea's gaze, Geoffrey "importantly, defensively" produces Yvonne's letters (which grow "clearer" through his dark glasses, which now shut out the surroundings of hell), perhaps to prove that he too is in touch with powerful occult forces. It was still "only a quarter to seven. Time was circumfluent again too, mescal-drugged." The illiterate sailor continues his religious ramblings, which are interspersed in Geoffrey's mind with passages from Yvonne's letters to form a kind of litany. " 'Without you I am cast out, severed. I am . . . a shadow.' " * Now the words of the letters become a choral commentary on Geoffrey's present situation: cast out, a shadow, no longer even a man, no less a powerful magician—all of which assumes greater relevance because of the role of the white magician-hero in restoring his severed world to the Sephirotic tree in a superhuman effort.

The American then introduces himself as Weber, Hugh's enemy and a member of the Foreign Legion (the legion of devils). " 'We ask nobody no questions because down there we don't run.' "

* Cf. Señora Gregorio's earlier statement.

Against this are Yvonne's words of hope that those who have attained the *upper* spheres will pray and "strengthen us once more to nourish the flame which can never go out, but burns so fearfully low."

The incoherent sailor interrupts with an unwitting blasphemy: " 'Here to the off of God' "—he, like Geoffrey, "cuts off" from God when he means to say "love." Continuing the theme of severance and homelessness is the sudden voicing of the *non sequitur:* " '—de la Légion Etrangère. Vous n'avez pas de nation.' "

The struggle between the demons of despair and the message of hope grows more forceful, the two sides taking part battling with the Consul at its center. On the one hand, Yvonne as the departed *Shekinah* implores Geoffrey to change his direction to the very last:

You are one born to walk in the light. Plunging your head out of the white sky you flounder in an alien element. You think you are lost, but it is not so, for the spirits of light will help you and bear you up in spite of yourself and beyond all opposition you may offer. . . . Seize the immense potential strength you fight, which is in your body and ever so much more strongly within your soul [the magician's power is derived largely from the microcosmic equivalent of the divine fluid, or "Od"], restore to me the sanity that left when you forgot me, when you sent me away, when you turned your footsteps towards a different path, a stranger route which you have trod apart . . .

Weber's onslaught does not weaken either; and he launches into a sadistic history and description of hell and a grim predictive portrait of Geoffrey and Yvonne's deaths:

"He turreted out this underground place. . . . The sun parches the lips and they crack. Oh Christ, it's a shame: the horses all go away kicking in the dust. . . . They plugged 'em too."

—"I am perhaps God's loneliest mortal. . . . Help me, yes, save me, from all that is enveloping, threatening, trembling, and ready to pour over my head" [cries Yvonne from the past, present and future all at once].

". . . You got to study deep down to know that Mozart writ the Bible. But I tell you, you can't think with me. I've got an awful mind. . . . And I hope you the same. I hope you will have good. Only to hell on me," . . . and suddenly despairing, this sailor rose and reeled out.

This has all been a confused warning, perhaps the personification of the Consul's own shattered mind in the form of an unsuccessful Freemason, another God-intoxicated offender giving warning as he embraces hell.

A strange radio blares out the question "Do you wish that Christ should be our King?" and is followed by an abrupt "No" from somewhere in the midst of the chaos. This is the first of the three denials of Christ, two more to be uttered at later intervals. As though it had been Yvonne whose voice is now totally merged with the entreaties of the *Ofanim,* there follows immediately:

—"Geoffrey, why don't you answer me? I can only believe that my letters have not reached you. . . . I cannot, I will not believe that you have ceased to love me, have forgotten me. Or can it be that you . . . are sacrificing yourself . . . ?"
". . . Where are you, Geoffrey? . . . Where did we go, I wonder? In what far place do we still walk, hand in hand?"—[But she is interrupted by the] voice of the stool pigeon [which] now became clear, rising above the clamour—the Babel . . . the confusion of tongues. . . ."

The stool pigeon, or bird of the place of excrement, and the dove(Yvonne), now compete for the Consul's attention—the pimp in a disgusting parody of Yvonne's plea for Geoffrey's love.

". . . Give me cigarette for me. Give me match for my. My Mehican war gone for England all tine—"
—"Where are you Geoffrey? . . . [My] life is irrevocably and forever bound to yours. Never think that by releasing me you will be free. You would only condemn us to an ultimate hell on earth. You would only free something else to destroy us both [something he has already begun, for it is he who will unleash the horse that kills her]. . . . And my God, what do you wait for? What release can be compared to the release of love? . . . The emptiness of my body is famished for the need of you. . . . If you let anything happen to yourself you will be harming my flesh and mind. I am in your hands now. Save—"

Here she is cut off permanently, both her offer of salvation and her cry for help canceled out by the pimp's intrusion, which diverts Geoffrey just long enough for him to pocket the letters and thereby condemn her to permanent silence. Christ is denied for the second time.

A fiddler (possibly the guitar-playing Hugh transformed once

again as a "helping hand"), a "patriarchal toothless old Mexican,"
is loudly playing the "Star-Spangled Banner" (a reminder of heaven
and the zodiac zone). He turns out, moreover, to be still another
messenger from above: he is a potter, in fact (creator of the Cabbalistic "vessels" that Geoffrey has destroyed in Chapter Ten), who
warns the Consul to get out and offers him sanctuary. The potter is
followed by an old woman (Gregorio, Yvonne, mother) who
warns Geoffrey: "They diablos. Murderers. He kill ten old men"
(the uprooting of the ten upper *Sephiroth* by Samaël). But the
Consul remains; and the confusion mounts into a *Walpurgisnacht*
frenzy of "marijuana" and "raw alcohol." The pimp continues to
cling to him offering "life" for his pipe; but it is the wrong pipe
(his favorite one having been appropriated by Diosdado) and the
wrong "life," for the magic fire of heaven is no longer available to him.

To get rid of the pimp he says: "I happen to be American, and
I'm getting rather bored by your insults," as Christ is denied for
the third and final time. Someone launches into "It's a long, long
way to Tipperary" and counts significantly, "One, two, tree, four,
five, twelve, sixee, seven," immediately after which the serious persecution of the Consul begins.

This turn of the action is another ironic sidelight on the "long
way" down into the abyss prefaced by the hint that the Consul's
time has come. The placing of the number 12 (especially in light
of its Cabbalistic relation to 7 and all its ramifications) after 5 and
before 7 indicates that the twelve initiatory degrees have been
traversed from 7:00 to 7:00 and Geoffrey's trial is about to end.
Reinforcement of the finality of the process comes as "the bar was
emptying . . . yet a handful of mysterious strangers had already
entered to take the others' places. No thought of escape now
touched [his] mind. Both his will, and time . . . were paralysed."
The demons of sexuality, drugs, and confusion depart, making way
for the inner circle of accusers. Among these is the driver of the
bus to Tomalín.

The police begin by pulling papers out of Geoffrey's pockets (cf.
the initial stage of the final descent is the Consul's loss of identity
prepared for on the infernal machine that afternoon). There is, of
course, the inevitable self-incriminating evidence, Hugh's telegram,
which "the Consul, baffled, was reading . . . himself: '. . .

German behind . . . interiorwards. . . . news . . . jews . . .
country belief . . . power ends conscience . . . stop Firmin.' "
Lowry uses the telegram as a brief and frantic synopsis of the danger Geoffrey is in with regard to the political situation, in its correspondence to the esoteric struggle for power between good and
evil. On seeing the telegram, the police refer to him as a Jew and a
"cabrón," meaning both cuckold and he-goat, the sacrificial victim
of the Jewish ritual sacrifices. Although he disclaims the name
"Firmin" and calls himself Blackstone,* he has unwittingly assumed his brother's identity, for Hugh's anarchist membership
card is also removed from his pockets. As the actual physical torture begins, "the rabbit [is] having a nervous convulsion, trembling all over . . . ," and Geoffrey's inner fear is being enacted
by his alcoholic familiar. The old woman had remained "loyally.
. . . She was shaking her head at him, frowning sadly . . . she
was the same old woman who'd had the dominoes." (*Binah,* the
mother, is present both in the morning—birth—and at night—
death.)

    " 'You say your name is Black. No es Black. . . . You are no
a de wrider, you are de espider [scorpion]. . . . You Al Capón
[impotent cuckold].' " He is recognized now among the fiends with
whom he had been associating in all the cantinas of hell as not
being *truly* "Black," not one of them but a "Jewish" spy (a rene-
gade Cabbalist).

    The radio again desperately conveys a message

like orders yelled in a gale of wind, the only orders that will save
the ship: "Incalculable are the benefits civilization has brought us.
. . . Inconceivable the marvellous creations of the human sex in
order to make men more happy, more free, and more perfect. Without parallel the crystalline and fecund fountains of the new life
which still remains closed to the thirsty lips of the people who follow
in their griping and bestial tasks."

Here is the voice of judgment reciting Geoffrey's mystical crimes,
his self-imposed isolation from life, and his unworthy and blasphemous use of the sacred wine, whose source is the fountain of paradise itself—the paradise he had lost through his misapplication of

---

* At this point, the name may be read as an attempt on Geoffrey's part
to prove that he is one of them, a *black* stone. Cf. the numerous references
to "the stone" in Chapter Ten.

sexual functions, his attraction to the world of matter, his "bestial" life.

Then he sees the cock of doom "clawing and crowing," and as the announcement of his end dawns, the Consul springs into belated action by striking the Chief of Gardens and shouting, " 'Give me those letters back!'. . . but the radio drowned his voice [the accusations once filed, he now is entirely stripped of any remaining magical power], and now a peal of thunder drowned the radio."

At this point, Geoffrey opens his declaration against evil: " 'You killed that Indian.' . . . The clock outside quickly chimed seven times. The cock flapped before his eyes. . . ." As the initiatory ordeal reaches its climax, the Consul-magician denounces his tormentors in a state of drug-induced ecstasy, brandishing an imaginary sword in a final identification with the redeemer: " 'Only the poor, only through God, only the people you wipe your feet on, the poor in spirit, old men carrying their fathers and philosophers weeping in the dust . . . only the beggars and the accursed. . . . You stole that horse.' " *

Geoffrey now understands that the destroyers have stolen the power of God (the horse) in the manner in which he has himself stolen the sacred fire. The Chief of Rostrums continues:

"What the hell you think you do around here? You pelado, eh [a reversal of the role of the thief on the bus being characteristic of the upsidedown world]? It's no good for your health. I shoot de twenty people. . . . We have found out—on the telephone—is it right?— that you are a criminal. You want to be a policeman? I make you a policeman in Mexico."

The Consul's "criminal" record has been transmitted from the recording angel (an echo of the scrivener of the morning) to the demons by means of the telephone that connects above and below. The prosecutor taunts him with the possibility that he might become a "policeman," a guardian in hell.

Geoffrey sees the horse, "the number seven branded on its rump, the stud behind the saddlebuck glittering like a topaz. . . . [And he] tore frantically at the horse's bridle." Staggering toward God, by means of the blazing light of *Tiphereth,* Geoffrey

---

* "The god must first descend into the abyss and must emerge triumphant if humble folk are to possess assurance of immortality." Spence, *The Myths of Mexico and Peru.*

has determined, though too late, the means to salvation, the reason for his coming there that had so eluded him before. Sensing the Consul's positive inclination,

The Chief of Rostrums pushed the Consul back out of the light, took two steps forward and fired. Lightning flashed like an inchworm going down the sky [the lightning path to God], and the Consul, reeling, saw above him for a moment the shape of Popocatepetl, plumed with emerald snow and drenched with brilliance [Netzach, Victory]. The Chief fired twice more, the shots spaced, deliberate [3 is the number Achad designates as representative of Venus, Netzach]. Thunderclaps crashed on the mountains. . . . Released, the horse reared; tossing its head, it wheeled round and plunged neighing into the forest.

The power of God, now reversed, becomes *Chavajah,* power of destruction. Dying rather cinematically, the Consul "felt a queer relief. . . . 'Christ, . . . this is a dingy way to die' "—the death of the world fool entails a paradox combining the heroic and the base. "A bell spoke out: *Dolente . . . dolore!"*

As the purifying rain begins to fall he sees nothing but the face of the old fiddler, "a mask of compassion" as his own life goes "slivering out of him like liver . . . into the tenderness of the grass." All the Consul's hatred (in Cabbala, the liver is the organ of hatred) passes into love and tenderness.

Now the dying Indian in the guise of the old potter, calls to the Consul:

"Compañero—" . . . And it was as if, for a moment, he had become the pelado, the thief—yes, the pilferer of meaningless muddled ideas out of which his rejection of life had grown. . . . But someone had called him "compañero" too, which was better, much better. It made him happy. These thoughts . . . were accompanied by music he could hear only when he listened carefully. . . . Finale of the D minor quartet by Moses [the celestial music that accompanies the final degree of the Cabbalist's initiation].

And then he hears a guitar (Hugh's instrument) and "what sounded like the cries of love." The cries of death and love merge for him as he seems to recall gradually the essence of his previously "muddled ideas"—that only love is as strong as death.

Suddenly his astral body begins to emerge from his dying physical body, and he finds himself in Kashmir, "lying in the meadows

near running water among violets . . . the Himalayas beyond
. . . [but he is also] setting out with Hugh and Yvonne to climb
Popocatepetl." He hears both Yvonne and the police chief warning
against spiders (himself) as the various planes of existence merge.
His soul longing for the ascent, he painfully "trudged the slope of
the foothills toward Amecameca alone. . . . He could go no farther. Exhausted, helpless, he sank to the ground. No one would
help him even if they could. Now he was the one dying by the wayside where no good Samaritan would halt." But he falsely hears
what, still enlisted in the struggle of the soul to escape from the
body, he imagines to be help: "an ambulance shrieking through
the jungle . . . racing uphill . . . toward the peak—and this
was certainly one way to get there!"—a final comment on the indirect course of his entire quest. Penitently, therefore, he repeats:

"No se puede vivir sin amar." . . . How could he have thought so
evil of the world when succour was at hand all the time? And now
he had reached the summit. . . . Strong hands lifted him. Opening
his eyes, he looked down, expecting to see . . . those peaks of his
life conquered one after another before this greatest ascent of all
had been successfully, if unconventionally, completed.

Although he is deluded as to the actual events in the physical
world where he is not being saved but lifted up only to be cast
down, on another level, perhaps, the Consul's soul has loosed itself
from his tormented humanity and achieved a flash of enlightenment.
In his physical self-sacrifice he becomes the Messiah for one short
but eternal moment by experiencing in his own person all the horrors of the war to come:

But there was nothing there. . . . Nor was this summit a summit
exactly: it had no substance. . . . It was crumbling too [i.e., the
world] . . . while he was falling, falling into the volcano, he must
have climbed it after all [the initiate must maintain the constant desire to unite with *Kether*, especially if he is to descend, for it provides
him with the courage to undergo even hell itself] . . . now there was
this noise of foisting lava in his ears . . . it was an eruption, yet no,
it wasn't the volcano, the world itself was bursting . . . into black
spouts of villages catapulted into space, with himself falling through
it all, through the inconceivable pandemonium of a million tanks,
through the blazing of ten million burning bodies, falling, into a

forest, falling— . . . [The trees] were crowding nearer, huddled together, closing over him, pitying . . .

Somebody threw a dead dog after him down the ravine.*

Lowry's vision of destruction here is a consequence of the symbolic crashing glass of Chapter Ten. The breaking of vessels is a Cabbalistic analogy for the destruction of the world as a result of the Fall. The Cabbalist's view of this Day of Judgment, according to Serouya, is of the world ending in the sixth millennium

after portents like great storm and lightning, war and dictatorship, natural and planetary disturbances—all resulting in the loss of many lives, all of which will bring the Messiah down from his place at God's throne for the salvation of humanity.†

Lowry's last sentence of the novel reflects this prophecy: "You like this garden which is yours? Don't let your children destroy." ‡ Geoffrey "sees" these words as he plunges to his death, an ironic reminder that this black magician, though he dies for us all, has been too late in locating his own secret path out of hell.

---

* The Aztec Indians always included a dog with the corpse of the sacrificed god so that the spirit could swim on the dog's back over the water of the dead: "The departed was to take a little dog with him . . . and, after four years of passage, he arrived with it before the god, to whom he presented his papers. . . . Whereupon he was admitted together with his faithful companion to the 'Ninth Abyss.'" Spence, *The Myths of Mexico and Peru.*

† Serouya, *La Kabbale.*

‡ The epilogue is included in all editions but the 1966 Signet paperback.

# APPENDICES

# APPENDIX A

## *Cabbalistic and Occult Works Read by Lowry**

Achad, Frater. *The Anatomy of the Body of God.*
————, ed. *Equinox Magazine.*
————. *An Essay on Number in the Temple of Solomon the King.*
————. *A Note on Genesis.*
————. *QBL, or The Reception of the Bride.*†
————. *The Sefer Sephiroth.*
Agrippa, Cornelius. *The Philosophy of Natural Magic.*
"Astrology." Authors and titles unknown.
Blake, William. *Collected Poetry.*
————. *Prophetic Books.*
Böhme, Jakob. *The Aurora* (?).
Browne, Sir Thomas. *Religio Medici.*
Burnet, Thomas. *The Sacred Theory of the Earth.*
Crowly, Aleister. *Magick.*
Dunne, J. W. *An Experiment with Time.*
*The Egyptian Book of the Dead.* Edition unknown.
Fort, Charles. *The Book of the Damned.*
————. *Lo!*
————. *Wild Talents.*
Goethe, Wolfgang von. *Faust.*
*Goetia, or Lesser Keys of Solomon.* Edition unknown.
Hesse, Hermann. *Demian.*
————. *Steppenwolf.*
Huxley, Aldous. *Beyond the Mexique Bay.*
————. *Essays on Drug Experience.*

———

* According to *Under the Volcano,* notes, letters, Mrs. Lowry, University of British Columbia—Lowry Collection.
† In requesting Harvey Burt to send him some belongings from Dollarton to Sussex, Lowry asks only for Frater Achad's books and Melville's *The Confidence Man.* See Lowry, *Letters.*

*I Ching.* Edition unknown.

James, William. *The Varieties of Religious Experience.*

Jung, Carl. *Modern Man in Search of a Soul.*

―――. *Psyche and Symbol.*

Kafka, Franz. *The Castle.*

―――. *The Trial.*

Lévi, Eliphas. *Transcendental Magic: Its Doctrine and Ritual.*

―――. *The History of Magic.*

*Mahabharata.* Edition unknown.

Mann, Thomas. *Dr. Faustus.*

Marlowe, Christopher. *Dr. Faustus.*

Mathers, S. L. MacGregor, ed. *The Book of the Sacred Magic of Abra-Melin, the Mage.*

―――. *The Kabbala Unveiled.*

Ouspensky, Peter. *A New Model of the Universe.*

―――. *Tertium Organum.*

Paracelsus.

Pascal, Blaise. *Pensées.*

Poe, Edgar Allen. Stories, poems, criticism.

*Ramayana.* Edition unknown.

*Rig Veda.* Edition unknown.

Rimbaud, Arthur. *Un Saison d'Enfer.*

Saint John. *Revelations.*

Sandivogius, Michael. *The Hermetical Triumph* (Alchemy).

Singer, Charles. *From Magic to Science.*

Spence, Lewis. *The Myths of Mexico and Peru.*

Spinoza, Benedict.

Swedenborg, Emanuel. *Heaven and Its Wonders, and Hell.*

*Tibetan Book of the Dead.* Edition unknown.

*Upanishads.* Edition unknown.

Villars, Abbé de. *Comte de Gabalis.*

―――. *Sub-Mundanes or Elementaries of the Cabbala.*

Westcott, W. W., *The Sefer Yetziroth,* tr. Robert Fryar.

Yeats, William Butler. *Poems.*

―――. *A Vision.*

*Yoga Manual.* Author unknown.

# APPENDIX B

## Glossary of Cabbalistic Terms

*Adam Kadmon*—Jewish Cabbala: physical reflection of God; Christian Cabbala: Christ.

*Adam Tahton*—Microcosmic man.

*Assiah*—The world of matter that contains *Malkuth*.

*Aziluth*—First triune world of the *Sephiroth*, comprising *Kether, Chokmah,* and *Binah*.

*Beriah*—Second triune world, containing *Chesed, Geburah,* and *Tiphereth*.

*Binah*—Wisdom; female (mother), emanating from *Kether*.

*Cabbala*—Secret oral tradition of the Jews encompassing diversified "theosophical" systems (Hebrew *Kibbel,* "to receive").

*Chavajah*—Lévi's horse symbol denoting the unleashed power of Jehovah.

*Chesed*—Mercy; male.

*Chokmah*—Intelligence; second, masculine *Sephirah* emanating from *Kether*.

*En (Ain) Soph*—Boundless; highest unknown aspect of God.

*Etz Chaim*—Tree of Life; on which the *Sephiroth* are placed.

*Gai-hinnom*—Hell.

*Geburah*—Judgment; female.

*Gematria*—Manipulations of Hebrew letters and numbers for magical and prophetic purposes.

*Gilgul*—Metempsychosis.

*Hod*—Splendor; female.

*Kelipah*—Abyss within *Malkuth;* hell (*Gai-hinnom*).

*Kether*—Crown; first manifestation in the tree of life.

*Malkuth*—Kingdom; earth.

*Merkabah*—Earliest traces of Jewish Cabbala, centered on symbolism of the heavenly throne.

*Nefesh*—Moral soul.

*Neshama*—Rational soul.

*Netzach*—Triumph; male (legitimate Cabbala). Modern practical Cabbalists consider it synonymous with Venus; female.

*Notarikon*—Manipulations of Hebrew letters and numbers for magical and prophetic purposes.

*Ofanim*—Angels who intercede for man in *Malkuth*.

*Practical Cabbala*—Magic; introduced largely by the school of Isaac Luria; mistaken for speculative Jewish mysticism by Christians.

*Ruah*—Moral soul.

*Samaël*—Satan.

*Sefer Yetzirah*—Book of Formations; author unknown, written during Geonic period; promulgates essential doctrine of Cabbala: *Sephiroth*, or emanations from God.

*Sephiroth*—The planes of creation analogous to Plato's *logoi*.

*Shekinah*—God's feminine essence.

*Shin*—Hebrew letter that, because of its shape, is identified by theosophists as the magic trident, or the evil pitchfork.

*Shiur Komah*—Anthropomorphic description of the measure of the body of God composed during the *Merkabah*, or earliest period of Jewish mysticism.

*Sod*—Secret (equated by Lowry with mystical wine).

*Temurah*—Manipulations of Hebrew letters and numbers for magical and prophetic purposes.

*Tetragrammaton*—Mighty name of God, which is not to be uttered in vain.

*Tiphereth*—The sun, beauty; home of sacrificed gods.

*Tzimzum*—God's contraction, which is the cause for creation of all things.

*Yesod*—Foundation.

*Yetzirah*—*Creation;* the third triune world, composed of *Netzach, Hod,* and *Yesod*.

# APPENDIX C

## *Glossary of Motifs in* Under the Volcano *in order of prominence*

*Animals*—Birds (cock, eagle, vulture, pigeon), horse, serpent, cat, bull, scorpion, dog, goat, and various monsters both man and beast.

*Mountain*—Popocatepetl, Ixtaccihuatl, Himalayas, Parson's Nose in Wales, Alps.

*Wheel*—Ixion's wheel, infernal machine, windmill, Siva's wheel, Ezekiel's wheels within wheels.

*Tree/Wood*—Magic forest, Sephirotic tree, tree of death, cross, Casino de la Selva.

*Allegorical Numbers, Colors, Names*—7, 12, 666, 999, 4, 34; blue, red, white, green (the colors of the four beasts in Ezekiel's vision) purple; Vigil, Firmin, Laruelle, Cervantes, Fructuoso Sanabria, Diosdado, Quincey, Zuzugoitia.

*Gardens*—Mr. Quincey's garden, Geoffrey's ruined garden; Maximilian's ruins; public gardens, Canadian paradise, hell's garden.

*Wine*—Mescal, the synthesis of all joys ancient and sacred, as well as all sufferings; tequila, Scotch; also wine as "fire" of heaven.

*Elements*—Lightning (symbol of supreme reward or punishment), fire, air, water, earth in various guises, mines, the sea.

*Light/Darkness*—Mexico-Canada, lighthouse, cantina, fire/water, planets.

*Cinema and Billboard Advertisements Transformed into Occult Messages*—*Las Manos de Orlac*, 666 insecticide, toilet notices for syphilis cure, Arena Tomalín events, menus, calendar.

*Communications*—Telephones, railroad, telegraph messages, letters, telepathy.

*Tower*—Jacques' home, Babel, Farolito, prison watchtower.

# APPENDIX D

## *Orphic and Dionysian Elements in Eleusinian Mysteries Relating to Symbols in* Under the Volcano

1. A sanctuary dedicated to the "Bean" man.

2. Worship of the northern region connected with worship of mother.

3. Initiated mystic holds a club.

4. Bull sacrifice represents rebirth.

5. Semele—the thunderstruck mother in union with the Divine.

6. During descent into darkness, the lyre player (Orpheus) meets Dionysus, the raging one.

7. A ceremonial tenderness to animals is displayed by Pythagorean initiates.

8. Ritual of the wheel—used for purification, freeing oneself from the wheel of birth; then on to penance, punishment. The initiate passes with eager feet over the ring, or circle, entering a sacred enclosure. In the highest rite, the man is given a new name and sinks into the underworld. His burial is regarded as a mystic marriage, from which he emerges anew.

# APPENDIX E

## Unpublished Notes from Lowry's Journals*

*(Intended for future novels of intended series of seven.)*

### Outward Bound

This story, a chapter from a novel entitled *October Ferry to Gabriola,* concerns the diabolical possession by fire and storm of a tormented alcoholic lawyer. The young man's wife is the daughter of Angus McCandless, "a white magician," an "Old practitioner of ceremonial magic," who is writing a book about the world of "shells and demons."

Cinema is used as a mystical reflection of life throughout the notes. A recurring motif begins when a screen character says: "—But are we going to heaven, or hell?" and is answered by ". . . Ah, But they are the same place, you see" (p. 10).

The hero marvels at "the eerie significance of cinemas in our life— as if they related to the after-life, as if we knew, after we are dead, we would be conducted to a movie house where, only half to our surprise, is playing a film named: The Ordeal of Ethan Llewelyn . . ." (p. 11).

Jacquelyn Llewelyn, his wife, says: "My father is a magician . . . a *good* magician, a white one" (p. 12).

She explains further: "Daddy's [Angus McCandless's] had the idea that people like him are needed to combat the evil side of it all, that he maintains is flourishing now more than it did in the Middle Ages. He's got a bee in his bonnet about Hitler, for example."

"But he says that on this side too there're evil forces at work—and that there're some alchemists too among scientists, like an old wizard friend of his in Cleveland—and that in a few years they'll have the power to blow the whole world to smithereens—it sounds crazy, doesn't it?" (p. 15).

* For this material, I am especially grateful to Margerie Bonner Lowry, who, in addition to all the personal guidance and friendship which she extended to me, so graciously provided me with her husband's precious notes and manuscripts.

"It was not only that the McCandless . . . literally thought of nothing else but the great 'Plan' of the universe (what was more extraordinary here was perhaps that the average person never reflected, unless solipsistically, about such matters at all) but thought of himself . . . as a single factor whose conduct vitally effected it" (p. 15).

## Ghostkeeper

This story is about a writer who is having difficulty writing. In addition to his earthly problems, he is being distracted by a "presence" from the netherworld called Henrik Ghostkeeper. This draft is composed of actual material intended for the story and author's commentary. It opens in a wintry park where people are performing summer activities such as swimming and tennis:

1. "The point of all this is a certain duality of appearance in the picture: which balances the duality within the theme, and of existence. The picture is wintry, but it is also summery. This is like a nightmare, but it is also extremely pleasant."

2. "One theme is, or should be, rebirth."

3. (The hero sees a boatwreck.) "The wreck: symbol of something, perhaps bad omen. Or worse—presage of some catastrophe, or death of someone."

4. "Perhaps moon is omen too."

5. (The central image of the novel is a mysterious watch with the name "Henrik Ghostkeeper" inscribed on it.) It "is like a symbolic band or nexus relating him [Goodheart] to humanity."

6. "All this [i.e., the problems created by his finding the watch] ties in with the kaleidoscope of life, the complexity, flying saucers, the impossibility of writing good short stories."

7. (Goodheart wants to write about the mysterious watch, but he can't.) "For where did Ghostkeeper come in? Perhaps he wouldn't be able to use the name Ghostkeeper at all, which was an uncommon name, just as he wouldn't be able to use his own name Goodheart, that was too much like Pilgrim's Progress. . . . But what was the relation between the owner of the watch and the name on the wreck? Why should the Englishman he'd spoken to by the wreck have lost his watch too? And what was the relation between this and the watch he'd restored to the blind man by the anteater's cage? Why had the wreck seemed a bad omen? . . . And what was the relation between all these watches in general and the invisible watch in the movie. . . . etc."

8. (Here Lowry describes and explains the story and part of his

own creative process as well.) "That this situation must be in some sense a universal one (even though it is not generally recognised) is what I count on to provide the excitement. What we need too—or rather therefore—is not merely imagination, but hard boiled logical thinking. . . . In any case Goodheart is now standing within the possibilities of his own story and of his own life—something like Sigbjorn [author of *Under the Volcano* within the seven-novel framework] in relation to the Volcano, though this is both more complex and of course less serious. The point seems to be that all these possibilities, of his story (as of his own life) wish in some way to fulfill themselves, but what makes it terrifying is that the mind or intelligence that controls these things, or perhaps does not control them, is outside Goodheart and not within. If this intelligence (that which *we* mean when we say 'they're on the job') the *name* Henrik Ghostkeeper is the symbol. (sic) In himself (or themselves) of course Ghostkeeper is many things at once, and many persons, including a child, and so is incomprehensible to human thought. Perhaps what happens is something like this. The minute an artist begins to try and shape his material—the more especially if that material is his own life—some sort of magic lever is thrown into gear, setting some celestial machinery in motion producing events or coincidences that show him that this shaping of his is absurd, that nothing is static or can be pinned down, that everything is evolving or developing into other meanings, or cancellations of meanings quite beyond his comprehension. There is something mechanical about this process, symbolized by the watch: on the other hand the human mind or will or consciousness or whatever, of which the owner knows nothing at all, yet which has a will of its own, becomes automatically at such moments in touch as it were with the control tower of this machinery. (This brings me to Ortega—'A man's life is like a work of fiction, that he makes up as he goes along: he becomes an engineer for the sake of giving it form, etc.') I don't think any of the above should appear in the story—or do I?—of course and indeed now I've written it I scarcely know what it means. But that I am on the right track I am certain—at least to the extent that the lies, literal falsehoods in this story, such as the name Ghostkeeper on the wreck, the falling tree house seem valid, as produced by my unconscious. They merely parallel other coincidences we haven't space for such as Dylan Thomas, etc. In any case the average short story is probably a very bad image of life, and an absurdity, for the reason that no matter how much action there is in it, it is static, a piece of death, fixed, a sort of butterfly on a pin; . . . But the attempt should be—or should be here—at least to give the illusion of things—appearances, possibilities, ideas, even resolutions—in a state of perpetual metamorphosis. Life is indeed a sort of delirium perhaps that should be contemplated however by a sober "healthy" mind. By sober and healthy I mean of necessity limited. The mind is not equipped to look at the truth. Perhaps people get inklings of that truth on the lowest plane when they drink too much or go crazy and become delirious but it can't be stomached, certainly not from that sort of upside-down and reversed position. Not that the truth is 'bad' or 'good': it simply *is*, is incomprehensible, and though one is part of it, there is too much of it to grasp at once, or it is ungraspable, being perpetually Protean. Hence a final need probably for an acceptance of one's limitations, and of the absurd in oneself. So finally even this story is absurd which is an important part of the point if any, since that it should have none whatsoever seems part of the point too."

9. (The Yeatsian demon here visits the short story writer.) " 'Yes, yes, that is very nice, very touching, Mr. Goodheart, it is just as you say,' he seemed to hear yet another voice, as from half way up in the air, saying 'No, no, Mr. Goodheart, that is very lousy, what did I tell you? What about the King? What about Canada? What about the blind man? What about Segovia? What about the invisible watch? And the young Frenchman? What about the wheels within wheels, Mr. Goodheart, and not merely the wheels within wheels, but the wheels within wheels within wheels, Mr. Goodheart, that are even now still turning and evolving newer, yet more wonderful and more meaningless meanings—'

"And yet within himself he knew there was a meaning and that it was not meaningless.

". . . Who else, up there, was writing? Suddenly before his eyes the tree house crashed down on the bench again. And tell strange stories of—who else was writing, up there, about Kings dying, Elizabethans, invisible watches, flying saucers, blind men, mandarin ducks . . . Henrik Ghostkeeper! If only one could be sure he were playing a game!

"What did we know? And into his mind again came a vision of the ghostly ballet, seen through the half cleaned windows, on the pier at the entrance to the park. If one could only be sure!

"But suddenly his fear was transformed into love, love for his wife, and that meaningless, menacing fear was transformed into a spring wood bearing with it the scent of peach blossoms and wild cherry blossoms.

"Pray for them!"

# BIBLIOGRAPHY

## Works by Malcolm Lowry Appearing in Periodicals

"The Bravest Boat," *Partisan Review,* 21 (May 1954), 275–288.
"The Element Follows You Around, Sir!" *Show Magazine* (March 1964), pp. 45–103.
"Garden of Etla," *United Nations World,* 4 (June 1950), 45–47.
"Hotel Room in Chartres," *Story,* 5 (September 1934), 53–58.
"Lunar Caustic," *Paris Review,* 8 (Winter–Spring 1963), 12–72.
"On Board the 'West Hardaway,' " *Story,* 3 (October 1933), 12–22.
"Preface to a Novel," *Canadian Literature,* 9 (Summer 1961–Spring 1962), 23–29.
"Under the Volcano," *Prairie Schooner* (Winter 1963–64), 284–300.

## Books by Malcolm Lowry

*Dark as the Grave Wherein My Friend Is Laid.* New York, 1968.
*Hear Us O Lord From Heaven Thy Dwelling Place.* New York, 1961.
*The Selected Letters of Malcolm Lowry,* eds. Harvey Breit, Margerie Lowry. New York, 1965.
*Selected Poems.* San Francisco, 1962.
*Ultramarine.* London, 1933.
*Under the Volcano.* New York, 1947.

## Secondary Sources

Abelson, J. *Jewish Mysticism.* London, 1913.
Achad, Frater. *The Anatomy of the Body of God.* Chicago, 1925.
Agrippa, Henry Cornelius. *Occult Philosophy or Magic,* ed. Willis F. Whitehead. New York, 1887.
———. *The Philosophy of Natural Magic.* Chicago, 1913.
Aiken, Conrad. *Ushant.* New York, 1952.
Allen, Walter. *The Modern Novel in Britain and the United States.* New York, 1964.
———. "Review of *Under the Volcano,*" *New Statesman and Nation,* 34 (December 1947), 455–456.
Astre, Georges-Albert. "Review of *Under the Volcano,*" *Critique,* 46 (March 1951), 271.

Atwood, M. A. *Hermetic Philosophy and Alchemy.* New York, 1960.

Bakan, David. *Sigmund Freud and the Jewish Mystical Tradition.* Princeton, 1958.

Bayley, Harold. *A New Light on the Renaissance.* London, 1919.

Benz, Ernst. *Die Christliche Kabbala.* Zürich/Stuttgart, 1958.

Birney, Earle. "Against the Spell of Death," *Prairie Schooner,* 37 (Winter 1963–1964), 328–333.

Blau, Joseph. "The Cabala in English Literature," *The Review of Religion,* 6 (January 1942), 146–168.

———. *The Christian Interpretation of the Cabala in the Renaissance.* New York, 1944.

Blavatsky, Helene. *The Secret Doctrine.* London, 1888.

Bodkin, Maude. *Archetypal Patterns in Poetry.* New York, 1958.

Böhme, Jakob. *Dialogues on the Supersensual Life,* tr. William Law. New York, n.d.

Breit, Harvey. "Introductory Note, Lowry's *Through the Panama,*" *Paris Review,* 23 (Spring 1960), 84.

Buber, Martin. *Tales of Angels Spirits and Demons.* New York, 1958.

Bunyan, John. *Grace Abounding to the Chief of Sinners,* ed. Roger Sharrock. Oxford, 1962.

Burnet, Thomas. *The Sacred Theory of the Earth.* 2 vols. London, 1699.

Butler, E. M. *The Myth of the Magus.* Cambridge, England, 1948.

———. *Ritual Magic.* Cambridge, England, 1949.

Butler, W. E. *Magic and the Qabalah.* London, 1964.

Campbell, Joseph. *The Hero with a Thousand Faces.* New York, 1956.

Clark, Eleanor. "Review of *Under the Volcano,*" *Nation,* 164 (March 1947), 335–336.

Colville, W. J. *Kabbalah.* New York, 1916.

D'Astorg, Bertrand. "Review of *Under the Volcano,*" *Esprit,* 18 (November 1950), 702–707.

Day, Douglas. "Letters of Malcolm Lowry," *Shenandoah Review,* 15 (Spring 1964), 3–15.

———. "Of Tragic Joy," *Prairie Schooner,* 37 (Winter 1963–1964), 354–362.

Dodds, E. R. *The Greeks and the Irrational.* Los Angeles, 1951.

Dunne, John S. *The City of The Gods—A Study in Myth and Mortality.* New York, 1965.

Dunne, J. W. *An Experiment with Time.* New York, 1937.

Eliade, Mircea. *The Forge and the Crucible,* tr. Stephen Corrin. New York, 1962.

————. *Patterns in Comparative Religion.* New York, 1963.

Estang, Luc. "Review of *Under the Volcano,*" *Figaro Litteraire,* 14 (January 1961), 14.

Flint, R. W. "Review of *Under the Volcano,*" *Kenyon Review,* 9 (Summer 1947), 474–477.

Fort, Charles. *The Books of Charles Fort,* ed. Tiffany Thayer. New York, 1959.

Fortune, Dion. *The Mystical Qabalah.* London, 1935.

Fouchet, Max-Pol. "Non se puede . . . ," *Lettres Nouvelles,* 8:5 (July–August 1960), 21–25.

Francillon, Clarisse. "Malcolm, mon ami," *Lettres Nouvelles,* 8:5 (July–August 1960), 8–19.

————. "Souvenirs sur Malcolm Lowry," *Lettres Nouvelles,* 5:54 (November 1957), 588–603.

Frazer, Sir James. *The Magical Origin of Kings.* London, 1920.

Fuller, J. F. C. *The Secret Wisdom of the Qabalah.* London, n.d.

Gadienne, Paul. "Review of *Under the Volcano,*" *Cahiers du Sud,* 32 (February 1951), 519–522.

Garoffolo, Vincent. "Review of *Under the Volcano,*" *New Mexico Quarterly,* 17 (Summer 1947), 264–265.

Gaster, Moses. *The Asatir—The Samaritan Proof of the "Secrets of Moses."* London, 1927.

Ginsburg, Christian. *The Kabbalah: Its Doctrine, Development, and Literature.* London, 1920.

Ginzberg, Louis. *On Jewish Law and Lore.* Philadelphia, 1955.

Goethe, Wolfgang von. *Faust.* Munich, 1960.

Hardwick, Elizabeth. "Review of *Under the Volcano,*" *Partisan Review,* 14 (March–April 1947), 198–200.

Hays, H. "Review of *Under the Volcano,*" *The New York Times Book Review,* February 23, 1947, p. 5.

Heilman, Ronald. "The Possessed Artist," *Canadian Literature* 8 (Summer 1960–Spring 1961), 7–16.

————. "Review of *Under the Volcano,*" *Sewanee Review,* 55 (Summer 1947), 483–492.

Henderson, Joseph, and Maude Oaks. *The Wisdom of the Serpent.* New York, 1963.

Hopkins, Arthur John. *Alchemy, Child of Greek Philosophy.* New York, 1934.

Hopper, Vincent. *Medieval Number Symbolism.* New York, 1938.

Humboldt, Charles. "The Novel of Action," *Mainstream,* 1 (Fall 1947), 392–393.

Huxley, Aldous. *Beyond the Mexique Bay.* New York, 1934.

James, William. *The Varieties of Religious Experience.* New York, 1902.

Jung, Carl. *Psyche and Symbol.* New York, 1958.

Kafka, Franz. *Diaries 1910–1913,* ed. Max Brod. New York, 1965.

Kirk, Downie. "Glimpses of Malcolm Lowry," *Canadian Literature* 8 (Summer 1960–Spring 1961), 31–38.

Knickerbocker, Conrad. "Malcolm Lowry in England," *Paris Review,* 10 (Summer 1966), 13–38.

——. "The Voyages of Malcolm Lowry," *Prairie Schooner,* 37 (Winter 1963–1964), 301–314.

Knoche, Grace Frances. *The Mystery Schools.* Point Loma, Calif., 1940.

Laurence, L. W. de, ed. *The Lesser Key of Solomon: Goetia.* Chicago, 1916.

Lawrence, D. H. *Mornings in Mexico.* London, 1956.

Lévi, Eliphas. *The History of Magic,* tr. A. E. Waite. London, 1963.

——. *The Paradoxes of the Highest Science.* Adyar, Madras, 1922.

——. *Transcendental Magic: Its Doctrine and Ritual,* tr. A. E. Waite. New York, 1938.

Lewy, Hans, ed. *Three Jewish Philosophers.* New York, 1960.

Magnus, Albertus. *On Union With God.* London, 1911.

Mann, Thomas. *Doctor Faustus,* tr. H. T. Lowe-Porter. New York, 1948.

Marquette, Jacques de. *Introduction to Comparative Mysticism.* New York, 1949.

Mathers, S. L. MacGregor, ed. *The Book of the Sacred Magic of Abra-Melin, the Mage.* Chicago, 1948.

Mayberry, George. "Review of *Under the Volcano,*" *New Republic,* 116 (February 1947), 35–36.

Moore, William Joseph. *A Study of the Concept of the Mighty Word in Ancient Hebrew Literature.* Chicago, 1940.

Müller, Ernst. *History of Jewish Mysticism.* Oxford, 1946.

Myer, Isaac. *Qabbalah.* Philadelphia, 1888.

Myrer, Anton. "Le Monde au dessous du volcan," *Lettres Nouvelles,* 8:5 (July–August 1960), 59–66.

Ouspensky, P. D. *A New Model of the Universe.* New York, 1931.

——. *Tertium Organum.* New York, 1959.

Pancoast, S. *The Kabbala: or the True Science of Light.* New York, 1883.

Papus (Encausse, Gerard). *La Cabbale.* Paris, n.d.

——. *The Tarot of the Bohemians.* London, 1892.

Paracelsus. *Selected Writings,* ed. Jolande Jacobi, tr. Norbert Guterman. New York, 1951.

Pick, Bernhard. *The Cabala: Its Influence on Judaism and Christianity.* Chicago, 1913.

Praz, Mario. *The Romantic Agony.* New York, 1956.

Prescott, Orville. "Outstanding Novels," *The Yale Review,* 36 (Summer 1947), 765–768.

Purucker, G. de. *Occult Glossary.* London, 1933.

Raglan, Lord. *The Hero.* New York, 1956.

Read, John. *The Alchemist in Life, Literature and Art.* London, 1947.

Regardie, Israel. *The Art and Meaning of Magic.* Great Britain, 1964.

Rony, Jerome-Antoine. *A History of Magic.* New York, 1962.

Rosenroth, Knorr von. *The Kabbalah Unveiled,* tr. S. L. MacGregor Mathers. New York, 1907.

Saurat, Denis. *Literature and Occultism,* tr. Dorothy Bolton. London, 1930.

Schnur, Harry. *Mystic Rebels.* New York, 1949.

Scholem, Gershom. *Major Trends in Jewish Mysticism.* New York, 1961.

————. *On the Kabbalah and Its Symbolism,* tr. Ralph Manheim. London, 1965.

————. "Religious Authority and Mysticism," *Commentary,* 38 (November 1964), 31–39.

————. *Zohar: The Book of Splendor.* New York, 1963.

————. *Zur Geschichte der Anfänge der Christlichen Kabbala.* Privately printed pamphlet, November 1954.

Schorer, Mark. "The Downward Flight of a Soul," New York *Herald Tribune Book Week,* February 23, 1947, p. 2.

Senior, John. "The Occult in Nineteenth-Century Symbolist Literature." Ph.D. dissertation, Columbia University, 1957.

————. *The Way Down and Out.* Ithaca, N.Y., 1959.

Serouya, Henri. *La Kabbale.* Paris, 1947.

Simpson, R. G. "Review of *Under the Volcano,*" *Northern Review,* 1 (August–September 1947), 37–38.

Spence, Lewis. *The Myths of Mexico and Peru.* New York, 1913.

Spriel, Stephen. "Le Cryptogramme Lowry," *Lettres Nouvelles,* 8:5 (July–August 1960), 67–81.

Spurgeon, Caroline. *Mysticism in English Literature.* Cambridge, England, 1913.

Starkie, Enid. *Baudelaire.* New York, 1958.

————. *Rimbaud.* New York, 1961.

Steiner, Rudolf. *Theosophy,* tr. Henry B. Monges. New York, 1946.

Stenring, Knut. *The Book of Formation (Sepher Yetzirah)*. London, 1923.

Summers, Montagu. *The History of Witchcraft*. New York, 1956.

Swedenborg, Emanuel. *Heaven and Its Wonders, and Hell*. Philadelphia, 1880.

Symonds, Arthur. *The Symbolist Movement in Literature*. New York, 1958.

Tindall, William Y. *D. H. Lawrence and Susan His Cow*. New York, 1939.

————. "James Joyce and the Hermetic Tradition," *Journal of the History of Ideas*, 15 (January 1954), 23–29.

————. "Many Leveled Fiction: Virginia Woolf to Ross Lockridge," *College English*, 10 (November 1948), 65–71.

Underhill, Evelyn. *Mysticism*. New York, 1960.

Vaughan, Thomas. *The Magical Writings*. London, 1888.

Villars, Abbé de. *Comte de Gabalis*, tr. Lotus Dudley. New York, 1922.

Waite, A. E. *The Holy Kabbalah*. New York, n.d.

Walker, D. P. *Spiritual and Demonic Magic from Ficino to Campanella*. London, 1958.

Watts, Alan W. *The Two Hands of God—the Myths of Polarity*. New York, 1963.

Westcott, W. W. *Numbers: Their Occult Power and Mystic Virtues*. New York, 1911.

————. *The Sepher Yetziroth*, tr. Robert Fryar. Bath, 1887.

White, Helen C. "The Mysticism of William Blake," *University of Wisconsin Studies in Language and Literature*, 23. Madison, 1927.

Wilhelm, Hellmut. *Eight Lectures on the I Ching*, tr. Cary F. Baynes. New York, 1960.

Woodcock, George. "Malcolm Lowry as Novelist," *British Columbia Library Quarterly*, 23–24 (April 1961), 25–32.

————. "Malcolm Lowry's *Under the Volcano*," *Modern Fiction Studies*, 4 (Summer 1948), 151–156.

————. "On the Day of the Dead," *Northern Review*, 6 (December–January 1953–1954), 15–21.

————. "Under Seymour Mountain," *Canadian Literature*, 8 (Summer 1960–Spring 1961), 4–12.

Yates, Frances. *Giordano Bruno and the Hermetic Tradition*. Chicago, 1964.

Yeats, W. B. *A Vision*. New York, 1961.

Young, Vernon. "Review of *Under the Volcano*," *Arizona Quarterly*, 3 (Autumn 1947), 281–283.

# INDEX

## ABOUT THE AUTHOR

PERLE EPSTEIN was born in New York City, where she now lives with her physician husband. Although not yet thirty, she has already had a rich and rewarding career, combining a doctorate from Columbia University, theatrical journalism, teaching at New York University, membership in the American Recorder Society, and work on a novel. She is a descendant of Baal Shem-Tov, the eighteenth-century Cabbalist, and firmly believes in Cabbala.